the Eloquence *of*
Mary Astell

the Eloquence *of*
Mary Astell

Christine Mason Sutherland

UNIVERSITY OF
CALGARY
PRESS

Published by the
University of Calgary Press
2500 University Drive nw
Calgary, Alberta, Canada t2n 1n4
www.uofcpress.com

We acknowledge the financial
support of the Government of Canada,
through the Book Publishing Industry
Development Program (BPIDP), and the
Alberta Foundation for the Arts for our
publishing activities. We acknowledge the
support of the Canada Council for the Arts
for our publishing program.

This book has been published with the help
of a grant from the Canadian Federation
for the Humanities and Social Sciences,
through the Aid to Scholarly Publications
Programme, using funds provided by the
Social Sciences and Humanities Research
Council of Canada.

Library and Archives Canada
Cataloguing in Publication

Sutherland, Christine Mason

The eloquence of Mary Astell / Christine
Mason Sutherland.

Includes bibliographical references and
index.

ISBN-10 1-55238-153-6
ISBN-13 13-978-1-55238-153-3

1. Astell, Mary, 1668-1731—Literary art. 2.
Astell, Mary, 1668-1731—Political and social
views. 3. Women—Education,
Higher—England. 4. Feminism—Great
Britain. I. Title.

HQ1595.A88S87 2005   305.42'092
C2005-905554-5

Design & typesetting, Mieka West.

This book is printed on New Leaf Eco 100
natural, 100% post consumer waste paper.
Printed and bound in Canada by AGMV
Marquis.

To the best of teachers:
Dorothy F. Bartholomew
and the late Kathleen M. Lea

Table of Contents

Acknowledgements

This book has been published with the help of a grant from the Canadian Federation for the Humanities and Social Sciences, through the Aid to Scholarly Publications Programme, using funds provided by the Social Sciences and Humanities Research Council of Canada.

Grateful acknowledgements also go to the following: The Killam Trust for the Resident Fellowship that allowed me to work on this book; the University of Calgary Research Services Committee for awarding me the original starter grant to embark on this research; and the Faculty of Communication and Culture at the University of Calgary for the sabbatical fellowship that gave me the time to finish it. My thanks also go to Tania Smith for helpful suggestions on the influence of Bernard Lamy; to Isobel Grundy for sharing the information given in Appendix B; to Isabella Mihai and Kimberley Belton for help with editing; to Joyce Hildebrand for her most useful questions and comments; and especially to Christine Sopczak for her expert assistance with documentation.

Lastly, thanks go to Margaret and Joseph Mason, James, Richard, Timothy, Joel, and Aphra Sutherland, Dawn Bryan and Julia Hoover for their loving support.

Introduction

Mary Astell is not a well-known figure. Something of a celebrity in her own day, she had fallen out of fashion by the time of her death in 1731, and although her memory was revived and preserved for a time by George Ballard in the 1750s, she quickly faded once more from view. Not until Florence Smith's important biography of her was published in 1916 was interest in her once more aroused, and even since then the recovery has been slow. Astell was a political writer, a philosopher and an educationist as well an eloquent advocate for women, but it was principally as a feminist that she was brought forward again by Ruth Perry in her magisterial biography of 1986, *The Celebrated Mary Astell*. As for historians of rhetoric, they ignored her entirely until the 1980s, and even now she is not as well-known as she ought to be.[1] Since the assumed audience for this book is rhetoricians and students of rhetoric, as well as, I hope, some feminists and even general readers, the first task must be to introduce Mary Astell and to explain why it is important for us to study her. Why, after nearly three centuries of neglect, should we pay attention to her now? In particular, why should she be studied by rhetoricians and historians of rhetoric? Answering these questions is the purpose of the present enquiry.[2]

Astell was a native of Newcastle, a city in the far north of England.[3] She was born in 1666 to a middle-class family that was coming down in the world. The family belonged to the gentry – they had the right to bear arms. At the time this was an important social distinction. Her standing as a member of the gentry affected not only her sense of her own identity but also her opportunities for employment. Peter Astell, Mary's father, belonged to a highly prestigious guild known as the hostmen, associated with the coal industry, as was the family of her mother, Mary Errington.[4] Peter Astell had served a long apprenticeship, and in fact qualified as a hostman only a few years before his early death. There were only two children in the family, Mary and her younger brother Peter. It was common practice at the time for girls to be included in the primary education provided for their brothers, and Peter and Mary

Astell were taught by their uncle, Ralph Astell, an Anglican clergyman of a nearby parish. However, when Mary was thirteen her uncle died, and so far as is known she received no further formal education. From our point of view in the twenty-first century, it may appear that Mary's education was cut short almost before it had begun. We must remember, however, that during the Renaissance young boys proceeded to university when they were not much older than Mary was when her uncle died. Francis Bacon went up to Cambridge at the age of twelve, Philip Sidney at fourteen. Astell, despite the end of her formal education, continued to read and to educate herself, though it appears that there was no one to direct her.

During her teenage years, Astell suffered many losses that determined the course of her future. Her father had died a year before her uncle, leaving the family not well provided for. Besides the children, there were two women to support, Mary's mother and her aunt, another Mary Astell. Such small funds as could be saved would have had to be put aside for Peter's education. Little if anything was available for Mary's dowry, and without an adequate dowry a gentlewoman could not hope to marry well, if at all.[5] Some young women, naturally, were able to charm men considerably richer than themselves into marriage, but Mary Astell was not one of them. No portrait of her remains, but such evidence as we have suggests that she was not particularly attractive. Lady Mary Wortley Montagu's granddaughter records her as having been "in outward form [...] rather ill-favoured and forbidding," though Astell was long past her youth when this observation was made (Louisa Stewart, qtd. in F. Smith 16). Furthermore, Astell had not only a keen intelligence but also a biting wit and a sharp tongue. Tender as she was with the women of her acquaintance, she could be unsparing in her attack upon men, and there is nothing to suggest that she would have made a happy or successful wife to a man of her time.

Without adequate funds to support her, Mary Astell moved to London at the age of twenty-one to seek her fortune, trying to earn her living by her pen. This project was difficult at the time even for men, and not surprisingly, Astell soon found herself close to destitution. In this exigency, she appealed for help to William Sancroft, the Archbishop of Canterbury, a man known for his charity, and he did not fail her. Ruth Perry quotes Astell's letter of appeal to Sancroft:

My Lord,

I come to [your] grace as an humble petitioner being brought to very great necessaty threw some very unfortunate cercumstances [that] I have Laine under for some time I have pawned all my cloaths & now am brought to my Last Shift [that] is to desire charity of [your] grace & some others of [the] bishops, my Lord, I am a gentlewoman & not able to get a liflyhood, & I may say with [the] steward in [the] gospelle worke I cannot & to beg I am ashamed, but meer necessaty forces me to give [your] grace the trouble hoping [your] charity will consider me, for I have heard a very great and good character of [which] charity you have done & do dayly, so [that] I hope for [your] pitty upon my unhappy state, & if [your] grace please to admit me to speak to you I will give you a very just account of my cercumstances [which] is to Long to do in writing so I humbly beg [your] admittance to

My Lord
[your] graces
most humble & most
devoted servant (qtd. in Perry, Celebrated 66)

Even in her destitution, Mary Astell shows a saucy wit, making jokes that the archbishop would certainly have relished. If he did not, perhaps, entirely approve of the punning of "brought to my Last Shift," he would certainly have enjoyed Astell's comparison of herself to the *unjust* steward of Luke 16:3. Similarly, when she thanks him for his help by sending him a booklet of her own poems, sewn together by herself, she refers to it derogatorily as "but of Goats hair and Badger skins"; but as Sancroft would immediately have recognized, it was of goats' hair and badgers' skins that the Holy Tabernacle of the Israelites was made.

Aided by Sancroft, Astell was able to find a bookseller, who commissioned some of her works, and she also made a number of friends among the ladies of the nobility some of whom became her patrons. She made her home in Chelsea, then little more than a village but within easy reach of London by road or water. It was a pleasant place of gentlemen's estates, with numerous gardens, and inhabited, it seems, by many of the intellectuals of the day. Mary Astell found congenial friends there, and except for one brief period when she lived by the sea, she stayed in Chelsea for the rest of her life, supported in part by her patrons. Patronage was commonly practised at the time, and in receiving it Mary Astell was doing no more than most of the writers who were her contemporaries. What is interesting about Astell's patrons, and perhaps unusual, is that they were also her close friends. Lady Ann Coventry, Lady Elizabeth Hastings and Lady Catherine Jones were women who shared Astell's High Church piety and her interest in the education of women. Like Astell, they were, with the exception of Lady Ann Coventry, unmarried, preferring the independence provided them by their fortunes to the loss of freedom and fortune that marriage at that time entailed. It is probable that Astell met most of these ladies in Chelsea, possibly at church, though only one of them was permanently resident there.[6] This was Lady Catherine Jones, the friend to whom Astell dedicated her published correspondence with John Norris and, some years later, her *magnum opus*, *The Christian Religion*.

At least one of her friends, however, was not well-to-do. This was Elizabeth Elstob, of all Astell's friends the most intellectual, and like her, a native of Newcastle. Working with her brother, an Oxford scholar, Elstob published in 1709 a translation from the Old English of the *Homily on the Birthday of St. Gregory*. Owing to its success she was encouraged to produce an Anglo-Saxon grammar, written in contemporary English rather than Latin so that the language could be made available to women. This was published in 1715. In 1702 she had moved from Oxford to London, where her brother was rector of St. Swithin's and St. Mary Bothaw. Here she became part of Astell's circle of friends, and two of the subscribers to Elstob's book were Astell's friends and patrons, Lady Elizabeth Hastings and Lady Catherine Jones[7] (Reynolds 174). Elstob's career as a scholar came to an end with the death of her brother. Although she was never in a position to act as Mary Astell's patron, in one respect she made a greater contribution to Astell than any of her other friends, for it was she who provided much of the information for Astell's eighteenth-century biographer, George Ballard.

These, then, were the friends, companions, and patrons among whom Astell worked and shared her life. She was fortunate to find women who shared so many of her interests, some of whom were also able to provide for her financially. In this setting she prospered, developing as a scholar and a writer. Between 1694 and 1709, she published nine works, one of them in collaboration: not a large output, but of a quality that ensured her status as a celebrity at the time and enabled her to put into practice one of her most cherished projects, the education of girls. For after 1709, Astell abandoned her career as a writer to undertake the headship of a charity school for girls in Chelsea, a position she held until 1724. In her last years, she lived with her great friend and patron, Lady Catherine Jones, and it was in her house that Astell died of breast cancer in 1731.

During the early part of the eighteenth century, Astell was a noted figure in the intellectual world of London, engaging in politics (she wrote four political pamphlets supporting the Tory position) and promoting the cause of women whenever she could. She had a certain reputation for eccentricity: George Ballard records that

> when she had accidentally seen needless visitors coming, whom she knew to be incapable of discoursing upon any useful subject, but to come for the sake of chat and tattle, she would look out at the window and jestingly tell them [...] "Mrs Astell is not at home," and in good earnest keep them out, not suffering such triflers to make inroads upon her more serious hours. (385)[8]

Another incident related by George Ballard demonstrates not only Astell's intellectual powers but also her peculiar position as a woman of greater ability than many men. One of her friends was the wife of Dr. Francis Atterbury, later Bishop of Rochester. Atterbury gives the following account of his humiliation by Astell in a letter to Dr. Smalridge:

> I happened about a fortnight ago to dine with Mrs Astell. She spoke to me of my sermon (which I suppose by what follows, is that which he preached and afterwards printed, against Bishop Hoadley's Measure of Submission) and desired me to print it; and after I had given the proper answer, hinted to me that she

should be glad of perusing it, I complied with her, and sent her the sermon the next day. Yesterday she returned it with this sheet of remarks, which I cannot forbear communicating to you, because I take them to be of an extraordinary nature, considering they came from the pen of a woman. Indeed one would not imagine a woman had written them. There is not an expression that carries the least air of her sex from the beginning to the end of it. She attacks me very home, you see, and artfully enough, under a pretence of taking my part against other divines, who are in Hoadley's measure. Had she had as much good breeding as good sense, she would be perfect; but she has not the most decent manner of insinuating what she means, but is now and then a little offensive and shocking in her expressions; which I wonder at, because a civil turn of words is what her sex is always mistress of. She, I think is wanting in it. But her sensible and rational way of writing makes amends for that defect, if indeed anything can make amends for it. I dread to engage her, so I only wrote a general civil answer to her, and leave the rest to an oral conference. (qtd. in Ballard 387)

The letter is more revealing than Atterbury could have guessed, and not only of Astell. Obviously he, as a man of his time, believed that Astell's superior intellect did not entitle her to the respect due to an outstanding intelligence: he, as a man, and a cleric, expected to be treated with deference rather than honesty. One wonders how he would have responded had his critic been another man. Particularly telling is his decision to "leave the rest to an oral conference." In person, he would have all the advantages of stature, dress, and voice to support him: she would have her intelligence alone. One longs to know what happened. In fact, he would have done well to pay attention to her criticism: Hoadley was far more skilled than Atterbury in argumentation, and the advice of Astell, the skilled polemicist, would have been invaluable.

Mary Astell, then, was a considerable figure in her own time, though like many other women writers she was ignored by the public for nearly two centuries after her death. Ruth Perry calls her an early feminist, as indeed she was, if outrage at the plight of women and eloquence on their behalf qualify her. Yet some modern feminists find her an uneasy heroine. She was a Tory, a Royalist, fully supporting the Stuarts and the Anglican church.[9] She believed not only in the divine right of kings but also in the divine right of husbands. The idea that a woman might speak in public as a lawyer, a politician, or a preacher seemed to her little short of insane. On the other hand, she championed the cause of women's education and gave the latter part of her life to it. Devout, charitable, and hardworking, she devoted her life to the alleviation of that ignorance which in her view was responsible for much of women's suffering. Most of her writing was intended to support this cause.

This brings us to the second question: why is Mary Astell so important in the history of women's rhetoric? She was not the first to publish her work, and although she was in the context of her own time a feminist, she was certainly not the first to plead on behalf of women. Nor is she particularly well known as a woman writer. The fame of Katherine Phillips ("Matchless Orinda"), of Aphra Behn, even of Margaret Fell Fox, the Quaker, far exceeds hers. Nevertheless, I believe Mary Astell contributed to women's rhetoric in a way that makes her the most important woman rhetorician of her time. For Astell excelled in a number of ways, all of them important to the history of women's rhetoric. First, she was a highly accomplished practitioner. Her various works are models of rhetoric in argumentation, structure, accommodation of the audience, and style. Then, she was not only a practitioner of rhetoric, but also a theorist – and a theorist, moreover, who anticipated the rhetoric of care of the late twentieth century. Beyond this, it is important to study her career as a writer because it demonstrates the progress from one kind of rhetoric to another, a path taken by many other women writers, both in her own time and since.

What were these kinds of rhetoric, and why do they matter? Until fairly recently it was assumed that women were absent from the history of rhetoric, that there was no record of their having had any importance as public speakers or writers on public affairs. This assumption has been successfully challenged in the last two decades by women scholars who have shown that, although not prominent, women were by no means absent. These scholars include, among many others, Andrea Lunsford, Molly Meijer Wertheimer, Jan Swearingen, Patricia Bizzell, Jane Donawerth, and Cheryl Glenn, whose *Rhetoric Retold* is a landmark in the scholarship of women's rhetoric. The chief concern of such scholars has been to show that there have indeed been women speakers, writers, and teachers of rhetoric as far back as the time of Plato, and even before that.

However, these scholars have chiefly addressed the kind of rhetoric known as *contentio*, or public speech, typical of the law courts and the legislative assemblies. *Contentio* in fact has been the subject of most of the histories of rhetoric as it was practised and theorized from before the time of Plato.[10] It has traditionally been regarded as the whole of rhetoric: it was assumed that rhetoric meant public discourse, usually with an adversarial flavour, a battle of words. The forensic model of rhetoric was particularly strong in the Roman period, when most politicians worked their way up to power through the law courts. Yet there was, and has always been, another form of rhetoric, one acknowledged by Cicero himself: *sermo*. This is what he has to say about it:

> The power of speech in the attainment of propriety is great, and its function is twofold: the first is oratory; the second, conversation. *Contentio* is the kind of discourse to be employed in pleadings in court and popular assemblies and in the senate; *sermo* should find its natural place in social gatherings, in informal discussions, and in intercourse with friends; it should also seek admission at dinners. There are rules for *contentio* laid down by rhetoricians; there are none for *sermo*, and yet I do not know why there should not be. (qtd. in Tinkler 284)

The root meaning of *sermo* is conversation, and conversation is a kind of discourse that has always been practised by women, in which, indeed, they have often surpassed men. If *sermo* is taken seriously as an essential part of rhetoric, it is obvious that even the greatest orators received their early rhetorical training from hearing the conversation of their mothers: *sermo*, in fact, is anterior to *contentio*. Sermocinal culture, as John Tinkler points out, "inevitably operated on the margins of instituted power" (295). And it is on the margins, of course, that women have usually operated. Often influential, they have seldom held great political power, and their voices have not often been heard in public. Yet increasingly in the seventeenth century, this marginalized form of discourse was moving toward the centre, becoming more important in the formulation of ideas about both politics and art. Indeed, conversation itself was becoming an art, and by the late eighteenth century it had become formalized, with its own set of rules (Redford 3). Furthermore, the art of conversation, especially as it developed during the seventeenth century, was the particular province of women. It was in the salons of seventeenth-century France that women had a particularly significant role to play. Carolyn Lougee asserts that "the salon of seventeenth-century France centred on women" (qtd. in Donawerth, "As Becomes" 305). The key figure here is Madeleine de Scudéry, who "develops a rhetorical theory [for women] by modeling discourse on conversation rather than on public speaking" (Donawerth, "As Becomes" 307). Scudéry's "On Conversation" is an especially important document in the history of women's rhetoric. In fact, as Jane Donawerth points out, Scudéry "revisioned the tradition of masculine public discourse for mixed gender 'private' discourse in salon society, emphasizing conversation and letter writing" (304).

Conversation and letter writing: the connection between these two forms of *sermo*, the oral and the written, is especially important in the history of women's rhetoric.[11] The familiar letter may be said to be a form of conversation: Samuel Richardson calls it "the converse of the pen" (qtd. in Redford 1). Like conversation, the letter was a form of discourse particularly appropriate to the circumstances of women's lives, essential in maintaining family relationships at times when travel was particularly difficult. Of all the forms of discourse, it was the one most useful to women, and one that did not carry the restraints imposed on their public speaking. In a private context, and among their families and friends, women did not need a public reputation in order to get a hearing. Conversation was their particular province, and letter writing, because it was originally conceived of as a private form, usually having an audience of only one, was also open to them. As early as the fifteenth century, women engaged in correspondence, a practice not only allowed but also positively encouraged by their men folk: "[I]n this period [the fifteenth century] men both tolerated and positively expected women to partake in letter-writing" (Truelove 44). And even women who were not literate could and did write letters by dictating them. Madeleine de Scudéry is again important here, specifically her *Conversation on the Manner of Writing Letters*, in which she opens up for discussion and theorizes the writing of letters by women as well as men.

However, although originally a private form of discourse, the letter could be made public, and was in fact often intended for publication. Cicero himself had used the form in this way: *De Officiis*, for example, takes the form of a private letter to his son.[12] Furthermore, as Judith Rice Henderson explains, during the Renaissance the letter became a highly important form for the dissemination of scholarship: "At a time when there were no learned journals in which scholars could have their articles published, letters, whether intended to be printed or merely to be circulated in manuscript, served much the same purpose" (339). This tension between form and intention – a private form used as a public vehicle – provided for women an opportunity to move from the private to the public sphere of activity, from *sermo* to *contentio*.

Mary Astell was one of those who made such a transition. Her first experience as a writer was as a correspondent of John Norris, and when a few months later she wrote *A Serious Proposal to the Ladies*, she again used the form of a letter, as she did also for *A Serious Proposal, Part II* and even for her major work, *The Christian Religion*. A recurring theme throughout this book will be Astell's gradual move from *sermo* to *contentio*, a move she completed with her political tracts, the last of which she wrote in 1709. Her mastery of letter writing, a form of *sermo*, contributed to the success of her published work. Similarly her skill in the art of conversation, another form of *sermo*, was the foundation of her style. She provided in her home a "sort of minor learned salon" (Reynolds 304). And it was this experience of conversation that rendered her style voiced, usually intimate, and often even colloquial.[13] Astell's career, then, demonstrates how it was possible for a woman of her time to move out of the private into the public sphere, using her expertise in private and semi-private forms and conventions to address a wider public.

A word of explanation about my method and organization: I have used a rhetorical perspective. I deal with questions of *inventio*, how Astell finds her subject matter and how she uses her sources and supports her arguments; of *dispositio*, the organization of her work, including considerations of genre; and of *elocutio*, matters of tone, diction, and the use of rhetorical devices. Above all, a rhetorical perspective involves the study of rhetorical situation and audience: Mary Astell must be seen in the context of her own time and in terms of the interests and assumptions of her contemporary audiences. To understand her achievement, therefore, it is necessary to know something of the political, philosophical, and cultural issues of her age, and I have accordingly given some attention to these matters. The book is organized in three parts. Part I gives the background to women's writing. The first chapter demonstrates some of the peculiar difficulties experienced by women writers during the late seventeenth century. In chapter 2, I discuss Mary Astell's own approach to these problems of *ethos*. Part II, the longest section, discusses each of Astell's works in turn as instances of her rhetorical practice. I have used this chronological scheme in order to highlight her progress as a rhetorician. Part III, consisting of two chapters, deals with her rhetorical theory. I have organized the material in this rather unusual way because I want to highlight the fact that Astell was an important theorist of rhetoric as well as a fine practitioner. Her theory forms part of *A Serious Proposal to the Ladies, Part II*. I discuss this work, then, in the second part, and again in the third, with a different focus. Astell's theory demands sustained discussion, and therefore, I believe, requires separate treatment. Several themes recur throughout the book. One of these, as I have suggested, is the development of *contentio* out of *sermo*, Astell's progress from semi-private to fully public discourse. Another is her feminism, most apparent in *Some Reflections Upon Marriage*, but present to some extent in nearly all of her writing. Since it is important to note these characteristics in each of the works, the reader will notice a certain amount of recursiveness.

The study of Astell's rhetoric is, I am convinced, not of antiquarian interest only. Certainly it is important to remember and celebrate women writers of the past, especially those as eloquent as Astell. However, a study of her work has a more practical application. Much of her advice is still relevant in the twenty-first century, and as Erin Herberg has pointed out, it is as useful to men as to women (156). If Astell's rhetorical practice can still serve as a model for eloquence that few of us can equal, her theory also is timeless. Serious study of her technical expertise as a writer, as well as of her guiding principles in her craft, can benefit aspiring writers even today.

Part I

Mary Astell's Context

1

The Problem of *Ethos*

For the Renaissance woman," writes Tita Baumlin, "*ethos* is [...] problematic, since any use of public language risked the destruction of both her public image and her private virtues" (230). Thus in the very act of drawing upon her *ethos* in order to engage in public discourse, the woman destroyed it. Such was the paradoxical situation in which the seventeenth-century woman writer found herself. This chapter will be devoted to an exploration of the elements of *ethos*, and why a woman was thought to be necessarily deficient in them. Since the method used here is the rhetorical one of placing texts and writers within a context, we shall have to take into consideration a number of beliefs and traditions, some of them at odds with one another. Nevertheless, in order to understand the challenges met by Mary Astell, it is important to understand the underlying values and convictions of her time.

Since the time of Aristotle, rhetorical theory has recognized the crucial importance of *ethos*: any speaker or writer must begin by securing an audience, a readership, of those who are prepared to trust his or her judgement. A speaker or writer who has no strong *ethos* is unlikely to be persuasive and may not even get a hearing; the audience has at the very least to be willing to pay attention if the discourse is to be heard at all. The address to considerations of *ethos* is to be found in the work of most classical rhetoricians. It is theorized in Aristotle: "We believe good men more fully and more readily than others: this is true whatever the question is, and absolutely true where exact certainty is impossible and opinions are divided" (*Rhetorica* 1.2.1354). Probably better known in the Renaissance, however, were Cicero's and Quintilian's teachings on this subject. Quintilian calls it authority: "For he, who would have all men trust his judgment as to what is expedient and honourable, should both possess and be regarded as possessing genuine wisdom and excellence of character" (3.8.13). *Ethos* is held to be of two kinds: intrinsic and extrinsic. Intrinsic *ethos* is that which is generated during the course of reception: the text, or speech itself, carries with it an authority or credibility that engages the recipient and exercises persuasion. This kind of *ethos* is considered in general more reliable because it is less open to manipulation. Extrinsic *ethos*, on the other hand, derives from the already-established reputation of the speaker or writer. Nearly all rhetoricians since antiquity have recognized its power. Here, for example, is what the ancient teacher of rhetoric, Isocrates, had to say about its importance: "[T]he man who wishes to persuade people will not be negligent as to the matter of character; no, on the contrary, he will apply himself above all to establish a most honourable name among his fellow-citizens"[1] (49). Aristotle agrees: "It is not true, as some writers assume in their treatises on rhetoric, that the personal goodness revealed by the speaker contributes nothing to his powers of persuasion; on the contrary, his character may almost be called the most effective means of persuasion he possesses" (Aristotle, *Rhetorica* 1.2.1356). The drawback, of course, is that it is possible to create a false *ethos*: witness the spin-doctors of our own day. Extrinsic *ethos* works most reliably in small communities where the person is familiar and manipulation more easily detected. It is least reliable in contexts of mass communication.

Of the two, intrinsic *ethos* was by far the easier for women to achieve in Astell's day. If the written discourse was allowed to speak for itself without reference to prior reputation, it was possible that it could impress its audience very favourably. This indeed is what occurred in respect of the writing of various women in the seventeenth century who published anonymously: if it showed sufficiently high quality, it was admired, though ironically the consequence often was that its authorship by a woman was disbelieved on the grounds that no woman could write so well. Owing to this frequently practised anonymity, the success of intrinsic *ethos* did not, as it would in the case of a man, contribute to a woman's extrinsic *ethos*. Mary Astell's *Some Reflections Upon Marriage* was so well written that a man actually claimed to have produced it himself, and Astell was obliged to refute his claim in a preface to the edition of 1706 in order to defend herself, even though she remained anonymous, divulging only her sex (8).

Within classical and Renaissance theories of *ethos*, there are three categories: considerations of intelligence, integrity, and goodwill. The speaker or writer must be seen to have authority to speak upon this particular subject to this particular audience. That is, he (the public speaker in classical rhetoric is assumed to be a male) must be well informed so far as the subject matter is concerned, as well as being demonstrably a rational human being. The second component of *ethos* is integrity, or moral reliability. This element is especially important in the theory of Quintilian, who denies the title of orator to the immoral speaker; but it is also of course important to Christian rhetoricians such as Augustine, who makes the point that the preacher must practise his own precepts if he is to be believed: "How do they say something with words which they deny with deeds? The Apostle did not say vainly, 'They profess that they know God, but in their works they deny him'" (4.19.62). What this moral reliability means differs, of course, according to the values of the particular culture: for Quintilian, virtue means civic virtue, that which contributes to the public good; for Augustine, it means the practice of the specifically Christian virtues, especially love of God, one's neighbour, and oneself. The third element of *ethos* is goodwill for this particular audience at this particular time. It is, naturally, highly contextual, and it is accordingly hard to generalize about it. Goodwill also is one of the categories of response: if the rhetorician is perceived as rational, well-informed, ethically sound, and motivated by goodwill for this particular audience, that audience will respond by reciprocating the goodwill. They will also respond to the rationality and command of the subject matter displayed by the speaker, and to his projection of an ethical persona, by showing attentiveness to his arguments and a willingness to give them favourable consideration.

In two of these elements, women during the Renaissance (and at most other times in the history of Western civilization) were thought to be deficient by nature. The ideology of the later medieval period, still very strong in the Renaissance, was influenced by the philosopher Thomas Aquinas, who took over from Aristotle the idea that woman was a deficient form of man: "It seems that woman ought not to have been produced in the original production of things. For Aristotle says that the female is an incomplete version of the male" (qtd. in Maclean 8). Nonetheless, Aquinas rather puzzlingly concludes that with reference to the species as a whole the female is not deficient but "according to the plan of nature" (9). What this means is that although women in general are part of nature, and necessary for procreation, the individual woman is to be seen as defective. And she was seen as particularly defective in reason.

This deficiency in reason – or intelligence, the first element in classical *ethos* – involved necessarily a deficiency also in morality, or integrity, the second element. Reason was supposed to govern the passions; if, therefore, reason was deficient, it could not control the passions as it ought. Thus woman was thought to be at the mercy of her emotions. This conviction is well demonstrated in a passage from a commentary on Genesis 2 by the Dominican Thomas de Vio, Cardinal Cajetan (1469–1534):

> What philosophers have said about the production of woman [that she is a botched male] is recounted metaphorically by Moses. There is a great difference between the point of view of the philosophers and that of Moses; for the former considered the production of woman only in relation to sex, whereas Moses considered the production of woman not only as it concerns sex but also with regard to moral behaviours as a whole [*universam vitam moralem*]. Therefore he used a complex metaphor [...] as the sleep of Adam should be understood metaphorically, Adam is described asleep, not being woken up or keeping vigil. A deep sleep is sent by God into the man from whom woman is to be produced, and this defect of male power bears a likeness from which woman is naturally produced. For a sleeping man is only half a man; similarly the principle creating woman is only semi-virile. It is for this reason that woman is called an imperfect version of the male by philosophers. (qtd. in Maclean 9)

This perception of woman as morally deficient has a long history. It is found in the works of some of the early church fathers, but it goes back even further. Despite de Vio's ingenious reading of the account of the creation of woman given in Genesis 2, prejudice against women is not typical of the writings of the Old Testament, and although certain prophets were celibate, the traditional view of marriage in Judaism is positive. The prejudice therefore most probably derives originally from traditions outside both Christianity and Judaism. David S. Wiesen cites two such traditions: "Of course, asceticism was [...] subject to many non-Christian influences. The severe ethic of the Stoa and the extreme dualism of the Gnostic world view gave powerful encouragement to the ascetic rejection of the flesh" (154). He continues: "Proponents of such austere views looked with horror upon women as sensuality incarnate and in their exhortations in behalf of chastity naturally attacked marriage as the destroyer of holiness." Wiesen concludes that "Jerome's satiric attacks on women and marriage are revealed as a Christian continuation of the anti-feminism of certain pagan thinkers" (154).

Given this background in the Fathers and Aquinas, it is not surprising to find a great outcry against women in the sermons of medieval preachers.[2] These negative views of women were slow to change, even in the Reformation. Martin Luther states that "it is evident [...] that woman is a different animal to man, not only having different members, but also being far weaker in intellect" (qtd. in Maclean 10). And again, or still, this rational deficiency makes woman morally unreliable:

> [L]acking reason to guide her, she is governed by passions alone. [...] [W]e are prepared to hear of "the nine thousand, nine hundred and ninety-nine forms of malice" that plague the world in the shape of women. Like a blotter she has absorbed them all. Beginning with the Seven Deadly Sins the catalogue runs to great length [...]: licentiousness, instability, intractability to God's express commands, drunkenness and gluttony, pride, vanity, avarice, greed, seditiousness, quarrelsomeness, and vindictiveness, and evidently the most irritating of all, talkativeness. To end with the favourite summary of weary cataloguers: if all the seas were ink, and fields parchment, trees pens, and all who knew how to write were to write without ceasing, all the evil in women could not be expressed. (Kelso 11–12)

The conviction that women were deficient in reason, and consequently in morality, is demonstrated in some of the literature of the Renaissance. For example, in Heywood's *A Woman Killed with Kindness* and Middleton's *Women Beware Women* and *More Dissemblers Besides Women*, the female characters fall into sin with a suddenness that exceeds (for a later age) dramatic credibility. The women do not go through the process of wrestling with temptation: they simply fall. This depiction of women as undergoing an instantaneous transformation, however unbelievable in the twenty-first century, was quite consistent with the view of women that denied them their full share of rationality. Because at the time resisting temptation was seen as a matter of bringing to bear the light of reason upon the inclination of the passions, women were naturally at a disadvantage: they had so little with which to resist

temptation. It was partly this conviction about the extreme vulner-
ability of women to such temptation that led many moralists to
recommend that women stay safely at home, out of harm's way.
It was indeed one of the controversies of the time whether or not
the virtue of women should be put to the test. Juan Luis Vives
believes that it should: "[A]s St Hieronyme sayth she is chast
in dede that may do ivell and she liste and wull nat" (n.p.). Of
course, women had their defenders: one of the favourite rhetorical pastimes of the period was the famous "Querelle des Femmes,"
exercises in the epideictic rhetoric of praise and blame, using this
question as the subject.[3] Not everyone believed that women were
deficient in morality, or in reason either. Nevertheless, the weight
of opinion was against women – certainly enough to bring their
ethos into question should they dare to speak in public or venture
into publication.

In all three elements of *ethos*, therefore, women were seen as
deficient: they lacked the full measure of rationality possessed by
males, and as a consequence, they also lacked moral reliability. As
for the third category, goodwill: if the audience had no faith in a
woman's reason or in her morality, it was unlikely that they would
perceive her as having goodwill toward them. What good could
she do them? Hence, they would not extend their goodwill to her.

But woman's lack of *ethos* was not only a matter of her supposed
deficiency in reason and therefore in morals. It was also a question of decorum, a very strong element in rhetorical theory
from ancient times. In the third book of *Rhetorica*, for example,
Aristotle comments: "Even in poetry, it is not quite appropriate that fine language should be used by a slave, or a very young
man" (3.1.1404). In the Renaissance, considerations of decorum,
or propriety, were of the greatest importance, and it is not easy
to distinguish between the linguistic and the social. As Heinrich
Plett says: "Decorum has always comprised both a socio-ethical
and a socio-esthetical component" (366). In support of this claim,
Plett refers to George Puttenham's *The Arte of English Poesie*, where
the chapter on stylistic decorum is followed by another on social
decorum, "Of Decencie in behaviour which also belongs to the
consideration of the Poet or maker." Puttenham comments on the
difficulty of drawing a clear distinction between literary and social
decorum:

[A]nd there is a decency to be obserued in every mans action and behauiour aswell as in his speech and writing, which some peradaventure would thinke impertinent to be treated of in this booke, where we do but informe the commendable fashions of language and stile; but that is otherwise, for the good maker or poet, who is in decent speech and good termes to describe all things, and with prayse or dispraise to report of euery mans behauiour, ought to know the comelinesse of an action aswell as of a word, & thereby to direct himselfe both in praise and perswasion or any other point that perteines to the Oratours arte. (181)

Puttenham is, of course, giving advice to the writer of fiction, but the principles he uses are drawn from contemporary codes of manners.

What one could do or say in public, then, was constrained by considerations of social status. The extent to which society depended upon the observance of "degree" is something that we with our democratic ideology find hard to understand. For a later age, democracy seems to guarantee freedom, something to which modern Western societies attribute the highest value. At the beginning of the seventeenth century in England, however, security seems to have been valued far more than individual freedom, and "degree" was thought to undergird that security. This conviction is well expressed in the speech Shakespeare puts in the mouth of Ulysses in *Troilus and Cressida*:

> *Take but degree away, untune that string,*
> *And hark what discord follows! Each thing melts*
> *In mere oppugnancy: the bounded waters*
> *Should lift their bosoms higher than the shores,*
> *And make a sop of all this solid globe;*
> *Strength should be lord of imbecility,*
> *And the rude son should strike his father dead;*
> *Force should be right; or rather, right and wrong –*
> *Between whose endless jar justice resides –*
> *Should lose their names, and so should justice too.*
> *Then everything includes itself in power,*
> *Power into will, will into appetite;*

And appetite, an universal wolf,
So doubly seconded with will and power,
Must make perforce an universal prey,
And last eat up himself. 1.3.109–24)

It is the loss of degree that John Donne laments in the famous passage from "An Anatomie of the World: The First Anniversary":

And new Philosophy calls all in doubt.
The Element of fire is quite put out,
The Sun is lost, and th'earth, and no man's wit
Can well direct him where to looke for it.
And freely men confesse that this world's spent,
When in the Planets and the Firmament
They see so many new; they see that this
Is crumbled out againe to his Atomies.
'Tis all in peeces, all cohaerence gone;
All just supply, and all Relation:
Prince, Subject, Father, Sonne, are things forgot,
For every man alone thinkes he hath got
To be a Phoenix, and that there can bee
None of that kinde, of which he is, but hee. (214)

Decorum was not just a trivial matter of "who goes first": indeed the observance of decorum in apparently trivial matters, such as the order of precedence, enacted and so reinforced that system which, it was thought, stood between civilization and the ultimate barbarity of "might is right." To quote Heinrich Plett:

Anyone who infringes them [the restraints normative] is not only violating a prevailing social convention but is ultimately calling the entire social and political system into question. The ruling monarch is the guarantor of its stability; the hierarchy of norms borne by him reflects feudal habits of thought. [...] Each of the three estates is accorded a style appropriate to it, be it in depiction, address, or self-expression: "the nature of the subiect" has ordained it thus. Nature in this case has the character of a topos used to sanction the existing hierarchy of values and society. (366–67)

Part of the prejudice against women's engaging in public discourse, then, was derived from this strong sense of the importance of observing decorum. Such observance entailed a recognition of one's place in the order of things, and in the Protestant England of the seventeenth century the proper place of a woman was in the shadow of her husband. It was almost the only place available to her.

It had not always been so. The situation had been very different in the Middle Ages. In a study of a woman of the early Enlightenment period, it may seem unnecessary to discuss the medieval status of women; however, Mary Astell drew her inspiration from medieval ideologies and institutions as well as from some of the philosophy current in her own time. It is important, then, to understand something of medieval ideas of the status of women and how they came to change. Few if any medieval women enjoyed full control over their lives – but then very few men did either. During the Middle Ages, however, in spite of the strictures of Aristotle via Thomas Aquinas, women were not thought of exclusively in terms of their service to men. In "Equality of Souls, Inequality of Sexes," an essay whose title nicely encapsulates the fundamental paradox, Eleanor Commo McLaughlin explains how medieval Christianity perceived the standing of the sexes and shows that in some respects, the medieval view gave women greater freedom than in subsequent centuries. It would, of course, be outrageous to suggest that the position of women in the Middle Ages was in general an enviable one. Women were both feared and despised, and they seldom had rights equivalent to those of the men of their class. Nevertheless, according to McLaughlin, the doctrines of Christianity, revolutionary at the beginning of the Christian era, had some effect upon a society which, in theory at least, upheld them. And Christian doctrine taught that, whatever might obtain in the secular and temporal world, in the spiritual and eternal state of things in the world to come, men and women were equal. St. Paul states: "In Christ there is no male or female" (Galatians 3:28). According to McLaughlin, there were thought to be two "orders": the order of creation, in which woman was subordinate to man, and the order of resurrection, in which she was his equal. In the society of the medieval period, which took matters of faith seriously, this distinction had some practical consequences. What it meant for women was that they were not seen exclusively as supporters of men, or helpmates, but spiritually, as persons in their own right, standing before God not as somebody's daughter or wife, but as themselves. Furthermore, marriage was not, in the spiritual hierarchy of the Middle Ages, the position of highest status for women. First came virginity; widowhood came second, with marriage a poor third.

It is important not to overrate the degree of respect accorded to women on these spiritual grounds. Practically, it often made very little difference; when a woman enjoyed respect, it was usually because of her social rather than her spiritual standing. Virgins were not always thought of as necessarily holy simply because they were unmarried, and widows had a bad time of it for the most part, though there is evidence that some of them, particularly among tradesmen and craftsmen, achieved a degree of independence.[4] Nevertheless, there were some advantages to be found in consequence of theologically held positions: for example, some at least of the virgins and widows found refuge in the life of the religious, a life that, especially in the earlier Middle Ages, offered possibilities for self-development. Probably as significant as any practical benefit, however, was a general state of mind that to some extent took a woman seriously as a person in her own right, not the mere adjunct of the man.

If in the spiritual scheme of things women enjoyed some recognition of their independence from men, in high feudalism they enjoyed, to a certain degree, both privilege and power. Of course, this power and privilege applied only to women of the nobility; yet it had implications, perhaps, for other women too. "Feudalism, as a system of private jurisdiction, bound power to landed property; and it permitted both inheritance and administration of feudal property by women. Inheritance by women often suited the needs of the great landholding families, as their unremitting efforts to secure such rights for their female members attest" (Kelly-Gadol 144). Not only might a woman on occasion inherit property: during her lord's absence, which frequently occurred during times of warfare, she acted as his deputy. She became, in his absence, the lord to whom vassals owed allegiance.

Reflecting this feudal relationship of vassalage, there arose the phenomenon of courtly love, in which the lover was the servant and the lady was spoken to as "midons," a form of address used in feudalism by the vassal to his lord (Lewis 2). Now it is perhaps true that courtly love existed primarily as a literary convention; nevertheless, literature and life impact upon each other, and some of the ideals of courtly love have survived even into twenty-first-century social practice. At the time, the convention of courtly love served to some degree to raise the profile of the lady and to give her some emotional and even spiritual significance. At a time when marriages were arranged to suit the concerns of landholders to maintain and increase their property, with little regard to the feelings of either the woman or the man, courtly love served to humanize the relation between the sexes. Joan Kelly-Gadol associates this phenomenon with the influence of Christianity, particularly its recognition of the importance of love, its key virtue.

> In Christian Europe *passion* acquired a positive, spiritual meaning that classical ethics and classical erotic feeling alike denied. Religious love and courtly love were both suffered as a destiny, were both submitted to and not denied. Converted by a passion that henceforth directed and dominated them, and for which all manner of suffering could be borne, the courtly lovers, like the religious, sought a higher emotional state than ordinary life provided. (143)

It is this insistence upon love, indeed, that characterizes the accommodation of classical rhetoric to the new Christian culture, achieved by St. Augustine of Hippo in *On Christian Doctrine*.[5] It must be recognized, of course, that the strong adulterous element to be found especially in the earliest manifestations of courtly love was in direct conflict with Christian morality. Nevertheless, as a means of providing an ideology in which women were seen as powerful figures, commanding not only respect but also devotion, even obedience, courtly love was a powerful force in the Middle Ages.

This state of affairs was disturbed – even challenged – in the first instance not by the Reformation but by the Renaissance. As Régine Pernoud has argued, what really distinguished the Renaissance was not so much the rediscovery of ancient texts as a new attitude toward classical civilization, one that took classical culture as a model to be followed. This was associated with a move to replace the ideal of the *via contemplativa* with the *via activa*.[6] The men of the Renaissance, following Cicero, saw the ideal human being as one fully engaged with the world. For women, according to Pernoud, this meant a return to classical ideas about their function and position that entirely disregarded their standing as spiritual entities. Kelly-Gadol, on the other hand, associates the decline in women's status with the rise of the nation-state: as the feudal system weakened and gave place to statism, the power of the nobleman dwindled into that of a mere courtier, seeking only to influence his prince. In the same way, the power of the lady receded until her major role was only to exercise charm: she too possessed now only the ability to influence, rather than to exercise power (Kelly-Gadol 150).

To some extent, the effects of the return to the values of classicism and the rise of statism were mitigated so far as women were concerned by Christian humanism. Important in this movement were certain royal and aristocratic women who served as patrons of the new learning and encouraged the education not only of boys but of young girls as well. For example, Isabella of Castile (patron of Christopher Columbus) employed Beatrix Gelindo, a female professor of rhetoric at the University of Salamanca, to teach her daughter, Catherine (Donawerth, "Politics" 316). Catherine became the first queen of Henry VIII of England. Educated herself, Catherine was concerned that her daughter Mary (later Mary I) should receive the best available instruction. She therefore invited to England, as tutor for her daughter, the Christian humanist scholar Juan Luis Vives, who had worked with Erasmus and had indeed written *The Instruction of a Christen Woman* for Catherine while she was still a young princess; for Princess Mary he wrote *Plan of Study for Girls* (Glenn 129). Like other notable Christian humanist scholars of his time – Desiderius Erasmus, Thomas More, and Thomas Elyot – Vives believed that girls should be educated. All these men wrote on the subject, questioning the traditional belief that women were incapable of receiving a fully intellectual education. Sir Thomas Elyot, in *The Defence of Good Women*, denies that women are lacking in either reason or morality: "I see well inoughe that women beinge well and vertuously brought up do not onely with men participate in reason, but som also in fidelity and constancie be equall unto them" (22).

But it is dangerously easy to overestimate the significance of such support, and even its nature: Erasmus defends the education of women on the grounds that it prepares them for marriage, and Elyot's Widow Zenobia asserts that the chief value of the moral philosophy that she and her women friends studied was to teach them the importance of being obedient wives: they "learned to honour [their] husbands nexte after God; which honour resteth in due obedience" (qtd. in Woodbridge 20). Erasmus and Elyot, Luis Vives, and Sir Thomas More, in spite of believing that a woman can and should be educated, nevertheless do not believe that she ought to enter public life. Her proper (that is, appropriate) sphere of influence is the home. A letter from Sir Thomas More to his scholarly daughter, Margaret Roper, refers to her "singular love of virtue, the pursuit of literature and art." He continues:

> Content with the profit and pleasure of your conscience, in your modesty you do not seek for the praise of the public, nor value it overmuch if you receive it, but because of the great love you bear us, you regard us – your husband and myself – as a sufficiently large circle of readers for all that you write. [...] In your letter you speak of your imminent confinement. We pray most earnestly that all may go happily and successfully with you. May God and Our Blessed Lady grant you happily and safely to increase your family by a little one like to his mother in everything except sex. Yet let it by all means be a girl, if only she will make up for the inferiority of her sex by her zeal to imitate her mother's virtue and learning. Such a girl I should prefer to three boys. (155)

Even the enlightened Thomas More, then, still believed that women were naturally inferior to men, though he also believed that they could correct the deficiency by education. What comes out most clearly, however, is his conviction that his daughter should not make her scholarship public: it is for the benefit of her family alone. Erasmus too saw woman in terms of her family relationships, and although like More he recommended the education of women, he also, like More, believed that the function of the married Christian woman was to support and serve her husband.

But what of the Reformation? It has sometimes been assumed that women's position improved significantly under the Protestants. In some respects it did, but not in all. Both advantages and disadvantages were related to revolutionary Protestant ideas about marriage. The reformers challenged the asceticism of the Fathers and disputed the interpretation of Scripture with Roman Catholic theologians. The reforming theologians cited such passages as

Hebrews to support their view that marriage was a praiseworthy state, in no way inferior to virginity: "Marriage is honourable in all and the bed undefiled: but whoremongers and adulterers God will judge" (Heb.13:4). Whereas the medieval church had honoured virginity and celibacy in both sexes above marriage, the reformers, on the contrary, elevated marriage to a new dignity and status. Women's sexual activity was no longer seen as shameful. In a letter written to three nuns in 1524, Luther has this to say: "Women are ashamed to admit this, but Scripture and life reveal that only one woman in thousands has been endowed with the God-given aptitude to live in chastity and virginity. [...] God fashioned her body so that she should be with a man, to have and rear children. [...] No woman should be ashamed of that for which God intended her" (qtd. in O'Faolain and Martines 196).

Woman's predisposition toward sexual activity was affirmed – in marriage at least. But outside marriage, her opportunities were increasingly curtailed. In Protestant countries, there was no longer the refuge of the nunnery for the unmarried or the widowed, and within marriage, the woman's position was dictated by the idea of the unity of the flesh. This was of course not a new idea: it is, at least according to one interpretation, set forth in the account of the creation of woman in Genesis 2. However, at this time, among the early Protestants who denied the impurity of the sex act itself, it received a new emphasis. The mystical unity of man and wife appealed strongly to the reformers because they saw marriage as a metaphor for the relationship between Christ and the church. This draws upon the older use of the same metaphor to express the relationship between Yahweh and the people of Israel. The Christian metaphor is used by the writer of the epistle to the Ephesians to suggest to husbands that their treatment of their wives should be as self-sacrificial as was that of Christ for his bride, the church:

> Husbands, love your wives, even as Christ also loved the church, and gave himself for it; That he might sanctify and cleanse it with the washing of water by the word, That he might present it to himself a glorious church not having spot, or wrinkle, or any such thing; but that it should be holy and without blemish. So ought men to love their wives as their own bodies. He that loveth his wife loveth himself. For no man ever yet hated his own flesh; but nourisheth and cherisheth it, even as the Lord the church: For we are members of his body, of his flesh and

of his bones. For this cause shall a man leave his father and mother, and shall be joined unto his wife, and they shall be one flesh. This is a great mystery: but I speak concerning Christ and the church. Nevertheless, let every one of you in particular so love his wife even as himself; and let the wife see that she reverence her husband. (Eph. 5:25–33)

I have quoted the passage in full, in the version that would have been familiar to seventeenth-century Englishwomen. The writer expresses a kind of mutuality in the marriage relationship, which was innovative in his time – that is, the first century of the Christian era. However, it is the traditional subjection of the wife to the husband that was most often stressed by the moralists of the Reformation. The doctrine of the unity of the flesh was interpreted to mean that there was indeed one person, but that person was the husband. As Edmunde Tilney puts it in *The Flower of Friendshippe*, "the wise man may not be contented only with his spouse's virginity, but by little and little must gently procure that he maye also steale away her private will, and appetite, so that of two bodies there may be made one onely hart, which she will soone doe, if love raigne in hir" (32). Robert Burton's *Anatomy of Melancholy* demonstrates the same understanding of the marriage relationship:

> Such should conjugal love be, still the same, and as they are one flesh, so should they be of one mind, one consent, Geryone-like; the same. A good wife, according to Plutarch, should be as a looking-glass, to represent her husband's face and passion. If he be pleasant, she should be merry; if he laugh, she should smile; if he look sad, she should participate of his sorrow, and bear a part with him, and so they should continue in mutual love one towards another. (3:59)

Obviously, the instructions of the writer of Ephesians were interpreted in accordance with classical ideas of the wife's position, though there were some moralists who also stressed the husband's responsibilities. In the cultural values of the time, as in the law, the wife was subsumed under the person of the man. Woman had her place, but that place was in her husband's shadow.

What did filling that place entail? It meant that man and woman had different functions in the social scheme of things, functions that were complementary: he was to be concerned with the public world, she with the private. However, the situation was more complex than it might appear. As Ruth Kelso has shown, one of the inconsistencies of the period was not only that men and women were supposed to live by different codes, but also that the codes themselves derived from different traditions: "The moral ideal for the lady [of the Renaissance] is essentially Christian [...] as that for the gentleman is essentially pagan. For him the ideal is self-expression and realization. [...] For the lady the direct opposite is prescribed. The eminently Christian virtues of chastity, humility, piety, and patience under suffering and wrong, are the necessary virtues" (36). The pagan code referred to by Kelso was the Aristotelian code of magnanimity; but the Renaissance concept of the ideal citizen-orator, derived from classical models, was yet different from them in that it recognized the individual person as the ancients did not. As Tita French Baumlin says, "This new consciousness of self and of man's power to shape it characterizes Renaissance discourse" (231).[7] Language was beginning to be seen as the tool whereby a man created his image, and since the time of Machiavelli, it had been recognized that this public image might be to some degree a fabrication. "Seeming rather than being good is most crucial to the political success of the prince [...] for 'having [the qualities expected in a good and just ruler] and always conforming to them would be harmful, while appearing to have them would be useful'" (Baumlin 236). Part of the Renaissance gentleman's duty, then, was to fashion for himself a persuasive identity, to give himself, in other words, a voice:

> [I]f the English humanists never managed to produce a coherent rhetorical theory, and they didn't, at least through their mishmash of Ciceronianism and Christianity they showed people what voice is. In humanism, voice, character, self, and *ethos* all have the same meaning, for rhetorically they all come down to one quality: a sense of a person speaking to other people. (Sloane, qtd. in Baumlin 230)

But fashioning her own identity and finding her own voice were forbidden to the Renaissance woman. Her identity, as we have seen, was subsumed under that of her husband, and pre-eminent among the virtues she was supposed to possess was that of silence: it was the feminine equivalent of the masculine virtue of eloquence.

Indeed, in Aristotle's *Politics*, we read: "We must therefore hold that what the poet Sophocles said of woman 'A modest silence is a woman's crown' [...] contains a general truth, but a truth which does not apply to men" (44). This dictum was partially based on an assumed connection between speaking and sexual activity that dates back at least as far as Aristotle, and forward at least as far as Darwin, if not beyond. Aristotle held that mental activity depleted the strength women had available for their unborn children: "Children evidently draw on the mother who carries them in the womb, just as plants draw on the soil" (qtd. in Jamieson 68). And Darwin believed that whereas the female used her strength to form ova, the male expended "much force in fierce contests with rivals, in wandering about in search of the female, *in exerting his voice*" (italics added) (Jamieson 68). Quintilian also saw a connection between sexual activity and speaking:

> [P]hysical robustness is essential to save the voice from dwindling to the feeble shrillness that characterises the voices of eunuchs, women, and invalids, and the means for creating such robustness are to be found in walking, rubbing-down with oil, abstinence from sexual intercourse, an easy digestion, and, in a word, the simple life. (11.1.2, 19)[8]

Connected with this idea of the mutual exclusivity of fertility and eloquence was the association made between volubility and unchastity. In his *The Excellencie of Good Women*, Barnabe Rich asserts that "a Harlot is full of words" (qtd. in Woodbridge 77). It seemed to follow that one who was full of words was a harlot. Tita French Baumlin cites a number of sixteenth-century moralists who made this connection between loquaciousness and unchastity:

> As Thomas Bentley points out (1582) a woman who breaks "silence [...] is no more a maid, but a strumpet in the sight of God" (sig. A2). This sentiment is proverbial: "an eloquent woman is never chaste," appears from the fifteenth century on (Labalme 139, 150). [...] Robert Cleaver (1598) offers "her talke or speech, or rather her silence as a 'signe' denoting a woman's chastity" (95). (241)

A talkative woman was more likely to be accused of witchcraft than was a silent woman: "In Essex County, Massachusetts, more 'witches' were convicted of 'assaultive speech' than any other crime. [...] Encompassed in such assaults were 'slander,' 'defamation,' 'filthy speeches,' and 'scandalous speeches'" (Jamieson 75). The situation was similar in England. The punishment for inappropriate speech could thus be execution: "At the stake, fire, a metaphor for speech, consumed the witch and her ability to speak. Alternatively, fiery words were drenched permanently by drowning" (75). Less drastic, but still sufficiently unpleasant, were the ducking stool and the "Skimmington Ride": In the former, the loquacious woman was ducked in the local pond; in the latter, she was made to wear the brank, a sharp bridle, and was driven through the community to be mocked and vilified.

The woman who became an eloquent speaker or writer, then, was believed to be in some way betraying her sex. Sometimes she was accused of harlotry, sometimes even of witchcraft. At the very least, she might be seen as something less than, other than, a true woman – something unnatural. This sense of the woman as transgressing against her own gender comes out strongly in the references to speaking and writing women as androgynous. In her discussion of Ben Jonson's *Epicoene, or The Silent Woman*, Cheryl Glenn notes that the Collegiate Ladies were said to be "'rather hermaphroditical,' *epicoene*, in fact, monstrously unnatural. [...] So for Jonson, androgyny can be the only acceptable explanation for autonomous women. And misogyny is the only solution" (134). The "hermaphroditical authority" with which these women spoke was felt to be against nature (134). The hermaphrodite, according to Ian Maclean, was "firmly placed in the category of monsters by renaissance physiologists" (12). Women who stepped out of the stereotypical behaviour could be regarded as unsexing themselves. For example, when Lady Macbeth resolves upon a course of cruelty, thought to be untypical of women, she calls upon the spirits to "unsex me here" (1.5.40).

A woman could not normally retain the respect accorded to her gender if she transgressed against what were thought to be its characteristics. Kathleen Hall Jamieson shows that this prejudice goes back to antiquity:

> If a wife '*wants to appear educated and eloquent*,' noted Juvenal, '*let her dress as a man, sacrifice to men's gods, and bathe in the men's baths*.' This aspiration was not taken to be the sincerest form of flattery because, said women's rights opponents, '*when she*

unsexes herself, and puts on the habiliments and claims to exercise
the masculine functions of man in society, she has lost the position
which she should occupy. When woman violates the law which God
has given her, she has no law, and is the creature of hateful anarchy.'
(77)

Here we see clearly that insistence upon "degree," the hierarchical
placement of every creature, which during the Renaissance guaranteed a defence against the terrifying possibility of anarchy.

However, there was an exception to this rule: according to most
authorities, if the woman concerned were a monarch, she was
allowed, even expected, to act in accordance with the masculine
code of behaviour. "The princess is, as it were, a man by virtue of
her birth, and hence the masculine standard of morality applies to
her" (Maclean 62). Her status as a "prince," then, took precedence
over her gender; though even this dictum could be questioned, and
of course was questioned, notably by John Knox in his tract *The*
First Blast of the Trumpet against the Monstrous Regiment of Women.
What Knox is questioning here, however, is not specifically the
propriety of public speech by the female monarch, but the legiti-
macy of the female monarch herself. That a woman should rule
is, for him, "monstrous" – a distortion, a malformation, of the way
things should be. Elizabeth I, the finest and most successful of
Renaissance princes, was well aware of the gender confusion that
her position as monarch involved.[9] She not only negotiated it very
carefully; she even exploited it, so as to give herself the advantages
of both sexes at once. As Leah S. Marcus says, "We can observe
her building the myth of her own androgyny" (137). Consummate
politician that she was, she was able to appeal to her subjects'
loyalty on the ostensibly weak grounds that she was only a woman;
yet at the same time she claimed the heart of a king, "and a king of
England too" (qtd. in Thompson 392). In her Golden Speech, she
assumed the virtues, not just of queenship but also of kingship – an
almost perfect example of androgyny:

> To be a king and wear a crown is more glorious to them that
> see it than it is pleasure to them that bear it. For myself, I was
> never so much enticed with the glorious name of a king or royal
> authority of a queen as delighted that God hath made me this
> instrument to maintain His truth and glory, and to defend this

kingdom, as I said, from peril, dishonour, tyranny and oppression. (qtd. in Thompson 392)

Mindful that the first duty of a man, especially a king, was courage, she stressed her lack of fear, and praised God, "Who hath ever yet given me a heart which never yet feared foreign or home enemies" (393). However, she never forgot or denied that she was a woman; she acknowledged her gender and its disabilities frankly, and by doing so, turned them into strengths. The humility topos was never more effectively used. The paradoxical nature of her exploitation of both genders, of her manipulation of androgyny, is well expressed by Tita French Baumlin:

> In Elizabeth's textualized self, authority and Other are met in one. In her case, the cultural identifications of authority and alien oscillate: as a monarch she wields great power; yet as a woman, she is marginalized by the power she represents. Any assertion of her authority requires that she alienate herself and call attention to her alienness [...] that she invoke, ultimately to subvert, the rhetoric of silence enforced on her gender. (254)

Elizabeth I was able to negotiate her dual self, the sovereign and the woman, in part because she was a virgin: to some extent, a woman became exempt from the weaknesses of her gender by renouncing her sexuality. Although in the Protestant England over which Elizabeth ruled, the virgin was, in theory, no longer respected above the married woman, in practice Elizabeth was able to draw upon a long tradition of respect for the virgin, which added to the mystical qualities of kingship that other mystique that belonged to virginity. And of course her virginity, or at least her unmarried state, allowed her to retain the power in her own hands: had she married, that power would have been transferred to her husband. The difficulty of finding a husband who would be acceptable to her people may in part explain why she never married; however, it is just as likely that she wished to retain her power herself. Although Elizabeth died at the beginning of the seventeenth century, well before Astell's time, the legacy of her achievements was of inestimable value to the women of later generations. For Elizabeth had demonstrated, to put it crudely, that a woman could beat the men at their own game: one of the most successful of England's monarchs, she was also one of the most powerful women in Western history.

Women – and men – of succeeding centuries looked back to her reign as the golden age; and there is no doubt that her *ethos* was a source of confidence and strength to the women who came after her.[10]

In nearly every respect, then, a woman's personality and activity were to be different from a man's. And if the creation of his identity through language was one of the more important duties of the man, it was silence that characterized the good Renaissance woman.[11] The practice of rhetoric, therefore, was seen to be inappropriate in women, but some moralists – Leonardo Bruni, for example – held that they should avoid even the study of it. In a letter to Baptista Malatesta, outlining a suitable course of study for women, he specifically excludes certain kinds of study, among them rhetoric:

> You will be surprised to find me suggesting (though with much […] hesitation) that the great and complex art of rhetoric should be placed in the same category [of excluded studies]. My chief reason is the obvious one, that I have in view the cultivation most fitting to a woman. To her, neither the intricacies of debate nor the oratorical artifices of action and delivery are of the least practical use, if indeed they are not positively unbecoming. Rhetoric in all its forms – public discussion, forensic argument, logical defence and the like – lies absolutely outside the province of woman. (qtd. in Kersey 23)

As Ruth Kelso explains, rhetoric "was under suspicion as leading to vain exhibitions of mere verbal skill, clashing most of all with the desired unobtrusiveness of a woman who held her tongue" (76).

It must be remembered, however, that the rhetoric from which women were excluded so rigorously was *contentio*. Bruni himself was indeed one of the earliest scholars to promote this kind of rhetoric in the Renaissance. As John Tinkler observes, it was Bruni who, with Vergerio, "developed humanist oratory" (285). As we have seen, so long as they did not "go public" and draw attention to themselves before men, women were free to engage in the arts of *sermo*, whether in conversation or in the writing of letters.

To conclude then: deficient in all the requirements of *ethos* – rationality, moral reliability, and goodwill – and inhibited by considerations of propriety that denied her the right to go public, the woman writer of the Renaissance who wished to publish her work faced enormous obstacles. Nevertheless, an increasing number of women did indeed write and publish, making their voices heard in spite of the fact that they were not supposed to have any. By the time of Mary Astell, a significant number of women had published, most of them anonymously, and their work had received some recognition. The prejudice against women as public figures had by no means disappeared. Yet certain philosophical ideas current in the seventeenth century – some old and some quite new – encouraged women to develop a stronger sense of their own powers and gave them the confidence to participate in the intellectual life of the community. It was upon these philosophies that Astell drew in embarking upon her career as a thinker and writer at the end of the seventeenth century.

2

Mary Astell and the
Problem of *Ethos*

s we have seen, the consensus in the seventeenth century
was that women lacked all the requirements of *ethos*:
rationality, moral reliability, and goodwill.[1] In spite of
this prejudice, however, the number of women who wrote and
published their work increased significantly. These women faced
and solved the problem in a variety of ways. To mention only a
very few of them: Margaret Cavendish exploited it – notoriety
served her purpose of self-promotion; Bathsua Makin evaded it by
adopting the persona of a man; and Margaret Fell openly defied
it, justifying her position by providing alternative interpretations
of Biblical texts. But it was Mary Astell who argued cogently
against it.

The first requirement for any woman who thus transgressed
against accepted norms was necessarily a conviction that she had
both the right and the ability to publish her ideas. Surmounting the
many obstacles required an unusual strength of purpose, determination, and persistence, and without robust self-confidence, nothing could be achieved. Upon what strengths did women draw? The
women cited above resolved the problems of a woman's *ethos*, to their
own satisfaction at least, by identifying with a tradition other than
the Protestant bourgeois model of the private and silent domestic figure. Margaret Cavendish adopted the ideology of deliberate
display that belonged to the nobility; Bathsua Makin identified
herself with the Renaissance tradition of the learned woman that
developed in England in the sixteenth century; and Margaret Fell
considered herself to belong to the even older prophetic tradition
in which gender was irrelevant. Like other women, Astell refused
to align herself with ideals of silent and publicly inactive feminine
behaviour. Her inspiration and support derived from the ideas of
two schools of thought that dissented from the received opinion
of the time: on the one hand, she identified with the Christian
Platonists; on the other, she was supported in her belief in her own
powers as a woman by the Cartesians.

Astell derived her Christian Platonist ideas in the first instance, no doubt, from her uncle, Ralph Astell, who undertook her early education. Ralph Astell had been a member of Emmanuel College, Cambridge, the centre of the Cambridge Platonists, and there he had come under the influence of one of the most important of them, Ralph Cudworth. After the death of her uncle, Astell continued to read the works of the current Christian Platonists, in particular John Norris, with whom she corresponded. The influence of the Christian Platonist philosophy is apparent in all of Astell's works. It is particularly important in her resolution of the problem of *ethos*, for unlike the Aristotelians, the Christian Platonists had a high view of women.

Plato himself, in *The Republic* (and in the *Timaeus*) includes women among the guardians of the state, and makes no distinction between the sexes in their education:

> If then we are to employ women in the same duties as the men, we must give them the same instructions.
> Yes.
> To the men we gave music and gymnastics.
> Yes.
> Then we must train the women also in the same two arts, giving them besides a military education, and treating them in the same way as men. (*Republic V*, qtd. in Kersey 2)

Women, then, must be given the same education as men because they are expected to engage in the same kind of work and because they share the same nature: Socrates concludes that "we shall not have one education for men, and another for women, especially as the nature to be wrought upon is the same in both cases" (8).[2]

There is no question that Plato himself had a much higher opinion of women than did Aristotle. The Christian Platonists, however, had extended Platonic ideas by adding to them Christian principles. One of the Church Fathers who influenced their thought was Augustine of Hippo, who believed that "while woman might be inferior to man by nature, she was his equal by grace" (Schiebinger 169), and that in the mind "there is no sex" (Harth 3). Furthermore, the Christian Platonists believed that the feminine was an essential element in creation: "Neoplatonists [...] held that creativity – both intellectual and material – resulted from a union of masculine and feminine principles. The Neoplatonists described creation as the union of opposing male and female elements and made the joining of those elements the basis of all creativity. For Henry More, the masculine without the feminine was imperfect, incomplete" (Schiebinger 133). This view is obviously in contrast to the Aristotelian view, which, as we saw in chapter 1, holds that the male is perfect and the female deficient.

In asserting as she did the intellectual equality of the sexes, then, Astell had the full support of the tradition in which she was educated. And this strong sense not only of her own intellectual powers, but also those of women in general, had been strengthened by ideas arising from the philosophy of Descartes. Feminist opinion is deeply divided about the effect of Cartesian ideas on the position of women. Some modern feminists are inclined to see them as working against the interests of women.[3] Ruth Perry, however, argues that in the seventeenth century the effect of Descartes's philosophy was liberating. This is particularly true of Mary Astell. Perry goes so far as to claim that "Cartesian rationalism was the very cornerstone of her feminism" (Perry, "Radical Doubt" 491). Cynthia Bryson agrees: "What Astell sees in Descartes' method is the opportunity for self-determination, a goal which any individual who feels her or his social group has been denied it would wholeheartedly embrace" (43). These scholars support the view that Descartes did women a great service by dissociating the mind from the body. Women had been thought to be dominated by the body and its passions to such an extent that their reason was disabled. Descartes's philosophy allowed them to identify themselves with the rational and spiritual, to claim that the essential self was independent of the body altogether. If the intellect could thus be seen as disconnected from the body, women could challenge the prejudice that saw their reason as perpetually and inevitably inhibited and compromised by their emotions. As Bryson puts it, "The disembodied mind is the 'who' a person is, and the gendered body is meaningless to individuality and identity" (49). Furthermore, in challenging Aristotelian philosophy, Descartes began to unsettle the ancient doctrine of the humours that undergirded belief in women's inferiority: "The idea of man as a machine undermined the Aristotelian dictum that because women are colder than men they have a lesser reason" (Schiebinger 174). On a more practical level, Descartes helped to empower women by questioning the necessity of the long and complicated classical education and the process of traditional logical disputation as preliminaries to engag-

ing in the life of the mind. Furthermore, by his example he helped
to legitimize the use of the vernacular for scholarly purposes, thus
demonstrating that it was not necessary to be able to write in Latin
in order to engage in intellectual discussion. Astell certainly draws
upon Descartes's philosophy in her rhetorical theory. She also uses
his ideas to support her own sense of women's intellectual abili-
ties.[4]

Descartes himself, however, did not directly address the question of women's intellectual capacity; it was one of his followers
who applied Cartesian principles to this issue and in doing so
provided strong support for women engaging in scholarship and
particularly in rhetoric. François Poullain de la Barre (1647–1723)
was an ex-Jesuit who became converted to Cartesian thought in
1667. Thereafter, he devoted himself to working out some of the
implications of Descartes's ideas. His interest in the question of
women's intellectual powers arose from his perception that this
issue served as an effective demonstration of the utility of the
Cartesian method. As Daniel Frankforter and Paul Morman
put it, "[T]he issue of sexual inequality was an ideal vehicle for
[Poullain's] purpose. What better way to illustrate how social
custom – reinforced by the learned opinion of the ancients – creates
a heavy weight of prejudice that men (and women themselves)
accept as unquestioned fact?" (xxiii). In 1673 Poullain published *De
l'Egalité de deux Sexes*, in the preface of which he proposes to refute
both general and expert opinion. In the course of his argument,
he naturally considers the question of rhetoric. Girls, he claims,
have as much natural aptitude as boys, and are in many respects
superior:

> There is in their conversation the greatest vivacity, sprightliness
> and freedom. They more quickly comprehend what they are
> taught. When we pay them equal attention, girls are more dili-
> gent, and more patient at work, more obedient, more modest,
> and more self-controlled. In a word, we see in them to the high-
> est degree all the excellent qualities that are assumed when they
> are found in young men, to make these boys more fit than their
> fellows for great things. (35)

So far as articulacy is concerned, women, he believes, are definitely
superior. Of men, he says, "Only a few express themselves with
clarity, and the struggle they have to get their words out spoils

the flavour of whatever they can say [that is] of value" (37). He continues:

> Women, on the other hand, state what they know clearly and with order. Words cause them no trouble. They begin and continue as it pleases them. When they are at liberty, their imaginations are inexhaustible. They have the gift of presenting their ideas with a gentleness and good nature that works as well as reason in winning assent – while men, in their turn, usually employ a hard, dry style. (39)

Women, he says, express themselves gracefully. They acquire "more [knowledge] of language from practice alone than most men do from practice combined with study" (43). In fact, "no-one can dispute that eloquence is a natural talent peculiar to them. [...] There are women's letters on the topic of the passions, whose course constitutes the beauty and whole secret of eloquence. [...] All the rhetoric in the world could not give men this skill that costs women nothing" (45).

Women are competent in more than rhetoric, however. Poullain goes on to argue that they are, or could easily become, men's equals or superiors in medicine, philosophy, history, and law. In almost every respect, he believes, women are to be regarded as in no way inferior to men. The fact that they are so regarded he attributes to men's conspiracy to make them fearful, ignorant, and insecure:

> In everything that we make women learn, do we see anything that would contribute to instructing them soundly? On the contrary, it seems that we have agreed on this kind of education in order to diminish their courage, cloud their intellects, and fill their minds with nothing but vanity and foolishness – to stifle all the seeds of virtue and of truth in them, to render useless all the inclinations they might have to great things, and (by denying them the means) to deprive them of the desire to perfect themselves as we do. (157)

According to Ruth Perry, it was Poullain de la Barre's writings that "gave Astell her method of attack and thus prepared the way for both volumes of *A Serious Proposal*" (*Celebrated* 72). Poullain's *De l'Egalité des deux sexes* was published in 1673; in 1677 it was translated into English and published as *The Woman as Good as the Man.* But apparently the version that had the most influence in London was the 1690 French edition: "[I]t caused quite a stir in Paris, and in 1692 and 1693, parts of it were exported to London by a French Huguenot named Pierre Motteux. Astell may well have read these in *The Gentleman's Journal* or *The Ladies Journal*" (Perry, *Celebrated* 482).⁵ Supported, then, on the one hand by the conservative and backward-looking Neoplatonists and on the other by the forward-looking Cartesians, Astell challenges received opinion on the nature of woman: she denies that woman is inferior to man either intellectually or morally; she argues forcefully against the idea that the woman is made simply to serve the man; and she asserts that her talents are to be used in the public as well as in the private sphere.

Astell's most sustained argument for the full rationality of women is found in the Preface to the 1706, that is, the third edition of her *Some Reflections Upon Marriage.* Originally published in 1700, this work had drawn criticism, some of it based upon the conventional position that women were inferior to men. Astell set out to refute this claim, arguing from experience, from authority – that of Scripture – and from sheer reason, reinforcing her arguments by demonstrating the literal analogy between domestic and national governance. The constitutional crisis was the burning issue of the day. Astell's adroit association of the question of the status of women with the political question gave it prominence and immediacy.

Astell begins her argument for the full rationality of women by simply referring to experience. In this simple appeal to common experience, she shows her modernity. She does not appeal to ancient authorities, not even Plato, who had a relatively high opinion of women. Observe, she says. She declares that she was

> [i]gnorant of the *Natural Inferiority* of our Sex, which our Masters lay down as a Self-Evident and Fundamental Truth, She saw nothing in the Reason of Things, to make this either a Principle or a Conclusion, but much to the contrary. [...] For if by the Natural Superiority of their Sex, they mean that *every* Man is by Nature superior to *every* Woman, which is the obvious meaning, and that which must be stuck to if they would speak Sense, it wou'd be a Sin in *any* woman to have Dominion over *any* Man, and the greatest Queen ought not to command but to

obey her Footman, because no Municipal Laws can supersede or change the Law of Nature. (*Some Reflections* 9)

This argument had all the more force as Astell was writing during the reign of Queen Anne. She continues her appeal to common experience: "If they mean that *some* Men are superior to *some* Women this is no great Discovery; had they turn'd the Tables, they might have seen that *some* Women are superior to *some* Men" (10).

Astell goes on to give arguments from the authority of Scripture. These are in part conventional: she cites respected female figures from the Old Testament – Miriam, Deborah, Ruth, the Widow of Zarephah, Esther – in a way that had become standard since Christine de Pisan had written in defence of women in the fifteenth century.[6] However, some of Astell's citations of Scripture to defend her position are more original and show her powers of astute argumentation. In fact, she begins with an interpretation of certain debated texts from the New Testament epistles. Demonstrating her command of theology, she skilfully interprets these passages so that they support, rather than contest, the status of women. For example, she refers to I Corinthians 11:3, a verse that would appear to ground the inferiority of women in dogma: "But I would have you know, that the head of every man is Christ; and the head of the woman is the man; and the head of Christ is God." Here is what she says about it: "[N]o inequality can be inferred from hence, neither from the Gradation the Apostle there uses, that the Head of every Man is Christ, and that the Head of the Woman is the Man, and the Head of Christ is God, It being evident from the Form of Baptism, that there is no natural Inferiority among the Divine Persons, but that they are in all things Co-equal" (11). Thus arguing from the liturgy and the equality of the three persons of the Trinity, she establishes from the words of St. Paul himself that women are to be seen as the equals of men, spiritually speaking. In this she harks back to the Catholic theology of the Middle Ages, as influenced by St. Augustine, abandoning the sexism of the later Protestant approaches. She also adroitly argues from St. Paul's choice of specific words that women in general are not inferior to men:

But scripture commands wives to submit themselves to their own husbands; True, for which St Paul gives a mystical reason

(Eph. 5.22 etc.) and St Peter a Prudential and Charitable one (I St Peter 3) but neither of them derive that subjection from the Law of Nature. Nay, St Paul, as if he foresaw and meant to prevent this Plea, giving Directions for their Conduct to Women in general (I Tim. 2), when he comes to speak of Subjection, he changes his Phrase from Women, which denotes the whole Sex, to Woman, which in the New Testament is appropriated to a Wife. (*Some Reflections* 20)[7]

Astell does indeed accept the scriptural injunction that wives should obey their husbands, but she sees this as primarily a matter of convenience, saying nothing about their essential nature. The superiority is one of office only:

> We do not find that any Man thinks the worse of his own Understanding because another has superior Power; or concludes himself less capable of a Post of Honour and Authority, because he is not Prefer'd to it. How much time wou'd lie on Men's hands, how empty would the Place of Concourse be, and how silent most Companies did Men forbear to Censure their Governors, that is, in effect, to think themselves Wiser. Indeed Government wou'd be much more desirable than it is, did it invest the Possessor with a superior Understanding as well as Power. And if mere Power gives a Right to Rule, there can be no such thing as Usurpation; but a Highway-Man so long as he has strength to force, has also a Right to require our Obedience. (*Some Reflections* 16)

As is apparent in this quotation, Astell bases her arguments not only on Scripture, but also on the analogy of the government of the state.[8] Here she argues most strongly and compellingly, bringing to bear on the question of women's status the kind of reasoning that was constantly used at this time to determine political issues. Time and again, she draws a parallel between domestic and public economy. What goes for the one must surely be applicable to the other: "[W]hy is Slavery so much condemn'd and strove against in one Case, and so highly applauded and held so necessary and so sacred in another?" (19). The subjection of women is undeniable, but the fact that they are everywhere subordinate to men does nothing to prove their incapacity: "That the Custom of the World has put Women, generally speaking, into a State of Subjection, is not deny'd; but the Right can no more be prov'd from the Fact, than the Predominancy of Vice can justifie it" (10). That men have had a greater success in intellectual endeavours and public affairs Astell admits; but, like Poullain, she attributes this discrepancy to women's lack of the advantages of education: "For Sense is a Portion that God Himself has been pleas'd to distribute to both Sexes with an Impartial Hand, but Learning is what Men have engross'd to themselves" (21). She believes that given the same advantages of education, women would do much better. Finally, she argues that if indeed men believe that women are irrational, then they must treat them as they treat animals. To do otherwise is unfair: "But if Reason is only allow'd us by way of Raillery, and the secret Maxim is that we have none, 'tis the best way to confine us with Chain and Block to the Chimney-Corner" (29). It is unjust for men to declare that women have no reason, and then to expect them to behave reasonably.

If it is true that women are intellectually equal to men, what conclusions can be drawn about their purpose and their function? Astell argues that their primary function is to serve God: "['T]is certainly no Arrogance in a Woman to conclude, that she was made for the Service of God, and that this is her End. Because God made all Things for Himself, and a Rational Mind is too noble a Being to be Made for the Sake and Service of any Creature" (11). Milton, who was typical of the Puritans of his age, had thought otherwise: for him, even woman's spirituality is mediated by her husband. His Eve in *Paradise Lost* is subordinated to Adam: "He for God only,/ She for God in him" (4.299). He shows Eve as embracing this subordination willingly, even eagerly. When the Archangel Raphael and Adam are engaged in a philosophical discussion about astronomy, Eve withdraws to tend to her garden. But she does so, Milton is careful to explain, not because the intellectual level of the conversation is beyond her:

> *Yet went she not as not with such discourse*
> *Delighted, or not capable her ear*
> *Of what was high; such pleasure she reserv'd*
> *Adam relating, she sole Auditress;*
> *Her Husband the Relater she preferr'd*
> *Before the Angel, and of him to ask*
> *Chose rather. (8.48–54)*

For Milton, Eve's undisputed rationality does not preclude her absolute intellectual subservience to her husband. It is worth noting that in Milton's view this subservience dates from before the Fall: in the opinion of some moralists – referred to by Astell in *Reflections* (12) – woman's subjection was the result of the Fall, and her punishment for her part in it. But in *Paradise Lost* Milton grounds it deeply in her very reason for being.

For Mary Astell, on the other hand, service to a man is entirely subordinate to a woman's first responsibility, which is to serve God. How then is God to be served? The answer is interesting and a little unexpected from such a stern moralist as Astell: *"We ought as much as we can to endeavour the Perfecting of our Beings, and that we be as happy as possibly we may"* (*Serious Proposal, II* 83). Now it is true that she defines perfecting our being as including the patient endurance of trials (such as living with a cruel husband); but she also believes that a woman has an absolute duty to improve and develop the rational faculty that God has given her and that doing so will lead to her ultimate happiness:

> God does nothing in vain, he gives no power or Faculty which he has not allotted to some proportionate use, if therefore he has given to Mankind a Rational Mind, every individual Understanding ought to be employ'd in somewhat worthy of it. The Meanest Person shou'd think as Justly, tho' not as Capaciously, as the greatest Philosopher. And if the Understanding be made for the contemplation of Truth, and I know not what else it can be made for, either there are many Understandings who are never able to attain what they were design'd for, which is contrary to the Supposition that GOD made nothing in Vain, or else the very meanest must be put in the way of attaining it. (Serious Proposal, II 118)

However, the great gift of reason is not meant, she believes, to be used only for personal profit. It is also to be used for the benefit of the community:

> Our Faculties were given us for Use not Ostentation, not to make a noise in the world but to be serviceable in it, to declare the Wisdom, Power and Goodness, of the All-Perfect Being from whom we derive All our Excellencies, and in whose Service they ought Wholly to be employ'd. Did our Knowledge serve

no other purpose than the exalting us in our own Opinion, or in that of our Fellow Creatures, the furnishing us with Materials for a quaint Discourse, an agreeable Conversation, 'twere scarce worth while to be at the trouble of attaining it. But when it enlarges the Capacity of our Minds, gives us nobler Ideas of the Majesty, the Grandeur and Glorious Attributes of our adorable Creator, Regulates our Wills and makes us more capable of Imitating and Enjoying him, 'tis then a truly sublime thing, a worthy Object of our Industry: And she who does not make this the end of her Study, spends her Time and Pains to no purpose or to an ill one. (Serious Proposal, II 96)

This passage, although it provides us with a good grasp of Astell's fundamental convictions, is easy to misunderstand. In particular, her statement that we were put into the world "not to make a noise in it, but to be serviceable" seems to echo the bourgeois ideal of the silent woman. But the distinction she is making here is not between the silent, private woman and the public one, but between the woman who is merely ambitious for herself and the one who wants to serve her world. It is a question of motivation. "The true Christian," she asserts in *The Christian Religion*, "seeks a Reputation from Vertues of a public, not a private nature" (325). Astell in fact challenged the prejudice against women's participation in public affairs. Although she did not believe that women should engage in public speaking,[9] it is apparent from her own practice that she herself did her best to contribute to the public good. What she could not achieve in her own person, she accomplished through her writing. Andrew Hiscock has drawn attention to the importance of writing as a way of reconciling a woman's desire to contribute to the common good with society's determination to relegate her to the private sphere. Of Margaret Cavendish, he observes that she "appears to have been fascinated by the ways in which the printed word allowed her access to the stage of oratory without necessitating physical performance or presence" (411). The same is true of Mary Astell: she did not content herself with a private and domestic exercise of her powers, but entered into some of the most important political discussions of her day. For her, this was part of being serviceable in the world, something to which she believed she had been called. Her talents were such that they could not be fully used merely in a private capacity.

As for Astell's own views about *ethos*, it is not surprising to find that she takes a Platonic position. She makes her most explicit statement on this question in the Preface added to the 1706 third edition of *Some Reflections Upon Marriage*. There had been extensive speculation about the authorship of this work, which, like all of Astell's writing, was published anonymously. In fact she had heard that a certain gentleman had claimed to have written it himself (8). Astell is impatient of all such speculation:

> If any is so needlessly curious as to enquire from what Hand they [the *Reflections*] come, they may please to know, that it is not good Manners to ask, since the Title-Page does not tell them. [...] 'Tis a very great Fault to regard rather who it is that Speaks, than what is Spoken; and either to submit to Authority, when we should only yield to Reason; or if Reason press too hard, to think to ward it off by Personal Objections and Reflections. (7)

In this insistence on the importance of relying upon manifest truth rather than upon the reputation of the speaker, Astell's position is very close to that of Plato:

> [T]he priests in the sanctuary of Zeus at Dordona declared that the earliest oracles came from an oak tree, and men of their time, who lacked your modern sophistication, were simple-minded enough to be quite satisfied with messages from an oak or a rock if only they were true. But truth is not enough for you; you think it matters who the speaker is and where he comes from. (*Phaedrus* 275)

Concerned as she was to defend women and to establish their reputation as intellectually and morally the equals of men, Astell still believed that a text could, and should, carry its own authority within it. Its authorship by a woman – in her publications Astell often acknowledged her sex, though not her name – should not detract from its persuasive appeal, for this should be to reason, not to extrinsic *ethos*.

Mary Astell, then, addressed the question of woman's *ethos* by powerfully arguing the case for the full competence of women to engage in the life of the mind. She believed women to be no less intelligent and no less virtuous than men. If they appeared to be deficient in either mental grasp or moral behaviour, it was only because they had been denied the kind of education that would develop their potential. Women were made for God, not for men, and service to God implied the full use of God-given talents, not only for personal development in spirituality, but also for the common benefit of the world at large. In her own practice she acted upon her conviction that, at least for women like herself, using those talents would involve venturing beyond the private sphere of activity. Identifying herself with the Christian Platonists, and drawing upon Cartesians such as Poullain de la Barre for support, she offered one of the most compelling defences of women of her time.

Part II

Mary Astell's Rhetorical Practice

Letters Concerning
the Love of God

When in 1693 Mary Astell initiated a correspondence with John Norris, she was following a trend that had been developing throughout the seventeenth century.[1] As we saw in the last chapter, in the wake of revolutions in philosophy that discredited the necessity of years of formal education to prepare for the philosophical enterprise, a number of women began to study the works of philosophers and to engage in debate about them. Descartes and his followers had made it possible for women to indulge their interest in these matters without the benefit of an extensive education and even without leaving their own homes; the women found that they could engage in discussion and debate by means of correspondence.[2] Since letters were considered an acceptable genre for women, they could thus pursue their interests in philosophy without risking their reputation. Some of these correspondences were conducted between renowned scholars and ladies of the nobility: Descartes corresponded with his pupil and patron, Queen Christina of Sweden, and with Elizabeth, Princess of Bohemia; Henry More with Anne Finch, Viscountess Conway; and Joseph Glanville with Margaret Cavendish, Duchess of Newcastle. But by no means all the letter writers were eminent scholars or noble ladies. As Ruth Perry observes, at this time "learned correspondence became quite the rage" ("Radical Doubt" 476). According to Perry, Neoplatonists such as John Norris were especially devoted to these intellectual relationships conducted in letters (485). Before he embarked on the correspondence with Astell, he had already exchanged letters with Damaris Cudworth (later Masham) and had even dedicated a book to her, though she later repudiated his philosophy and adopted John Locke as her mentor. Norris had also corresponded with Mary, Lady Chudleigh. Both these women, and of course Astell herself, went on to publish their work. Perry suggests that this kind of learned correspondence served as a literary apprenticeship for many women who aspired to be writers (482). Certainly the correspondence with Norris gave

Astell, whose formal education had come to an end with the death of her uncle when she was thirteen, an experience of further education that we might compare with the modern graduate school. She was the kind of student every supervisor loves: highly intelligent, a critical thinker with independent judgement, not afraid to question and challenge the experts. She was already adept at argumentation, and Norris provided the challenge she needed to hone her skills and sharpen her wits still further. The opportunity of engaging in discussion with a noted scholar was crucial to her development as a writer: it was essential training in the process of scholarly enquiry. In this chapter, therefore, I shall first clarify the subject matter of the correspondence and then discuss in some detail what Astell learned from Norris.

The correspondence arose as the result of a question she addressed to him in September 1693. John Norris was eager to engage in such philosophical discussion, and the correspondence continued for the next year, overlapping with the writing and publication of her first book, *A Serious Proposal to the Ladies*. What was the objection that troubled Astell and led to her initiating the correspondence? The answer to this question involves some discussion of the tenets of the Cambridge Platonists, to whose philosophical principles, as we have seen, Astell had been introduced by her uncle. As an undergraduate at Cambridge, Ralph Astell had studied under Ralph Cudworth, one of the most famous of the Cambridge Platonists. These were a group of Anglican clergymen associated with Cambridge University, many of them connected with Emmanuel College, to which Ralph Astell belonged.[3] They were Platonists not in any strict sense of the word but in associating themselves with "the whole tradition of spiritualist metaphysics from Plato to Plotinus" (Copleston 54). The founder of this group known as the Cambridge Platonists, Benjamin Whichcote, reacted against the rather dour Puritanism of his upbringing and drew upon the Neoplatonic tradition of spirituality to assert a more optimistic view of human nature. Yet the Cambridge Platonists were also strongly Christian. They stood for the essentials of Christianity, with which all Christian sects could agree: "With regard to dogmatic differences, they [...] tended to adopt a tolerant and 'broad' outlook" (55). They stood, on the one hand, against the negative view of humanity represented by the Puritans, and on the other, against the growing atheism and materialism of their time. As Copleston says, "[T]hey were not in tune with either the empiricist or the religious movements of their time and country" (56). Here are some of their principal tenets:

1. A belief in "the inner light." One of the favourite sayings of the founder of the movement, Benjamin Whichcote, was a quotation from Proverbs 20:27: "The spirit of man is the candle of the Lord."

2. A belief in reason. This did not mean that they rejected revelation – quite the contrary. But they believed that God-given reason ("the candle of the Lord") was to be used in interpreting revelation. "Reason discovers what is natural; and Reason receives what is supernatural" (Whichcote, qtd. in Cassirer 40).

3. A belief in the fundamental importance of morality. Religion is not simply a matter of correct intellectual grasp; it must also be concerned with morality – that is, the will. Ernst Cassirer illuminates this position:

[T]he Cambridge conception of religious reason cannot be derived from the power of thinking alone. The presupposition shared by all these men is that the real instrument of religion is not to be looked for in thought and discursive inference. They combat logical as well as theological dogmatics, and dogmatics of the understanding as well as those of faith. For in both they see an obstacle to that pristine grasp of the divine which can spring only from the fundamental disposition of the will. These rationalists could also have assented to Pascal's famous definition of faith: [...] "[T]his is what faith is: God felt in the heart, not in the head." For like Pascal they distinguished sharply between the "order of the heart" and the "order of the understanding." In the former are the substance and real object of religion. (31)

4. The paramount importance of love. Here the Christian and the Platonic coincide, for Christianity holds love to be the most important of the virtues (I Cor. 13). Ultimately the relationship between God and humankind is one of love. Augustine, one of the influences on the Cambridge Platonists, enlarges on the importance of love not only in his *Confessions* but also in *On Christian Doctrine*. And for Plato, too, it is a key concept: for example, in the *Phaedrus*

and the *Symposium*, he makes clear his doctrine of the importance of love.[4] Cassirer believes that it is the centrality of love in the philosophy of the Cambridge Platonists that helps to distinguish them most clearly from the Puritans: "The outstanding peculiarity of Calvin's theology was that it conceived the relation between God and man not from the standpoint of love so much as from that of a rigorous justice" (75). Whichcote, on the other hand, believed that "the religious duty of man is fully exercised in the continuance of love" (74). Beyond the central dogmas, as put forward in the creeds, the Cambridge Platonists believed that dogmatic variation among Christians matters less than toleration, unity, and the maintaining of loving relationships.[5]

It was the study of love that engaged the most particular attention of the Cambridge Platonist, John Norris: "[T]he analysis of love was a subject that had interested Norris from the beginning of his literary career" (Acworth 154). By the time Astell wrote to him, he had already published several works on the subject. Since the death of her uncle, Astell had continued to interest herself in this philosophy and to adopt many of its principles. However, hers was a critical mind, and she did not passively accept any ideas that were put forward. Her letter to Norris reveals her procedure as a scholar: she makes it a practice, she says, "to raise all the Objections that ever I can, and to make [the books she studies] undergo the Severest Test my Thoughts can put'em to before they pass for currant" (Norris and Astell 3). As a result of this strenuous criticism, she had come upon a difficulty – something she could not accept: if, as Norris states, God is the author of all our sensations, and if, as he further states, we love him because he is the cause of our pleasure – what about our pains? Is not God the author of them also?

> For if we must Love nothing but what is Lovely, and nothing is Lovely but what is our Good, and nothing is our Good but what does us Good, and nothing does us Good but what causes Pleasure in us; may we not by the same way of arguing say, That that which Causes Pain in us does not do us Good, (for nothing you say does us Good but what Causes Pleasure) and therefore can't be our Good, and if not our Good then not lovely, and

consequently not the proper, much less the only Object of our Love? (5)

This was the problem that prompted Astell to write to Norris, and it was the first topic of their extended correspondence, eventually published as *Letters Concerning the Love of God*. Astell represents herself to Norris as a humble enquirer seeking instruction, putting herself in the position of a pupil addressing the master: "I have brought my unwrought Ore to be refined and made currant by the Brightness of your Judgment, and shall reckon it a great Favour if you will give your self the Trouble to point out my mistakes" (46). Norris, who seems to have been a natural teacher as well as a philosopher, welcomed the opportunity to engage in correspondence with one who obviously had a brilliant though untrained mind:

> *I find you thoroughly comprehend the Argument of my*
> *Discourse, in that you have pitch'd upon the only material*
> *Objection to which it is liable; which you have press'd so*
> *well and so very home, that I can't but greatly admire*
> *the Light and Penetration of your Spirit. One of your*
> *clear and exact thoughts might easily satisfie your self in*
> *any Difficulty that shall come in your way, as having*
> *brightness enough of your own to dispel any Cloud that*
> *may set upon the Face of Truth. (Norris and Astell 9)*

However, he also takes seriously her wish to be corrected. In the course of the correspondence, therefore, he not only engages with her ideas, but also corrects her philosophical procedure and her method in writing. This instruction was especially important to her development as a practising rhetorician, for from him she learned the importance of thorough and painstaking enquiry in writing as well as thinking.

Norris recognized that Astell's main experience in discourse up to this point had been in conversation. Her method, therefore, reflected the typical conversational style: frequent changes of subject with little extension or depth of treatment. Accordingly, he advises her not to embark upon a new topic before the old one has been thoroughly exhausted:

*I would have these Subjects well fitted and chosen, that so we
may not enter upon a new Argument till that which was first
undertaken be thoroughly discharged, whereby we shall avoid
a Fault very incident to common Conversation (wherein new
Questions are started before the first is brought to an Issue) and
which makes the Discoursings of the most intelligent Persons
turn to so little an account. But this Fault so frequent and
almost unavoidable in the best Companies, is easily remedied
in Letters, and therefore since we are now fallen upon a noble
and sublime Subject, I desire we may go to the Bottom of it,
and not commence any new Matter till we have gone over all
that is of material Consideration in this of Divine Love. (54)*

He goes on to give her a projection of the structure of the present
letter: "I shall therefore first of all set down what by comparing
the several Parts of your Letter together I take to be your Notion.
Which when I have stated and considered, I shall reflect upon
some single Passages in your Letter that relate to it. And in this
you have the Model of the Answer that I intend" (56). In outlining
his own procedure, he also tactfully gives her a model for her own
scholarly discourse.

Norris was diplomatic in the advice he gave, but he could also
be severe. Here is one example of his criticism of her philosophical approach: "[A]s I am not satisfied with the Grounds of your
Distinction, so neither am I with the Use and Application you
make of it" (63). Two of her passages, he says, require particular comment: "One is, that mental Pain is the same with Sin,
the other is, that Sin is the only true Evil of Man" (74). Sin, he
explains, is an act and pain a passion: they cannot therefore be
identical; it is necessary to distinguish sin from its punishment. He
thus encourages her to think philosophically, making definitions
and distinctions, engaging in thoughts of greater complexity at a
deeper level.

Astell was immensely grateful for the help he gave her. Her social
life, though it brought her into contact with congenial ladies who
admired and supported her, offered little in the way of intellectual
stimulation. She must have been by far the most able thinker of her
circle. The chance to enter into discussion with someone whose
superior scholarship and wide philosophical experience could

challenge her own ideas gave her the necessary preparation for the work she was later to undertake. Her intellectual isolation as a single woman living outside the society of men whose education might have sparked her own ideas had made her thirsty for exactly the kind of challenge that Norris gave her. Not only did he engage in serious philosophical discussion with her, correcting her procedures and clarifying her ideas; he also recommended books to her and on one occasion sent a book for her to read. She thanked him for recommending the philosophy of Malebranche and wished she could read him in the original language. Knowing how much she needed a mentor, she gratefully acknowledged his help in Letter V, dated December 12, 1693, when the correspondence had continued for some months:

> *I have hitherto courted knowledge with a kind of Romantic Passion, in spite of all Difficulties and Discouragements: for knowledge is thought so unnecessary an Accomplishment on a Woman, that few will give them selves the Trouble to assist them in the Attainment of it. [...] But now, since you have so generously put into my Hand an Opportunity of obtaining what I so greedily long after, that I may make the best Improvement of so great Advantage, I give my self entirely to your Conduct, so far as is consistent with a rational not blind Obedience, bring a free and unprejudiced Mind to receive from your Hand such Gravings and Impressions as shall seem most convenient, and though I can't engage for a prompt and comprehensive Genius, yet I will for a docile Temper. (79)*

It is in this letter that she specifically requests further instruction. She meekly accepts his criticism of her hastiness and asks that when he thinks "we have sufficiently examined the Subject we are upon," he will instruct her in proper philosophical procedure: "I desire you to furnish me with such a System of Principles as I may rely on to give me such Rules as you Judge most convenient to initiate a raw Disciple in the Study of Philosophy: least for want of laying a good Foundation, I give you too much Trouble, by drawing Conclusions from false Premises, and making use of improper Terms" (102). Norris responds by assuring her that she has already corrected her philosophical error and that "all is right and as it should be" (104). In fact, he gives her what amounts to an excellent report: "Your Hypothesis, as you now explain and rectifie it, runs clear and unperplext, and has nothing in it but what equitably understood challenges my full Consent and Approbation" (104).

Yet though she has professed in this letter to have "a docile Temper," it is worth noting that she reserves the right to disagree with him: she qualifies her intellectual subordination to his instruction by refusing to give up her own right to judge according to what seems to her rational. She does not always see things his way, and she is not afraid to challenge him. As the correspondence continues, she gains confidence in her own powers, and even after it is finished she adds an appendix that offers a telling critique of his philosophical position. So Platonic is Norris that he argues that the duty of the Christian is to die to the material world. God does not need it: he can give the experience of sensation bypassing the body altogether. Astell disagrees: such a position, she argues, "renders a great Part of God's workmanship vain and useless" (278). She believes that God's acting through the body contributes more to his glory than bypassing it would do (282). Norris, in a brief response, maintains that Nature is a mere chimera, but declines to continue the discussion further. Furthermore, in spite of her respect for him, and her deferential tone, she can be as direct as he can. For instance, when Norris objects to her division of the soul into inferior and superiors parts, she admits that she is confused, but says that she found the distinction in his own work, citing the text, *Christian Blessedness*, and even giving the page number, 158. Norris is forced to defend himself, acknowledging that he does "make use of this Scheme of Speech" (109) but asserting that he is only using common popular parlance and that the distinction must not be taken literally. His defence is, in truth, a bit lame: Astell, perhaps without precisely meaning to, has caught him out.

As in most good tutorial relationships, then, the instructor is learning from the student as well as the student from the instructor. Norris is honest and generous enough to acknowledge that he has benefited both morally and intellectually from the correspondence: he has received "not only Heat but Light, intellectual as well as moral Improvement" (Preface n.p.). He continues: "to my knowledge I have never met with any that have so inlightened my Mind, inlarged my Heart, so entered and took Possession of my Spirit, and have had such a general and commanding Influence over my whole Soul as these of yours" (Preface n.p.). This is no mere flattery: according to R. Acworth, Astell had contributed significantly to Norris's most cherished philosophical project, the refinement of the philosophy of love. He was "greatly assisted by Mary Astell, an admirer of his writings" (172), and it was in fact she who convinced him to change his position: "[A]lthough Norris at first rejected Mary Astell's reasoning, insisting that pain was a real evil and that God was to be loved in spite of, and not because of, being its author, he came in the course of their correspondence to accept her basic point" (173).

As the discussion moves on to other matters on which they obviously think alike, Astell is encouraged to express her opinions and confess her problems without restraint. In these letters, she displays a freedom that seldom appears in her later works. Confident of the superior intellectual powers of her correspondent and trusting his discretion, she obviously does not feel that she has to tailor her discourse to his interests and understanding in any way that restricts her, and the result is a kind of confessional intimacy usually more typical of the diary than of the letter. On occasion, she appears to be meditating on paper rather than communicating: the love of God is "so divine a Cordial, that the least Drop of it is able to sweeten and outweigh all the troubles of this present State [...] and were it but largely shed abroad in our hearts we should be out of reach of Fortune" (99). Her audience in these passages would appear to be herself, or perhaps God, rather than another human being. The tone of the *Letters*, then, is quite different from that of *A Serious Proposal to the Ladies*, begun a little later but while the correspondence was still in progress. In that work, she is the mentor, and the tone reflects the stance she adopts toward the audience. In the *Letters*, it is she who is being mentored, at least in her view, and her tone is one of deference to his greater knowledge – a deference, however, that does not preclude her arguing forcefully with him when she disagrees.

There can be no doubt that it was the experience of corresponding with Norris that established the genre that Astell made her own. In her subsequent works, she uses the genre of the letter in both parts of *A Serious Proposal* and in *The Christian Religion*. It is true that our sense of the discourse as a personal letter recedes further and further into the background in successive works. In *The Christian Religion*, aside from providing the occasion for introducing the topic and from the very rare addresses to Lady Catherine, the form of the letter is scarcely noticeable. Yet it seems that it is the letter genre that allows her to move gradually from *sermo* to *contentio*. From private letter, to public letter, from public letter to political pamphlet – this is the transformation to be observed in Astell's career as a writer. With each publication her audience broadens, until at last she addresses the great public world of political interest.

However, when she wrote her first letter to Norris, Astell had no thought of publication. The idea had never crossed her mind. It took all Norris's powers of persuasion to get her to allow him to publish their correspondence. While writing the letters, she had supposed that she was engaged in private discourse, and therefore felt free to discuss intimate problems concerning her own emotions that she certainly would not have aired before a public audience. For example, she confides to Norris how hurt she has been by the indifference and ingratitude of her friends: "But though I can say without boasting that none ever loved more generously than I have done, yet perhaps never any met with more ungrateful Returns" (50). As the context makes clear, Astell is speaking here as the disappointed teacher: "Fain would I rescue my Sex, or at least as many of them as come within my little Sphere, from the Meanness of Spirit into which the Generality of 'em are sunk" (49). Perhaps her own intellectual loneliness contributed to her desire to educate the women she met socially. In any event, it appears that her well-intentioned instruction was not well received: most of them, she thought, did not aspire to any "higher Excellency than a well-chosen Pettycoat, or a fashionable Commode" (49). She attempts to adopt the Augustinian position recommended by Norris – that "we may seek Creatures *for* our good, but not love them *as* our good" – but finds it hard to achieve. She confesses that she is still motivated by something other than pure benevolence and that her response in not wholly rational: "for there's no Reason that we should be uneasie because others won't let us do them all the good we would" (50).

In the context of a private correspondence, Astell felt free to confide to Norris some of her most intimate concerns. She dreads the consequences of publishing these personal reflections: "For truly Sir, when we expose our Meditations to the World, we give them the Right to judge, and we must either be content with the Judgment or keep our Thoughts at home" (Preface n.p.). This acknowledgement of the reader's right to judge does not, however, prevent her from complaining bitterly in *The Christian Religion* that she is being judged (by the writer of *A Discourse Concerning the Love of God*) on what was originally a private correspondence (131). She is in fact distressed by Norris's insistence that the *Letters* ought to be published. She protests that publication would compromise her privacy, referring to "my darling, my beloved Obscurity, which I court and doat on above all Earthly Blessings" (Preface n.p.).

This desire for obscurity is naturally related to her sense of what is proper for a woman. She shrinks, indeed, from the very publicity value that her gender gives to the correspondence. For Norris, it appears to be an advantage. Part of the interest of the *Letters* lies in the astonishing fact that they are written by a woman: he refers to those readers who "from the surprizing Excellency of these Writings may be tempted to question whether my Correspondent be really a Woman or no" (Preface n.p.). His fulsome praise of her writing, sincere though it undoubtedly is, is given in this context of surprise that a woman could write so well. He refers to "such Choiceness of Matter, such Weight of Sense, such Art and Order of Contrivance, such Clearness and Strength of reasoning, such Beauty of Language, such Address of Style, such bright and lively Images and Colours of things, and such moving Strains of the most natural and powerful Oratory" (Preface n.p.). To Astell this appears to be mere vulgar showmanship, useful only "to decoy those to Perusal of them, who wanting Piety to read a book for its Usefulness, may probably have the Curiosity to inquire what can be the Product of a Woman's Pen" (Preface n.p.). Far from wishing to attract admiration for her unusual achievement, she considers it a pity that "it should be any bodies Wonder to meet with an ingenious Woman" (Preface n.p.). In the end, however, she admits that publication of her letters might do some good: it might "excite a generous emulation in my Sex, perswade them to leave their insignificant Pursuits for Employments worthy of them" (Preface n.p.). Reluctantly, Astell finally gives her permission for the publication of the Letters, but only on condition that her name does not appear, even in initials. A further requirement is that the work be dedicated to someone she will in due course name. Her nominee is her friend Lady Catherine Jones.

There can be little doubt that Astell agreed to the publication of the *Letters* principally to attract a wider public for *A Serious Proposal to the Ladies*. This work, begun during her correspondence with Norris, was published in 1694. When the *Letters* came out the next year, 1695, she was identified on the title page only as the author of the *Proposal*: the full title of the published correspondence is *Letters Concerning the Love of God, Between the Author of the Proposal to the Ladies and Mr John Norris*. Shrinking from publicity for herself, she nonetheless desired it for the *Proposal*. The education of women was the project closest to her heart, and to promote it she was willing to risk the unwelcome publicity and self-exposure that the publication of the *Letters* would bring. *Letters Concerning the Love of God* was indeed bitterly attacked by none other than Damaris Masham, once the protegée of Norris, acting under the direction of John Locke. In due course, as we shall see, Astell found it necessary to reply in detail. Meanwhile, however, she was preoccupied by her project of working toward the establishment of her proposed Protestant monastery for women. Philosophy would have to wait. Although she responded in part to Masham's criticism in *A Serious Proposal to the Ladies, Part II*, it was not until 1705 that she finally brought out the work that fully answered the attack on the *Letters*. For the next few years she would be principally engaged in pleading the cause of women's liberation from ignorance and what amounted to slavery, and in political pamphleteering. The correspondence with Norris had been invaluable in preparing her for these undertakings.

A Serious Proposal to
the Ladies
Part I

W hile engaged in the correspondence with John Norris, Astell began to write the work that in 1694 launched her career as a practising rhetorician: *A Serious Proposal to the Ladies for the Advancement of Their True and Greatest Interest. By a Lover of Her Sex.*[1] The proposal takes the form of a letter, directly addressed to her audience and beginning in proper correspondence style, "Ladies," (5). The conversational style of the letter dominates throughout. As we have seen, the experience of engaging in serious correspondence with a noted philosopher no doubt honed Astell's writing skills and made her comfortable with the genre of the letter on serious subjects. She now adapts this form to a different and wider audience. In fact, she is beginning to make the great transition mentioned in the last chapter: she is going at least semi-public, moving from *sermo* to *contentio*. *Letters Concerning the Love of God* was addressed to one person and was originally not intended for publication. Like others before her (including Cicero), Astell now uses this originally private form as a means of addressing a more public audience. Still, it is addressed specifically to the ladies – that is, women of Astell's social class. She is not yet directly addressing the other sex.

The occasion of the proposal was Astell's perception of the enormous problems encountered by single women in a culture that had no place for them. The Protestant celebration of marriage necessarily disvalued the woman who failed to find a husband. She was seen as an anomaly – a burden to society in general and to her family in particular. Without a specific role to fulfill, she was deprived not only of sufficient income but also of a nourishing social community in which she might prosper. The unmarried lady, therefore, too often lived a life of poverty and loneliness. There was, for instance, Astell's friend, Elizabeth Elstob, the noted Anglo-Saxon scholar. As long as her brother lived she prospered, for he shared her interests, encouraged her scholarship, and supported her financially.

After his death, however, she endured long years of poverty before finding congenial work as governess to the daughters of the Duke of Portland.[2] Many other women fared even worse. Only because she had built upon the early education she had received from her uncle had Astell herself escaped destitution. She was determined to do what she could for other women in a similar situation. As she saw it, education was the key.

Yet the poverty that was too often the fate of the single lady was not the only social evil she addressed. Just as serious as the material destitution of the unmarried woman, in her view, was the spiritual and intellectual deprivation of many of the rich ladies in high society, whose lives were filled with the frivolities of pleasure-seeking and self-indulgence. As we saw in the previous chapter, she wanted to rescue other women from "meanness of spirit" (Norris and Astell 49). Bathsua Makin had addressed this problem as early as 1673 in her *Essay to Revive the Antient Education of Gentlewomen*. She had complained that young girls were encouraged to "trifle away so many precious minutes meerly to polish their Hands and Feet, to curl their Locks, to dress and trim their Bodies" (22). Twenty years later, the situation had not improved. Ruth Perry describes the self-indulgent life of the typical upper-class girl of the 1690s. She was offered no serious academic education, learning only to embroider and make sweetmeats, and perhaps to sing or play the flute (*Celebrated* 104). The fashionable women of high society spent their days dressing for sumptuous parties, engaging in illicit love affairs, and gambling. According to Dr George Hickes, most of them were functionally illiterate: "It is shameful, but ordinary, to see Gentlewomen, who have both Wit and Politeness, not able yet to pronounce well what they read. They are still more grossly deficient in Orthography, or in Spelling right, and in the manner of forming or connecting Letters in Writing" (qtd. in Perry, *Celebrated* 104). Astell saw such a life as demeaning, an abuse of talents and a waste of the divine gift of reason.

What Astell proposes is a complete reversal of such a lifestyle: she wants to turn these self-indulgent high-livers into serious scholars, given to prayer and good works. A greater change could hardly be imagined, nor one less likely to appeal to these ladies of fashion. What she is recommending would look to the average genteel lady of the 1690s to be little short of cruel and unusual punishment. How then is she even to get herself a hearing, let alone gain their support? She does so by introducing her topic very gradually – whetting the reader's appetite, luring her on by sheer curiosity. Instead of stating immediately the problem the proposal addresses, as Swift does, for example, in "A Modest Proposal," Astell first recommends it without actually disclosing what it is. She describes it as something that will "improve your Charms and heighten your Value [...] and fix that Beauty, to make it lasting and permanent, which Nature with all the helps of Art cannot secure" (5). Disingenuously, Astell denies using rhetoric, while at the same time taking advantage of every persuasive technique in her address to her readers: "And sure I shall not need many words to persuade you to close with this Proposal. [Readers still do not know what it is.] The very offer is a sufficient inducement; nor does it need the set-off's of Rhetorick to recommend it, were I capable, which yet I am not, of applying them with the greatest force" (6). Astell is wise thus to promote her proposal in advance of giving the least hint of what it is, or even the problem that it addresses. Only very gradually does she let the reader guess what she is about. First she introduces the unappealing words "Vertue" and "Wisdom." But she is careful not to frighten her readers off by suggesting any kind of self-denial: "No solicitude in the adornation of your selves is discommended, provided you employ your care about that which is really your *self*" (6). And she promises: "Neither will any pleasure be denied you, who are only desir'd not to catch at the Shadow and let the Substance go" (6). Next she appeals to their ambition and sense of competitiveness – neither a quality she particularly admires, as she will reveal later. For the time being, however, it seems that the promise of favourable attention may win over her audience. "You may be as ambitious as you please, so you aspire to the best things; and contend with your Neighbours as much as you can, that they may not out-do you in any commendable Quality. Let it never be said, that they to whom pre-eminence is so very agreeable, can be tamely content that others should surpass them in *this*, and precede them in a *better* World" (7). Precedence was of enormous concern to high-class ladies – and even to those of a lower class. Astell's appeal to this social value, therefore, is astute.

By degrees, Astell introduces the delights of the intellectual and spiritual life, appealing now to the ladies' sense of fashion: "For shame let's abandon that *Old*, and therefore one wou'd think unfashionable employment of pursuing Butter flies and Trifles" (7). Again saving their faces (something she will recommend in her rhetorical theory in *A Serious Proposal, Part II*), she attributes this pursuit of "Vanity and Folly" not to the choices made by the ladies themselves but to the cultural influences to which they are subject. She urges them to "break the enchanted Circle that custom has plac'd us in" (7) and to aspire to a style of life more worthy of them. Always considerate of the feelings of her female readers, she excuses herself for appearing to criticize them: "Pardon me the seeming rudeness of this Proposal, which goes upon a supposition that there is something amiss in you, which it is intended to amend." None of us is perfect, she reminds them: "To be exempt from mistake, is a privilege few can pretend to"; but she assures them: "I Love you too well to endure a spot upon your Beauties" (8). It nevertheless becomes increasingly apparent that Astell is bent upon reforming her ladies. Yet she offers every excuse she can think of for their frivolity, blaming men for denying women any escape from the ignorance for which they are despised – ignorance that Astell believes is "the cause of most Feminine Vices" (11). It is lack of education, not inherent inferiority, that is the problem. The soil (to use her own metaphor) is good, but it wants cultivating (10).

Having thus prepared her readers and stimulated their curiosity by analyzing the problem and its causes while postponing its solution, Astell finally makes her proposal simply and directly. It is to erect "a Monastery, or if you will [...] a Religious Retirement, and such as shall have a double aspect, being not only a Retreat from the World for those who desire that advantage, but likewise an institution and previous discipline, to fit us to do the greatest good in it" (18). Astell thus brings together the values of both the contemplative and the active life, in the way practised by some of the medieval monastic institutions. For her, the opportunity to "do the greatest good" (18) in the world is of equal importance with the nurturing of the soul; and this means for Astell intellectual activity as well as prayer, worship, and social service. In thus stressing the importance of intellectual activity, she is perhaps looking back to the example of some medieval monastic institutions for women where scholarship was encouraged. These, though rare in England, had existed. But scholarship in the Middle Ages had required the study of dialectic, and in the Renaissance of rhetoric, and both involved a good working knowledge of Latin. One of the great advantages of developments in the seventeenth century, Astell believed, especially the philosophical ideas of Descartes, was that it was now recognized that extensive professional education was not necessary in order to engage in the life of the mind. The human being, she asserts, following Descartes, is naturally endowed with intellectual and linguistic capacities. Nor do the ladies have to learn foreign languages in order to become educated: Latin is no longer the *sine qua non* of the scholar.

Astell, then, combines the best of the old with the best of the new: she wants to bring back the monasteries, but not exactly in their old form. Much more stress is to be put upon intellectual development: the ladies are to study Descartes and Malebranche, for instance – not exactly easy reading. Another important difference is that attendance is to be voluntary – there will be no binding vows to force the ladies to stay should they wish to leave: "And since Inclination can't be forc'd, (and nothing makes people more uneasy than the fettering themselves with unnecessary Bonds) there shall be no Vows or irrevocable Obligations, not so much as the fear of Reproach to keep our Ladies here any longer than they desire" (29). This provision was crucial to the proposal since the fear of bondage was very great. In fact, one of the legitimate fears about marriage was (for women) the impossibility of getting out of it. It was partly this constraint that led Mary Astell in a later work (*Some Reflections Upon Marriage*) to ask why women were born slaves.

Having described in some detail the principles according to which the ladies would live in the monastery, Astell follows the genre of the standard proposal by looking at some of the consequences and answering possible objections. In developing the advantages of her retreat, she details at some length the importance of giving women the right environment. She believes in the power of what she calls custom and we call cultural constraint, theorizing it (though she does not of course use these terms) as the social construction of reality. She sees the crucial importance of the context in which the ladies live and how hard it is for them to try to reform their lives and change their values while continuing to live among those who have no such aspirations. She represents the retreat, therefore, as an opportunity, as an escape: here they "may get out of that danger which a continual stay in view of the Enemy and the familiarity and unwearied application of the Temptation may expose them to" (18). What they are being offered is not a restriction of their freedom, but liberty itself: "You are therefore Ladies, invited into a place, where you shall suffer no other confinement, but to be kept out of the road of Sin" (19).

There follows what amounts to a panegyric on the delights of such a life – convincing because of its passionate sincerity. Astell is no sour moralist, trying merely to improve standards of behaviour; on the contrary, she is inviting her readers into a lifestyle that she obviously finds satisfying and joyful.

Next she turns to the possible objections her various readers might have to her proposal, dealing first with some of the anticipated reservations of the prospective students, the ladies themselves. Will they, for example, practise a life of unalleviated self-denial? By no means: the institution will "not only permit but recommend harmless and ingenious Diversions, Musick particularly, for 'Neither God nor Wise men will like us better for an affected severity and waspish sourness'" (26). Then there is the familiar objection that such religious retirement is unnecessary: "May not People be good without this confinement?" (40). She allows that they may; however, she points out that not everyone is strong enough to resist the corruption of the world: some degree of protection is advisable. She repeats once more her belief in the importance of the right social context for the practice of goodness.

Other objections that she anticipates are likely to be made by men. The proposal is addressed to the ladies, but Astell is astute enough to recognize that, since it is principally men who have the power and the money to set up her proposed institution, it is important to get them on side too. She therefore tries to anticipate, and answer, some of their possible objections. She refers, ironically, to the invasion of masculine privileged territory (a concern also addressed more than twenty years earlier by Bathsua Makin): "I know not how the Men will resent it, to have their enclosure broke down, and Women invited to tast of the Tree of Knowledge they have so long unjustly *monopolized*" (24). One fear she anticipates is that "a Learned Education [...] will make Women vain and assuming, and instead of correcting encrease their Pride" (41). She concedes that a smattering of learning might be dangerous – as it is, she pointedly remarks, for men. However, she does not propose that her ladies shall be superficially educated. Their knowledge will be in depth. They will therefore, like Socrates, recognize how little – relatively – they know.

Finally, there is the all-important question of money. In answering the assumed objection that such a retirement will cost too much, Astell first gives the pious answer – the objectors should get their priorities right: "Who will think 500 pounds too much to lay out for the purchase of so much Wisdom and Happiness?" (42). However, on a more practical level, she argues that well-educated women if and when they marry will not waste money on frivolities, and moreover will know how to run a household thriftily. Then there is the problem of dowries, a major concern for upper-class parents, for without an adequate sum to bring to her husband, a girl could not hope to make a good marriage. Astell goes into the question in some detail: "Five or six hundred pounds may be easily spar'd with a Daughter, when so many thousand would go deep; and yet as the world goes be a very inconsiderable Fortune for Ladies of their Birth; neither maintain them in that *Port* which Custom makes almost necessary, nor procure them an equal Match" (43). Another advantage is that the monastery would provide a safe retreat from fortune-hunters: "[H]ere Heiresses and Persons of Fortune may be kept secure, from the rude attempts of designing Men; And she who has more Mony than discretion, need not curse her Stars for being expos'd a prey to bold importunate and rapacious Vultures" (39). In an obvious appeal to the parents of such an heiress, she points out, "here she may remain in safety till a convenient Match be offer'd by her Friends, and be freed from the danger of a dishonourable one" (39). Astell, then, intends her monastery to serve both as a refuge for single women and as a school for young girls who will later become – she hopes – sensible wives and mothers, willing and able to give a suitable education to their own children, particularly their daughters.

The proposal ends with an appeal for funds: "Is Charity so dead in the world that none will contribute to the saving their own and their neighbours Souls?" (44). She summarizes her main arguments in the last paragraph, and ends on an optimistic note: "She who drew the Scheme is full of hopes, it will not want kind hands to perform and compleat it" (47). And since the proposal has been made in the form of a letter, she signs herself "Ladies, Your very humble Servant," but withholds her name.

Mary Astell's *Serious Proposal* created quite a stir in London: four editions were published in the next seven years; in fact, among all her writings it was this particular work that received the most attention during her lifetime[3] (Hilda Smith 137). The quality of the work no doubt justified this attention. Nevertheless, its popularity is surprising in view of the fact that what Astell proposed was by no means new. Astell herself was delighted to find support for her ideas in a work by Sir Henry Wotton, from which she quotes:

> Indeed a Learned Education of the Women will appear so unfashionable, that I began to startle at the singularity of the proposition, but was extremely pleas'd when I found a late ingenious Author (whose Book I met with since the writing of this [*Mr Wotton's Reflect. on Ant. and Mod. Learn. p 349, 350]), agree with me in my Opinion. For speaking of the Repute that Learning was in about 150 years ago: *It was so very modish* (says he) *that the fair Sex seem'd to believe that* Greek *and* Latin *added to their Charms; and* Plato *and* Aristotle *untranslated, were frequent Ornaments of their Closets. One wou'd think by the effects, that it was a proper way of Educating them, since there are no accounts in History of so many great Women in any one Age, as are to be found between the years 15 and 1600.* (22)

Besides Wotton, there had been many others who had thought this kind of serious education good for women. Some had even proposed a women's academy, others some kind of religious institution. In "A Refuge from Men: The Idea of a Protestant Nunnery," Bridget Hill gives an account of these proposals. One of the earliest suggestions came from Thomas Becon (1512–1567), during whose lifetime, of course, the monasteries had been dissolved by Henry VIII. Though a staunch Protestant, Becon proposed the foundation of schools for women and children like "the monasteries of solitary women whom we heretofore called nuns, built and set up, and endowed with possessions of our godly ancestors" (qtd. in Hill 110). Robert Burton, in his famous *Anatomy of Melancholy* (1621), suggests that "some time or other, amongst so many rich bachelors, a benefactor be found to build a monastical college for old, decayed, deformed, or discontented maids to live together" (qtd. in Hill 111). The idea was brought forward again by a character in a play by Sir William D'Avenant in 1636. In the mid-seventeenth century the same idea was used again in two plays written by Margaret Cavendish, *The Female Academy* and *The Convent of Pleasure*. The Protestant divine Thomas Fuller praised the institution of nunneries: "Yea, give me leave to say if such Feminine Foundations had still continued, provided no vows were obtruded upon them [...] haply the weaker sex [...] might be heightened to a higher perfection than hitherto hath been obtained" (qtd. in Hill 112).

Not only had the idea of a Protestant monastery often been suggested: it had even been tried. In the 1630s, there had been a famous settlement of women at Little Gidding under the direction of Nicholas Ferrar.[4] The women lived much the kind of life recommended by Mary Astell – devoting themselves to prayer, study, and good works (F. Smith 67).[5] Possibly inspired by the example of Little Gidding, Lettice, Viscountess Falkland conducted her own household on religious principles which also applied to her charity school. According to her biographer, John Duncon, she also had plans to set up something like nunneries, believing that there should be "places for the education of young Gentlewomen, and for retirement of Widows [...] hoping [...] that learning and religion might flourish more in her own Sex than hither-to-for" (qtd. in F. Smith 67). A similar lifestyle was practised by Mary and Anne Kemys, who established an Anglican sisterhood rather like that of Little Gidding at Naish Court.

Obviously, Astell's proposal was not new. It had been suggested, and tried, many times before. What was it, then, that seized public attention and made it famous in its own time? I suggest that it was the brilliance of Astell's rhetoric that made her proposal so arresting. As I have shown, her use of structure is masterly: she prepares the ground very carefully before setting forth her proposal, making full use of suspense, luring her audience to read on out of sheer curiosity. She knows and understands them extremely well, and introduces her project with the greatest tact and circumspection, anticipating their probable reservations, and offering convincing assurances that these are unwarranted. She is also shrewd enough to make her address directly to the ladies themselves. Bathsua Makin had made her proposal to the gentlemen, posing as a man herself. Astell, on the contrary, not only acknowledges her sex, but subtly empowers her audience of ladies by making her suggestions directly to them: let them take charge of their own destiny by insisting upon an education. She is not so foolish as to admit it, but what she is really calling for is something like a social revolution: by addressing the women, not the men, she is encouraging a revolt against the status quo. The very terms in which she rebukes men for withholding education from women are provocative: "Altho' it has been said by Men of more Wit than Wisdom, and perhaps of more malice than either, that Women are naturally incapable of acting Prudently, or that they are necessarily determined to folly, I must by no means grant it" (9). In fact, she challenges received wisdom and assumes an authority to protest against it that her society has by no means granted her. The fact that she is a woman, addressing women, gives added force to her proposal.

Her tone throughout is that of the caring mentor: affectionate, respectful but authoritative. It is utterly different from the tone she adopts in her earliest work, the correspondence with John Norris, *Letters Concerning the Love of God*, which she began in 1693. In that work she is deferential to her audience but she does not have to make allowances for ignorance or lack of self-esteem in her reader. The quite different audience of *A Serious Proposal* requires another rhetorical approach entirely. To accommodate her audience she must to some extent veil her powerful intelligence, avoid dazzling them with her superior intellectual capacity. Her tone in *A Serious Proposal*, then, demonstrates an important development in her craft as a rhetorician: she is equally able to address an eminent philosopher and a group of barely literate upper-class ladies. The tone in both works is intimate, but the intimacy is of very different kinds. That of her correspondence with Norris is the intimacy of two scholars who understand each other very well and are in substantial agreement. The address, though always respectful, is personal. The intimacy of *A Serious Proposal* is different. Here she sounds like a mother – loving, but strict – addressing her children. Never condescending to them, she addresses her women readers with genuine respect and affection, finding excuses for their ignorance and attributing to them the very best motives.[6] Determined on their moral reform, she is not so injudicious as to say so directly, at least not at first. She recommends her ideas in terms of the readers' values, not her own. And perhaps most persuasive in the tone of the work is her obvious sincerity: when she describes the delights of scholarship and holiness, she writes with emotional power:

> In a word, this happy Society will be but one Body, whose Soul is love, animating and informing it, and perpetually breathing forth it self in flames of holy desire after GOD, and acts of benevolence to each other. Envy and Uncharitableness are the Vices only of little and narrow hearts, and therefore 'tis suppos'd, they will not enter here amongst persons whose Dispositions as well as their Births are to be Generous. (27)

Finally, there is the attractiveness of her style: Astell was recognized as one of the finest stylists of her day. Here is an example of her writing at its best – nothing overstated, but with a satirical sharpness that makes it irresistible:

> Let those therefore who value themselves only on external accomplishments, consider how liable they are to decay, and how soon they may be depriv'd of them, and that supposing they shou'd continue, they are but sandy Foundations to build Esteem upon. What a disappointment it will be to a Ladies Admirere as well as to her self, that her Conversation shou'd lose and endanger the Victory her eyes had gain'd! For when the Passion of a Lover is evaporated into the Indifference of a Husband, and a frequent review has lessen'd the wonder which her Charms at first had rais'd, she'll retain no more than such a formal respect as decency and good breeding will require; and perhaps hardly that; but unless he be a very good Man (and indeed the world is not over full of 'em) her worthlessness has made a forfeit of his Affections, which are seldom fixt by any other things than Veneration and Esteem. (46)

For whatever reasons, Mary Astell's *Serious Proposal* made quite an impact on contemporary London, as she herself acknowledges in the introduction to *A Serious Proposal, Part II*. Some of the adverse criticism was probably motivated by jealousy: according to Bridget Hill, Bishop Gilbert Burnet, who was said to have persuaded a potential patron not to endow the proposed institution on the grounds that it sounded too Roman Catholic, shortly afterwards proposed something very similar himself, using the same terms: "[H]e expressed himself in favour of 'something like Monasteries without Vows which would be a glorious Design'" (Hill 118). Daniel Defoe said he admired her, but also asserted that his own scheme was quite different. In fact, he borrowed heavily from Astell, without acknowledgement (Springborg, *Mary Astell* xiii). Another writer of the time whom Astell believed to have plagiarized her was Richard Steele: Astell herself indirectly accuses him of doing so in the introduction to *Bart'lemy Fair*: he has, she says, "transcribed above an hundred pages into his Ladies Library, verbatim" (qtd. in Springborg, *Mary Astell* xxxviii n.49). However, it is now thought that the plagiarist was not Steele but George Berkeley (xxxviii n. 47, 48).

With the publication of *A Serious Proposal to the Ladies*, then, Astell became known to the world of the 1690s and launched her career as a rhetorician, a writer of persuasive discourse. Over the next few years, her work would become well known not only to the ladies whom she addressed, but also to the intellectual elite: philosophers, politicians, clergymen. Though known to have been produced by a woman, her ideas were respected, argued about – and against – plagiarized, and satirized. Within a few short years of her arrival in London to what threatened to be a life of poverty and despair, Astell had become a success.

—————— 5 ——————
A Serious Proposal to
the Ladies
Part II

By 1697 Mary Astell had by no means given up hope that her proposed Protestant monastery for women might eventually be founded, but she was becoming impatient. Above all, she wanted women to get started on their education without more delay.[1] In *A Serious Proposal to the Ladies, Part II*, therefore, she gives instructions about how the ladies might embark upon the project of educating themselves until such time as the institution she has proposed might be established. Tracking her progress as a rhetorician, I shall discuss in this chapter questions of audience and purpose and the philosophical grounding she provides for the instruction she gives before outlining the specific suggestions she makes in this second part of her proposal.

In spite of its title, which suggests that it is a mere continuation of Part I, Part II is in fact quite dissimilar from it, constituting another stage in Astell's progress from *sermo* to *contentio*. Part I is a simple proposal for a specific course of action. It is a relatively short work, addressed to ladies (that is, upper-class women), and although it also takes into account the interests of the gentlemen who might be expected to contribute financially, the arguments are almost exclusively directed to a female audience. Again in Part II, Astell uses the genre of the letter with its direct address to the audience, but it is a work of a very different kind. In the first place, it is more than twice as long — 114 pages as opposed to 42 (in the latest edition of 1997). It is also rather more formal: it does not address the ladies in the second person, except in the introduction. The most commonly used pronoun is the inclusive "we." But above all, the purpose is radically different. Part I falls into the category of deliberative discourse: fundamentally, it is persuasion. Part II, however, is primarily informative (though it is, of course, designed to be persuasive as well).[2] And although, like Part I, it is concerned with education, it includes long passages of philosophical discussion, a necessary background to the educational principles that

65

Astell sets forth. One might think that the intellectual level of the argument would go far beyond the capacity of barely literate women who have yet to embark seriously upon their education. Yet it is not so: Astell includes nothing that is not comprehensible to an uneducated but intelligent and interested audience.

On the question of the audience: the title implies that the audience of Part II is exclusively the ladies whose education Astell is concerned to promote. However, as with Part I, the ladies, though they constitute her primary audience, are probably not the only readers she has in mind. In fact, what we have here is at least a double audience. Besides the ladies, Astell is addressing such members of the general public as are interested in the current philosophical, theological, and political debate; for Part I of *A Serious Proposal* had created a great deal of interest, and not only among women.[3] Moreover, it is probable that she is also addressing the professional philosophers of the time, in particular John Locke and his followers, with many of whose ideas she strongly disagreed. Yet although she shows in this work her awareness of the Lockean position, I cannot agree with Patricia Springborg that the work is chiefly addressed to him (Springborg, *Mary Astell* xvi). Some discussion of this issue is necessary in order to clarify the important question of Astell's primary audience in *A Serious Proposal, Part II*.

As we have seen, Astell was strongly influenced by Neoplatonism and had engaged in correspondence with one of its foremost proponents at the time. *Letters Concerning the Love of God, Between the Author of the Proposal to the Ladies and Mr John Norris* had been published in 1695, one year after the first part of *A Serious Proposal*. Later in the same year, there was published, anonymously, *A Discourse Concerning the Love of God*, which attacked Norris's philosophy, and in particular the idea that we see all things in God. Since John Locke was known to be an opponent of the philosophy of John Norris, and the ideas expressed in *A Discourse* were very similar to those of Locke, Astell assumed that it was he who had written it. In fact, though no doubt he inspired it, it was written by his close friend, Damaris Masham, daughter of Ralph Cudworth. Ironically, Astell's *A Serious Proposal* had been attributed to Masham, for its Neoplatonist position seemed appropriate in the daughter of Cudworth, and she was known to be interested in education. Even more ironically, Masham had at one time been a correspondent of John Norris, who had dedicated a work to her. Now, however, under the influence of Locke, she had moved away from his ideas. The substance of Masham's criticism of Norris is that his conviction that we see all things in God promotes disengagement with the world, a selfish retirement into "hermitages" and a refusal to deal with the realities of human experience. A pupil, by now, of Locke, she finds the philosophy of Norris (and Astell) far too remote from human experience and the empiricism promoted by Locke.[4] *A Discourse* attacks Norris's ideas as put forward in *Reflections upon the Conduct of Human Life* (1690), as well as his joint work with Astell, *Letters Concerning the Love of God*. Masham refers to Astell obliquely, on page 120 of *A Discourse*:

> These Opinions of Mr. N. seem also to indanger the introducing, *especially among those whose Imaginations are stronger that their Reason*, a Devout way of talking; which having no sober, and intelligible sense under it, will either inevitably by degrees beget an Insensibility to Religion, in those themselves who use it, as well as others; By thus accustoming them to handle Holy things without Fear; or else will turn to as wild an Enthusiasm as any that has been yet seen; and which can End in nothing but *Monasteries and Hermitages*; with all those sottish and Wicked Superstitions which have accompanied them where-ever they have been in use. (italics added)

The possible references to Astell and her proposal are few. The focus of *A Discourse* is on the question of whether or not we see all things in God. Masham does not mention women's education as such at all. Yet Patricia Springborg believes that Masham's work so redirected Astell's focus in *A Serious Proposal, Part II* that a "revolution in her thought takes place between Part I and II" (*Mary Astell* xvi):

> [A]n important and undisclosed hiatus divides the first from the second part of *A Serious Proposal*. Into that gap stepped Lady Damaris Masham. As a consequence Astell's project changed course. What began as a fairly conventional proposal for a women's academy ended as a full-scale philosophical defence of women's intellectual equality and Cartesian epistemology that would support it. (xv)

Springborg, then, believes that "[u]nder the sting of criticism Astell turned a fairly conventional proposal for the education of women in a *Serious Proposal, Part I* into a major philosophical edifice in *Part II*. Education as such was no longer her project, but rather those deep background philosophical and theological assumptions which deny women the capacity for the improvement of the mind" (xvii). She therefore claims that Astell "disavows any intention of laying out a curriculum" (xvii) and that *A Serious Proposal, Part II* is a work of philosophy, not of education.

But if that is so, Mary Astell herself is mistaken as to the intention and nature of her work as set forth in the introduction. Far from being remote and withdrawn from the world into mystical contemplation, as Masham had charged (120), Astell was intensely practical. Her main concern in this work is to promote such education as the women may undertake in the absence of the institution she is still hoping one day to provide. She refers to the "favourable reception" of Part I, but complains that no steps have been taken to put the proposal into effect: "It were more to her [Astell's] satisfaction to find her Project condemn'd as foolish and impertinent, than to find it receiv'd with some Approbation, and yet no body endeavouring to put it in Practice" (72). She begins by blaming the ladies for not doing anything about it: "Why won't you begin to think?" she asks. "Why does not a generous Emulation fire your hearts and inspire you with Noble and Becoming Resentments?" (72). She concludes that the problem is not lack of motivation but uncertainty as to how to proceed: they "think that they've been bred up in Idleness and Impertinence, and study will be irksome to them, who have not employ'd their mind to any good purpose, and now when they wou'd they want the method of doing it" (76). She therefore proposes to give them more specific advice. Referring to Part I, she acknowledges that

> this was only propos'd in general, and the particular method of effecting it left to the Discretion of those who shou'd Govern and Manage the Seminary, without which we are still of Opinion that the Interest of the Ladies can't be duly serv'd, [yet] in the mean time till that can be erected and that nothing in our power may be wanting to do them service, we shall attempt to lay down in this second part some more minute Directions, and such as we hope if attended to may be of use to them. (78)

And she does in fact give the most minute directions. Springborg represents Astell as turning to the work of the Port Royal scholars in order to refute Masham/Locke, but she does not mention that the particular works that Astell draws on (as confirmed by her own marginal notes) are works on education: *The Art of Thinking* (by Antoine Arnauld and Pierre Nicole of Port Royal) and *The Art of Speaking* (by the Oratorian, Bernard Lamy). These two works form the basis of the quite specific instruction Astell gives in chapter 3: ninety-six pages (in the original edition) on the methods of logic and rhetoric. (The details of this rhetorical theory will be discussed in another chapter.) Ninety-six pages represent a good proportion – about one-third – of the whole work. As Springborg acknowledges, Astell was concerned to provide her academy "with sound epistemic, moral and Christian footings" (*Mary Astell* xviii). This philosophical discussion, however, does not displace the details of the educational programme: it underpins them. Such details have no force unless they are consistent with her philosophy of education. The exposition of this philosophy should therefore be seen as a necessary, if lengthy, preliminary. In "laying out the foundations of her metaphysics, ethics, philosophy of education and religion systematically" (*Mary Astell* xviii), then, she was concerned to support the "minute Directions" that she had promised in the introduction to give.

That said, there is, however, no doubt that Astell had read Masham's *A Discourse* (even if she probably attributed it to Locke), and she responds, though only briefly, to some of the objections made in it.[5] In the earlier part of chapter 3, and particularly at the end of chapter 4, one is aware of her taking into account this adverse criticism and the (as she sees it) too secular philosophy of Locke. In an illuminating note, Springborg shows that one particular passage, for instance, may be a direct reply to one of his tenets. I quote her note in full:

> Locke in *The Reasonableness of Christianity*, (1695 edn), p. 279, had argued from the impossibility of making 'the Day-Labourers and Tradesmen, the spinsters and Dairy Maids [...] perfect Mathematicians,' an equal impossibility of perfecting them 'in Ethicks' in the Neoplatonist mode (279). Astell turns the argument against him here. (Mary *Astell*, 187n.63)

What Astell says is this:

For the difference between a plow-man and a Doctor does not seem to me to consist in this, That the Business of the one is to search after Knowledge, and that the other has nothing to do with it. No, whoever has a Rational Soul ought surely to employ it about some Truth or other, to procure for it right Ideas, that its Judgments may be true tho its Knowledge be not very extensive. (*Serious Proposal, Part II* 105)

In short, as Astell says elsewhere, each person ought to exercise the mind according to its given capacity. (Incidentally, it appears here that Astell, the Tory, is more egalitarian than Locke, the Whig.) In this passage, and in others that defend piety and devotion to God (and not just to the observance of moral rules) as a necessary part of human experience and development, Astell shows her awareness of and resistance to the ideas of the Locke/Masham faction.

As for the charge of reintroducing monasteries, as Astell points out, it is quite clear from the text of *A Serious Proposal, Part I* that the life in her proposed institution is to be in most respects quite different from life in a nunnery. The women are to study in an academic programme, and they are not to take vows. The planned ministry of the ladies to the poor and the sick will, it is true, be shared by nuns, but will hardly be exclusive to them; and the daily services of morning and evening prayer were a common feature of great (secular) houses at the time. Astell is not here making excuses: she draws attention to facts as found in the text of Part I. She specifically addresses this criticism toward the end of chapter 4:

> They must either be very Ignorant or very Malicious who pretend that we wou'd imitate Foreign Monasteries, or object against us the Inconveniences that they are subject to; a little attention to what they read might have convinc'd them that our Institutions [*sic*] is rather *Academical* than *Monastic*. So that it is altogether beside the purpose to say 'tis too Recluse, or prejudicial to an Active Life; 'tis as far from that as a Ladys Practising at home is from being a hindrance to her dancing at court. For an Active Life consists not barely in *Being in the World*, but in *doing much Good in it*: And therefore it is fit we Retire a little, to furnish our Understandings with useful Principles, to set our Inclinations right, and to manage our Passions, and when this is well done, but not till then, we may safely venture out. (178)

Astell does, then, take some account of the charges made against her and Norris. However, as Springborg herself acknowledges, she postpones a full response to a later work, *The Christian Religion*, published in 1705.[6] To see *Part II* as primarily an address to Locke and/or Masham is to exaggerate her response to them beyond anything that can be supported by the text.[7]

If, as I have argued, the main (although not exclusive) address in this work is to the ladies, and its subject their self-education, how does Astell proceed? She begins, logically, with a discussion of the purpose of education, answering the implied question, "What is education for?" In Astell's view, it is to prepare us for life, not only in this world, but also in the world to come, in eternity. Part of this preparation consists in the practice of morality, and it is Astell's conviction that to engage in such practice demands not only obedience to rules but also an understanding of basic principles. True to her Neoplatonist beliefs, she asserts the interdependency of the understanding and the will. So crucial is this relationship between the intellectual and the moral that she makes a discussion of it the starting point of *A Serious Proposal, Part II*. The first of the four chapters of this work is entitled "Of the Mutual Relation between Ignorance and Vice, and Knowledge and Purity" (81). Astell discusses the reciprocity of the understanding and the will at the beginning of the first chapter:

> What are Ignorance and Vice but Diseases of the Mind contracted in its two principal Faculties the Understanding and Will? And such too as like many Bodily distempers do mutually foment each other. Ignorance disposes to Vice, and Wickedness reciprocally keeps us Ignorant, so that we cannot be free from the one unless we cure the other. (81)

If the reason and the will are thus mutually dependent, which takes priority? Where should we begin? On the one hand, Astell asserts that knowledge is primary: "There are some degrees of Knowledge necessary before there can be any Human Acts, for till we are capable of Chusing our Own Actions and directing them by some Principle, tho we Move and Speak and do many such like things, we live not the Life of a Rational Creature but only of an Animal" (82). On the other hand, however, the will is active in the human being long before the reason has developed. It is therefore necessary to be guided by the reason of others until our own is fully awake and functioning and ready to take charge. This is where education comes in. Astell contends that only a trained faculty of reason can be robust enough to counter the insistent claims of the passions. The traditional complaint that women are dominated by their passions, rather than by reason, Astell attributes to their lack of education. The apparent lack of the rational faculty, then, is not natural, but culturally induced: it is nurture, not nature, that makes women irrational. The training of the mind will promote the directing of the will: "Some Clearness of Head, some lower degrees of Knowledge, so much at least as will put us on endeavouring after more, is necessary to th'obtaining of purity of Heart." (84). In thus asserting the necessity of the exercise of the reason in living a good life, Astell is challenging the received opinion that women do not need to understand; they need only obey. She is in fact reiterating a conviction she stated in *A Serious Proposal, Part I* – that mere blind obedience to a set of rigid rules will not work:

> [A woman] is taught the Principles and Duties of Religion, but not acquainted with the Reason and Grounds of them, being told 'tis enough for her to believe, to examine why and wherefore, belongs not to her. And therefore, though her Piety may be tall and spreading, yet because it wants foundation and Root, the first rude Temptation overthrows and blasts it, or perhaps the short liv'd Gourd decays and withers of its own accord. (*Serious Proposal I* 16)

But if understanding should guide morality, morality must purify the understanding. The relationship is reciprocal: "She then who desires a clear Head must have a pure heart" (*Serious Proposal II* 82). Unfortunately, this is not easy to achieve:

> Indeed if we search to the bottom I believe we shall find, that the Corruption of the Heart contributes *more* to the Cloudiness of the Head than the Clearness of our Light does to the regularity of our Affections, and 'tis oftener seen that our vitious Inclinations keep us Ignorant, than that our Knowledge makes us Good. For it must be confess'd that Purity is not *always* the product of Knowledge; tho the Understanding be appointed by the author of Nature to direct and govern the Will, yet many times its head-strong and Rebellious Subject rushes on precipitately, not only without, but against its directions. When a

Truth comes thwart our Passions, when it dares contradict our mistaken Pleasures and supposed Interests, let the Light shine never so clear we shut our eyes against it, will not be convinc'd, not because there's any want of Evidence, but because we are *unwilling* to Obey. (84)

Reason and will must therefore work together, assisting and correcting one another. If women can receive an education, they will be in a position to practise virtue at a higher level and to a greater degree than is now possible for them. We should note here, too, that for Astell morality is not just a matter of social practice, but includes also the spiritual: a woman's first duty is to God. She is bound, therefore, to develop her spiritual capacities; such development is part of the responsibility to use all God-given talents that Astell sees as the primary business of human existence. Ultimately, the reason and the will work together to bring this about.

And afterward, when we have procur'd a competent measure of both, they mutually assist each other; the more Pure we are, the clearer will our Knowledge be, and the more we Know, the more we shall Purify. Accordingly, therefore, we shall first apply our selves to the Understanding, endeavouring to inform and put it right, and in the next place address to the Will, when we have touched upon a few Preliminaries and endeavour'd to remove some Obstructions that are prejudicial to both. (84)

Chapter 2, then, addresses these problems. Its heading reads as follows:

Containing some Preliminaries. As I. The removing of Sloth and stupid Indifferency. II. Prejudices arising. (1.) From Authority, Education and Custom. (2.) From Irregular Self-Love, and Pride. How to cure our Prejudices. Some Remarks upon Change of Opinions, Novelty and the Authority of the Church. III To arm ourselves with Courage and Patient Perseverance against (1.) The Censures of ill People, and (2.) our own Indocility. IV. To propose a Right End. (87)

She proceeds to give instructions on how to remove those moral failures that contribute to a faulty understanding and hence to deficient moral behaviour. They arise partly from societal and partly from personal conditions. In resisting certain traditional prejudices, Astell shows her modernity, but in tracing some of the most deep-seated deficiencies to personal imperfection, she demonstrates her allegiance to traditional Christian values.

As Astell herself notes at the beginning of the heading of chapter 2, these are *preliminary* remarks: she has not yet come to the heart of her discourse. This she reaches in chapter 3: *"Concerning the Improvement of the Understanding. I Of the Capacity of the Humane Mind in General. II Of Particular Capacities. III The most common Infirmities incident to the Undestanding and their Cure. IV A Natural Logic, And V. Rhetoric propos'd. VI The Application and Use of our Knowledge"* (99). Here she discusses the philosophy of mind as a necessary basis for understanding how to practise the clear thinking upon which she insists. She distinguishes among faith, science, and opinion. Particularly interesting is her discussion of the relationship between faith and science, in which she criticizes those who "wou'd make that the Object of Science which is properly the Object of Faith, the Doctrin of the Trinity" (100).[8] Having discussed the basic principles of enquiry and argumentation, and the premises that should be drawn upon in the different categories, Astell goes on to give instructions for the practice of logic and rhetoric. I will consider these in the context of her rhetorical theory in a later chapter.

As the last part of the heading of chapter 3 indicates, all her theorizing is meant to support application. In the fourth chapter, therefore, she returns to her starting point: the relationship between the understanding (which processes knowledge) and the will (the organ of moral choice); but now she actually applies the theory and gives specific advice. Chapter 4 is headed: *"Concerning the Regulation of the Will and the Government of the Passions"* (153). This chapter is less a philosophical disquisition than an exhortation with philosophical and in particular theological underpinnings. To a twenty-first-century mind, Astell perhaps appears to have strayed off the point. In terms of her own priorities, however, she has finally reached it, for the purpose of education is to promote happiness, and true happiness can be achieved only by finding and doing the will of God. The understanding assists in the finding, the will in the doing. Consistently throughout the work, Astell has emphasized that the two are mutually dependent. She ends by reiterating that conviction.

What then is Astell's achievement in *A Serious Proposal, Part II*? How successfully does she fulfill her purpose as stated in her introduction? How well does she respond to the rhetorical situation and accommodate her various audiences? In response to these questions it must be said at once that *A Serious Proposal, Part II* is a rhetorical *tour de force*, a balancing act, for as we have seen, her primary task is complicated by a subsidiary purpose and a double, if not triple, audience. Although, as I have argued, she does indeed see her main task to be providing those "more minute Directions" to which she refers in her introduction (79), she has as a subsidiary purpose an address to the more general public and to those philosophers who fundamentally disagree with her. Furthermore, in her advice to the ladies, she must walk a rhetorical tightrope: on the one hand, to support her specific advice she must lay the philosophical foundations of her theory; on the other hand, she must bear in mind their intellectual limitations. Although much of the subject matter – philosophy – might be considered beyond the interest of uneducated ladies, the clarity of her exposition makes it comprehensible and the manifest passion that underlies the arguments makes it attractive. At no point does Astell forget that she must remain accessible to her audience of women. She repeatedly draws back from too deep an engagement in discussions that they could not follow. For example, in her advice on the control of the emotions, she specifically undertakes "not to enter too far into the Philosophy of the Passions" (161). The short account she gives is fully comprehensible to her female audience and quite sufficient to support the practical advice on the options for dealing with emotional arousal.[9]

On the other hand, insofar as she does deal with philosophical issues, she does so superbly. As Springborg says, the work is "enormously wide-ranging in its capacity to syncretise contemporary philosophical debate" (*Mary Astell* xv). It offers "one of the most brilliant disquisitions of the age on Descartes 'clear and distinct ideas'" (xviii). Furthermore, though she postpones a full refutation to her later work, she sufficiently addresses some of Locke's theories to satisfy all her audiences in this work:

> Astell's critique of Locke's sensationalist psychology is devastating. She has caught him every which way. If sense experience is logically prior to reflection, as he claims, then he is in no position to claim for himself a privileged position in expound-

ing the truth. But if truth is a function of propositional logic, as he also maintains, he cannot claim the priority of sensational knowledge, which must be submitted to the criterion of reason. (Springborg, *Mary Astell* xxix)

To do all this without exceeding the capacity of her primary audience of women to follow her argument shows a truly unusual rhetorical skill.

This skill is also apparent in the tone she uses. She begins, indeed, by scolding her audience of women, trying to stir them up to start on their education: "Why won't you begin to think, and no longer dream away your time in a wretched incogitancy?" (72). But having – she hopes – aroused them, she addresses them with gentleness and understanding, making excuses for them, reassuring them, telling them that the methods of learning are not nearly as hard as they might suppose. In chapter 2, for example, she encourages the ladies not to be too hard on themselves:

As we disregard the Censures of ill People, so are we patiently to bear with our own backwardness and indocility. There goes a good deal of Time and Pains, of Thought and Watchfulness to the rooting out of ill-habits, to the fortifying our Minds against foolish Customs, and to the making that easie and pleasant which us'd to be irksome to us. (96)

Some of her readers may despair of ever having the mental grasp to undertake intellectual improvement. If they really find themselves incapable, she reassures them that they can still "do some Good in an Active Life and Employments that depend on the Body" (111). But before they give up, she asks them to consider whether they have correctly evaluated themselves. What they most probably lack is knowledge of the subject: "The way of Considering and Meditating justly is the same on all Occasions. 'Tis true, there will be fewest Ideas arise when we wou'd Meditate on such Subjects as we've been least conversant about; but this is a fault which it is in our power to remedy, first by Reading or Discoursing, and then by frequent and serious Meditation" (111).

Astell shows tenderness and consideration for her readers again in dealing with the mechanics of writing, which can be very daunting to the inexperienced. Particularly engaging is her advice about spelling: English women of the time had a reputation for being extremely poor spellers.

> And as to spelling which they're said to be defective in, if they don't believe as they're usually told, that its fit for 'em to be so, and that to write exactly is too Pedantic, they may soon correct that fault, by Pronouncing their words aright and Spelling 'em accordingly. I know that this Rule won't always hold because of an Imperfection in our Language, which has been oft complain'd of but is not yet amended; But in this case a little Observation or recourse to Books will assist us; and if at any time we happen to mistake by Spelling as we Pronounce, the fault will be very Venial, and Custom rather to blame than we. (144)

She goes on to discuss grammar, and here again she offers her female readers reassuring advice, as well as making a little jab at the men:

> And tho Women are generally accus'd of Writing false English, if I may speak my own Experience, their Mistakes are not so common as is pretended, nor are they the only Persons guilty. [...] [T]hose who Speak true Grammar unless they're very Careless cannot write false, since they need only peruse what they've Writ, and consider whether they wou'd express 'emselves thus in Conversation. (144)

If she is careful to reassure her insecure audience about their possible mistakes, she is also concerned to build up their confidence by drawing their attention to their talents. One of these is the quality of the voice: "Nature does for the most part furnish 'em with such a Musical Tone, Perswasive Air and Winning Address as renders their Discourse sufficiently agreeable in Private Conversation" (143). Since in Astell's opinion it is not appropriate for women to engage in public speaking, they do not need the harsh, more carrying qualities of the masculine voice. And in one particular respect, Astell considers women (in general) to be far superior to men – they are much more reliable as teachers of small children:

> Education of Children is a most necessary Employment, perhaps the chief of those who have any; But it is as Difficult as it is Excellent when well perform'd; and I question not but

that the mistakes which are made in it, are a principal Cause of that Folly and Vice, which is so much complain'd of and so little mended. Now this, at least the foundation of it, on which in a great measure the success of all depends, shou'd be laid by the Mother, for Fathers find other Business, they will not be confin'd to such laborious work, they have not such opportunities of observing a Child's Temper, nor are the greatest part of 'em like to do much good, since Precepts contradicted by Example seldom prove effectual. (150)

In conclusion, then, Mary Astell's rhetorical achievement in *A Serious Proposal, Part II* is considerable. She selects her material with due regard to the interests and capacities of her readers; she deals sufficiently, but by no means exhaustively, with the criticism of the Locke/Masham faction; and she takes into account not only the relative ignorance but also the lack of self-confidence of those who constitute her primary audience. The whole of the second part of *A Serious Proposal* is written with clarity and passion. Skilfully negotiating the various requirements of the rhetorical situation, Astell produces a document that is still capable of instructing, delighting, and persuading even an audience of the twenty-first century.

6

Some Reflections
Upon Marriage

By the time she came to write *Some Reflections Upon Marriage*, Mary Astell had had considerable success as a writer, having published both parts of *A Serious Proposal to the Ladies* and her correspondence with John Norris.[1] *Reflections* builds upon these achievements, but its purpose, its focus, and its audience are different. It was very well received in Astell's own day, running to five editions within her lifetime, and it remains one of the more accessible of her works to a twenty-first-century audience. In this chapter I shall use a discussion of *Reflections* to demonstrate Astell's expertise in what was for her a new kind of writing – epideictic, the rhetoric of praise and blame – and to track her further progress from *sermo* to *contentio*: here for the first time Astell engages in political discussion and also for the first time addresses a fully public audience.

To review briefly the discussion of audience in the previous chapters: her first work, *Letters Concerning the Love of God*, most of which was written, though not published, before *A Serious Proposal*, had an audience of one. The letters began as a private correspondence, and although they were later published, the address remains a private one. Astell's main challenges in *Letters* were to express her ideas with the utmost clarity and to sustain her arguments logically, providing support and accommodating rebuttal. Since her audience of one was highly intelligent, sympathetic, and well acquainted with the subject of their discussion, there were few other rhetorical challenges to meet.

In her continued development as a writer, we see her broadening her intended audience. *A Serious Proposal, Part I* is addressed primarily to the ladies – that is, to women of a certain social standing. She belonged to the same social stratum herself, and had suffered some of the same disadvantages as the women she addressed. In *Part I*, she accommodates – besides the women – parents and possible patrons. But the focus is always on the ladies, and nearly all her arguments are addressed to them. She has progressed from an audience of one to an audience of many, but the members of the audience are not diverse: they share most of their interests and values, and Astell is able to use these as material to promote her argument. In *A Serious Proposal, Part II* the audience is broader. There, though her primary audience is still the ladies, and though she still uses the convention of the letter, she clearly also has in mind other interested parties, including philosophers, in particular those who disagree with her fundamental convictions, and specifically John Locke and Damaris Masham.

In *Reflections* her audience is broader still. Unlike her previously published works, this one is not in the form of a letter. For the first time, then, Astell published a work that uncompromisingly belongs to *contentio*, to the full public discourse of oratory, not even in form using the much more permissible (for a woman) letter genre of *sermo*. Perhaps she made this change because she had no specific audience in mind. The audience is in fact the general public, all who take an interest in public welfare, and in particular leaders of opinion, formulators of cultural values in an age of change. Since the audience is fully public, then, it is appropriate that the form be a public one too. Her purpose in writing *Reflections* is given in the preface attached to the third edition of 1706: the *Reflections*, Astell states, "have no other Design than to Correct some Abuses, which are not the less because Power and Prescription seem to Authorize them" (7). In fact, she is launching an attack on the cultural values of her time, and in particular on those (chiefly, that is, the men) who perpetuate them. As in her other works, Astell withholds her name, though she makes no secret of her sex. As we have seen, she believes in the intrinsic *ethos* produced through rhetorical *logos*, rather than in extrinsic *ethos*: the text should speak for itself and should be evaluated on rational grounds.

In this work, then, Astell abandons the letter genre and goes fully public. Nonetheless, there are traces of the origins of the work in *sermo*. She uses throughout a style that in its immediacy derives from the conversational, though it is more controlled and focused, and it soars at times into full eloquence. The subject matter of *Reflections* embraces both the social domestic concerns of the ladies and the public and political issues that were under discussion by the gentlemen. What she clearly shows is that the two worlds – that of women and that of men, so sharply separated in the bourgeois ideology – must be seen as one.

Like all her works, this is an occasional piece; in this case, the occasion is the gossip aroused by the publication of *The Arguments of Mons. Mazarin against the Dutchess, his Spouse, and the Factum for the dutchess by Mons. St Evremont*. This document consisted of the legal briefs of the lawsuit brought by the Duke of Mazarin against his estranged wife (Perry, *Celebrated* 153). The work had been translated from the French and published in 1699, shortly after the death of the duchess. A notorious figure in late seventeenth-century London, the duchess had led the kind of life of which Astell strongly disapproved. They were near neighbours in Chelsea, and Astell must have been well aware of her questionable lifestyle. Nevertheless, she was sorry for her. The publication of the old legal briefs inspired Astell to read the duchess's memoirs and to compare the two accounts. The story of her trials and the claims made by the duke as to his right to insist upon her obedience illustrated exactly the kind of abuse that moved Astell to outrage and stimulated her considerable powers of vituperation.

The abuse of Hortense de Mancini had begun at the hands of her famous uncle, the Cardinal Mazarin. Approaching death, Mazarin had given Hortense to the Duc de Meilleraye et Mayenne on condition that he take the name of Mazarin. Unfortunately the duke, though passionately in love with Hortense, was mentally unstable. His abuse of her and his wasting of her considerable fortune finally provoked her to demand a separation, which the courts denied. Thereupon, she escaped to England and took refuge at the court of her friend, Charles II, who gave her a generous pension of four thousand pounds a year, her husband having cut off the allowance originally made her from her own large estates. Her lifestyle after her separation from her husband was somewhat irregular, and Astell did not approve of it:

> Had Madame Mazarine's Education made a right Improvement of her Wit and Sense, we should not have found her seeking Relief by such imprudent, not to say scandalous Methods, as running away in Disguise with a spruce Cavalier, and rambling to so many Courts and Places, nor diverting her self with such Childish, Ridiculous, or Ill-natur'd Amusements, as the greatest part of the Adventures in her Memoirs are made up of. (34)

But though her behaviour may not have been admirable, she was indeed an abused wife, and as such she drew Astell to her defence.

In *A Serious Proposal, Parts I and II* Astell's main concern was with the lot of unmarried women: it was for them that she planned the "Protestant monastery" that should serve both as a refuge and as an educational establishment. Now she extends her concern to embrace married women also. Though usually not reduced to such abject poverty as was often suffered by the unmarried, their position was in some respects even more pitiable. A woman had little power to choose her mate. She was, in theory, allowed to refuse the man her parents had chosen for her, but in practice such pressure was often brought to bear on her that in fact she had little choice. Once married, she was completely in her husband's power. She had no independent social or political status. Any money she brought to him as dowry became his to control, and if she left him for any reason at all, he retained it. Furthermore, he kept any children of the marriage. A woman who left her husband, therefore, lost everything: home, property, means of support, even her own children. A man might, in certain circumstances, obtain a divorce, but she could not. As Astell points out, "[I]f the Matrimonial Yoke be grievous, neither Law nor Custom afford that redress which a Man obtains" (46). At a time when the idea of the human right to freedom was growing, the total lack of it for the married woman was, Astell believed, particularly shocking. Her outrage is apparent throughout. It sets the whole tone of the discourse. For this is not primarily informative discourse, like *A Serious Proposal, Part II*, nor persuasive, like *Part I*: it falls into the epideictic category, the category of praise and blame. It is invective.

Reflections is Astell's most obviously feminist work. She is unsparing in her denunciation of the various parties responsible for the plight of women. There are three objects of Astell's attack: first the men, or to be more specific, the gentlemen, for as such they see themselves – gentlefolk, who lay claim to the virtues of courtesy and consideration that the term was supposed to imply. The second object is the ladies themselves, whom she indicts chiefly for their folly, and the third is the growing Whig faction, to which John Locke and his cohorts belonged. In this work Mary Astell goes beyond her earlier interests in philosophy and education and branches out into politics.[2]

Astell begins *Reflections* by giving the context, a short account of the life of Madam Mazarin, being careful not to excuse her faults. In beginning in this way, Astell shows that she is rhetorically astute: it is usually wise in a discourse of this confrontational kind to begin by making allowances to the other side. The concession to the opposition creates a sense of honesty and fair play, and thus creates a good intrinsic *ethos* for the writer. This is not to suggest, however, that Astell is not sincere in her condemnation of the conduct of the duchess. A strict moralist, she can in no way condone her behaviour. But having made these concessions she proceeds to her main task: "But Madam Mazarine is dead, may her Faults die with her; may there be no more occasion given for the like Adventures, or if there is, may the Ladies be more Wise and Good than to take it! Let us see then from whence the mischief proceeds, and try if it can be prevented" (36).

Astell proceeds by giving a defence of marriage as an institution. Everyone, she acknowledges, seems to complain about it, but it is in itself good, both by sacred and by secular standards: "The Christian Institution of marriage provides the best that may be for Domestic Quiet and Content, and for the Education of Children; so that if we were not under the tie of Religion, even the Good of Society and civil Duty would oblige us to what that requires at our Hands" (37). The trouble lies not in the institution but in the immoral practices of those who marry. As Astell traces faults in thinking and writing to moral flaws, so she attributes the sorrows of marriage to the failure of the partners to observe Christian standards of behaviour. Marriage requires, in the first place, mutual tolerance: "For he who would have every one submit to his Humours and will not in his turn comply with them, tho' we should suppose him always in the Right, whereas a Man of this temper very seldom is so, he's not fit for a Husband" (37).

Astell now launches into her attack on men: it is not surprising that so many men appear to be unhappy in their marriages, for they select their partners for all the wrong reasons. The first of these is money. Astell allows that the pair must have enough to live on in a manner appropriate to their social standing, but she denies that money ought to be the chief, much less the sole consideration. The intolerable burden of living with an uncongenial wife is a sorrow that many men bring upon themselves because they choose their wives only with a view to the fortunes they bring as dowry. Thus they often impose on themselves an exile from their own homes because they find they cannot live with their wives.

Marrying for money, however, is not the only cause of unhappy unions. What about those who marry for love of beauty? Astell considers this to be just as bad, just as indefensible, just as likely to lead to disappointment: "There's no great odds between his Marrying for the Love of Money, or for the Love of Beauty, the Man does not act according to Reason in either Case, but is govern'd by irregular Appetites" (41). Then there are those who choose their wives for their "wit" – their apparent cleverness. Surely this is unexceptionable? Not so, at least, not in the current social context: "But he loves her wit, perhaps, and this you'll say is more Spiritual, more refin'd; not at all if you examine it to the Bottom. For what is that which nowadays passes under the name of Wit? A bitter and ill-natur'd Raillery, a pert Repartee" (41): what we should now call smartness or cheekiness, or even caustic sarcasm. Again, Reason is to be the criterion: anything not consistent with "Decorum and Good Manners [...] is not just and fit, and therefore offends our Reason" (42). Here Astell digresses to assert that however disagreeable woman's wit may be, it can never match man's for sheer distastefulness. Yet a woman who is admired for her wit is likely to come as close as she can to this degraded standard. "A Man then cannot hope to find a woman whose Wit is of a size with his, but when he doats on Wit it is to be imagin'd that he makes choice of that which comes the nearest to his own" (42). Furthermore, "it is not improbable that such a Husband may in a little time by ill usage provoke such a Wife to exercise her Wit, that is her Spleen, on him, and then it is not hard to guess how very agreeable it will be to him" (43).

However, if men are to be blamed for marrying for all the wrong reasons, so are women: "But do the Women never chuse amiss? Are the Men only in fault?" (43). Astell is reluctant to blame women – she would rather pity them, she asserts. Even men must admit that the wife has "much the harder bargain. [...] [S]he puts her self entirely into her Husband's Power" (46). If he is unpleasant, neglectful, even abusive, she has no recourse in law. Astell points out that women cannot really be said to choose at all: all they have is the power of refusal. Yet in their failure to exercise this power, they show themselves to be foolish, even if they are not so much to blame as the men. She accuses them of being taken in by the courtship rituals of the time, according to which a man represented himself as the servant, even the slave, of the lady: "[H]e may call himself her slave a few days, but it is only to make her his all the rest of his Life" (44). Women, she thinks, are too susceptible to flattery, and men simply take advantage of their weakness, telling them lies and making false promises. If instead of flattering their ladies that they were already wise and good the men would attempt to make them so, those ladies might deserve the praise that is lavished on them. But such reformation is not likely: "[A]s long as Men have base and unworthy Ends to serve, it is not to be expected that they should consent to such Methods as would certainly disappoint them" (45). For the women would then see through the false protestations of their lovers, and refuse them. The worst offenders in using this deceitful discourse, then, are the least likely to reform.

Taken in by false flattery, believing literally that the lover is her "humble servant," which really amounts to nothing more than a form of words, the woman puts herself into the position of the unpaid labourer:

> A lover who comes upon what is call'd equal Terms, makes no very advantageous Proposal to the Lady he Courts, and to whom he seems to be a humble Servant. For under many sounding Compliments, Words that have nothing in them, this is his true meaning, he wants one to manage his Family, an Housekeeper, a necessary Evil, one whose Interest it will be not to wrong him, and in whom therefore he can put greater confidence than in any he can hire for Money. One who may breed his Children, taking all the care and trouble of their Education, to preserve his Name and Family. One whose Beauty, Wit, or good Humour and agreeable Conversation, will entertain him at Home when he has been contradicted and disappointed abroad; who will do him that Justice the ill-natur'd World denies him, that is in any one's Language but his own, sooth his Pride and Flatter his Vanity, by having always so much good Sense as to be on his side, to conclude him in the right, when others are so Ignorant, or so rude as to deny it. Who will not be Blind to his Merit nor contradict his Will and Pleasure, but make it her Business, her very Ambition to content him; whose softness and gentle Compliance will calm his Passions, to whom he may safely disclose his troublesome Thoughts, and in her Breast discharge his Cares; whose Duty, Submission and Observance, will heal those Wounds other Peoples opposition or neglect have given him. In a word, one whom he can intirely Govern, and consequently may form her to his will and liking, who must be his [for] Life, and therefore cannot quit his Service, let him treat her how he will. (51)

The woman is, in fact, little better than a slave.

This brings us to the question of Astell's political interests, and her use in *Reflections* of the language of politics and of law, including the vocabulary of slavery. Early in the preface to the 1706 edition, she institutes the parallel that she will continue to use throughout. "Far be it from her to stir up Sedition of any sort, none can abhor it more; and she heartily wishes that our Masters wou'd pay their Civil and Ecclesiastical Governors the same Submission, which they themselves exact from their Domestic Subjects" (8). The parallels continue:

> [I]f Absolute Sovereignty be not necessary in a State, how comes it to be so in a Family? or if in a Family, why not in a State; since no Reason can be alledg'd for the one that will not hold more strongly for the other? If the Authority of the Husband so far as it extends, is sacred and inalienable, why not of the Prince? The Domestic Sovereign is without Dispute Elected, and the Stipulations and Contract are mutual, is it not then partial in Men to the last degree, to contend for, and practise that Arbitrary Dominion in the Families, which they abhor and exclaim against in the State? (17)

In fact, the exercise of arbitrary power – that is, tyranny – is worse in the family than in the state, for it involves far more tyrants than merely one: every husband becomes a potential tyrant. The comparisons continue. Astell uses political language to represent the exercise of power within marriage: "Covenants between Husband and Wife like Laws in an Arbitrary Government, are of little Force, the will of the sovereign is all in all" (52). The woman "elects a Monarch for Life" and "gives him an Authority she cannot recall however he misapply it." This is a very timely comparison in the context of seventeenth-century politics: the rightful king, Charles I, had been beheaded for the alleged abuse of power, and his son James II had been forced to abdicate only a dozen years earlier. No such recourse was allowed to women. And in another passage, the question of rebellion is again raised:

> He who has Sovereign Power does not value the Provocations of a Rebellious Subject, but knows how to subdue him with ease, and will make himself obey'd; but Patience and Submission are the only Comforts that are left to a poor People, who

groan under Tyranny, unless they are Strong enough to break the Yoke, to Depose and abdicate, which I doubt wou'd not be allow'd of here. For whatever may be said against Passive-Obedience in another case, I suppose there's no Man but likes it very well in this; how much soever Arbitrary Power may be dislik'd on a Throne, not Milton himself wou'd cry up Liberty to poor Female Slaves, or plead for the Lawfulness of Resisting a Private Tyranny. (47)

Here we see Astell making use of the concept of freedom, so much under debate in her time, to represent the case of women. She has already used this idea in an earlier passage: "If *all men are born free*," she asks, quoting Locke, "how is it that all Women are born slaves? as they must be if the being subjected to the *inconstant, uncertain, arbitrary will of men be the perfect Condition of Slavery?*" (18).[3] The proper relationship between king and country, as between man and wife, Astell sees as a matter of service, not from the subordinates to the superior, but from the superior to the subordinates: "Nor will it ever be well either with those who Rule or those in Subjection, even from the Throne to every Private Family, till those in Authority look on themselves as plac'd in that Station for the good and improvement of their Subjects, and not for their own sakes" (56). And she goes on to point out that "he who shou'd say the People were made for the Prince who is set over them, wou'd be thought to be out of his Senses as well as his Politicks" (57). Yet it was commonly held that women were made only for the benefit of men.

It might appear from the parallels cited above that Astell is demanding that women be treated according to the democratic principles espoused by the political party of the Whigs: that she believes that hierarchy, whether in the state or in the family, is to be resisted. But in fact, Astell was a high Tory, a conservative, a Royalist, who believed in hierarchy as ordained by God: hierarchy in the state, where God had appointed the king as ruler; hierarchy in the church, where bishops had the right to rule; and hierarchy also within the family. She did not believe that all women were subordinate to all men, but she did believe in the divine right of husbands, as in the divine right of kings.[4] This apparent inconsistency has been the subject of considerable debate among Astell scholars. Hilda Smith thinks Astell implicitly contradicts herself at this point (118). Patricia Springborg contends that *Reflections* is not really about marriage at all, but about politics (*Astell, Political Writings* xxviii).

The question is highly complex. My own reading of this element in *Reflections* is as follows. Astell is becoming increasingly interested in politics. Her objections to the empiricism of Locke, begun in philosophy, have now moved to embrace politics as well. The two, after all, are very closely linked in seventeenth and early eighteenth-century thought. Objecting as she does to the political philosophy of the Whigs, she cannot forbear to point out that their application of it is inconsistent: if they truly believe in freedom, why not freedom for women as well as men? What applies in the one case applies equally in the other. Given their convictions, they ought to act to make available to women the same freedom that they are anxious to assert as the right of men. Unless they can prove that women, like animals, are deficient in reason, and hence ought to be "chained to the chimney corner" (29), they are bound by their own convictions to treat them as fully human; and this would necessarily involve giving them rights in the family.

But Astell's own solution to the problem of abused women is different, and it is typical of her:

> [I]f a Woman were duly Principled and Taught to know the world, especially the true Sentiments that Men have of her, and the Traps they lay for her under so many gilded Compliments, and such a seemingly great Respect, that disgrace wou'd be prevented which is brought upon too many Families, Women would Marry more discreetly, and demean themselves better in a Married State than some People say they do.[5] (74)

In fact, she reiterates the advice which she has given at length in *A Serious Proposal, Part II*: "[S]he shou'd be made a good Christian and understand why she is so, and then she will be everything else that is good" (*Some Reflections* 74).

Again, Astell stresses the importance of understanding: a woman cannot truly engage in moral behaviour unless she has understood its principles. Morality and comprehension work together. Once again, Astell argues that it is in men's best interests to provide education for women, for only so can they be sure of wives who are reliable, trustworthy, and good company. Properly educated, a woman would "duly examine and weigh all the Circumstances, the Good and Evil of a Married State, and not be surpriz'd with unforeseen Inconveniences, and either never consent to be a Wife, or make a good one when she does" (75).

From the parallels she draws between the political and the domestic, Astell does not derive what appears to the twenty-first-century feminist to be the obvious conclusion. For her, the authority of the husband is ordained by God, and even if it were not, common sense would dictate some hierarchy within the family: "Now unless this supremacy be fix'd somewhere, there will be a perpetual Contention about it, such is the love of Dominion" (15). All that Astell recommends is that women should cease to be fools and men cease to be villains. Until this state of affairs can be brought about, marriage for women will continue to be martyrdom. Yet if they enter into that state rationally, they have a better chance of happiness in this life and can be sure of reaping their reward hereafter.

It is the appeal to reason that characterizes the arguments throughout. The gentlemen should use their powers of reason in choosing a wife, the ladies in accepting a husband; the Whigs should be reasonable in applying the same political standards within the family and the state. And men in authority of any kind should recognize that it is in their own best interests to promote the understanding of those for whom they are responsible:

> Superiors don't rightly understand their own interest when they attempt to put out their Subjects Eyes to keep them Obedient. A Blind Obedience is what a Rational Creature shou'd never Pay, nor wou'd such an one receive it did he rightly understand its Nature. For Human Actions are no otherwise valuable than as they are conformable to Reason, but a blind Obedience is Obeying without Reason, for ought we know against it. (75)

In the importance she places on reason, both in her arguments and in her preference for *logos* over *ethos* as a means of persuasion, Astell shows herself as typical of the Enlightenment. Although she does not believe reason to be the only criterion, especially in matters of faith, she holds that the divine light – "the candle of the Lord" as the Neoplatonists called it – is innate in every human being, male and female alike. In *A Serious Proposal, Part II* she claims for women an equal share with men in this divine reason; here she is demanding that both women and men exercise that gift, using it to direct their behaviour.

What then are the most salient characteristics of Astell's achievement in this work? The most obvious one is that here for the first time she engages in a new kind of rhetoric. *A Serious Proposal, Part I* is deliberative rhetoric, the rhetoric of persuasion. *Part II* is forensic, the rhetoric of information. With *Some Reflections Upon Marriage* she completes her mastery of all three forms, for this work is epideictic, the kind of rhetoric that deals with praise and – as in this case – blame. It is important to recognize what Astell is about, for although this is her most strongly feminist work, contemporary feminists are likely to find it puzzling and unsatisfactory. Beyond suggesting that both men and women should become wise and good, Astell offers no real solution to the problem of gross injustice toward married women. She does not attempt to. For this is neither a proposal nor a philosophical discussion: *Reflections* is fundamentally a work of invective. It is vituperation. She does it very well, and is obviously enjoying herself.

An equally salient characteristic of *Reflections* is Astell's use of enthymemes.[6] She can assume that her audience will be both knowledgeable and interested in the current political debate, and she uses that knowledge and interest to her advantage. Particularly so far as the Whigs among her readership are concerned, she draws upon the assumptions that she can expect them to make, using that which to them is incontestable to force her point home. Her adoption of the political parallels, therefore, is designed both to engage the interest of the audience – for politics was the most discussed subject of the time – and to attack her political enemies. This use of current interests to strengthen her arguments is particularly astute, for among the general audience she here addresses there might be few seriously concerned about the plight of married women, but many for whom political convictions and allegiances are burning issues.

But above all, it is Astell's style that makes *Reflections* such excellent reading – still. Renowned for her eloquence in her own day, she brings to her invective a consummate rhetorical expertise. Her style is lucid, spare, the words exactly chosen, the sentence structures designed for maximum impact. Her language is deliberately wounding. She is devastating in her use of irony and sarcasm, some of it obvious, some more subtle. In her indictment of men she has recourse to an animal vocabulary: the husband who always insists upon having his own way "ought to be turn'd out of the Herd to live by himself" (37). Here with this simple choice of "herd" instead

of "community" Astell implies without stating it the beastliness of
the intolerant husband. A similar use of innuendo is found in the
veiled comparison of husbands with pigs in the preface added to
the third edition of 1706:

> ['T]is certainly no Arrogance in a Woman to conclude, that
> she was made for the Service of God, and that this is her End.
> Because God made all Things for Himself, and a Rational
> Mind is too noble a Being to be Made for the Sake and Service
> of any Creature. The Service she at any time becomes oblig'd to
> pay to a Man, is only a Business by the Bye. Just as it may be any
> Man's Business to keep Hogs; he was not Made for this, but if
> he hires himself out to such an Employment, he ought consci-
> entiously to perform it. (11)

Critical though she is of her political enemies, and at times even
of women themselves, it is in her indictment of men that she is
particularly unsparing. She expresses withering contempt for the
mindless aspiring beau: "A Husband indeed is thought by both
Sexes so very valuable, that scarce a man who can keep himself
clean and make a Bow, but thinks he is good enough to pretend to
any Woman" (66). She sarcastically dismisses the contemptuous
charge that women cannot keep a secret: "Some Men will have
it, that the Reason of our Lord's appearing first to the Women,
was their being least able to keep a Secret; a Witty and Masculine
Remarque, and wonderfully Reverent!" (27). More subtle is her
use of irony – the following is fair example of her mastery of this
trope:

> [I]t were ridiculous to suppose that a woman, were she ever
> so much improv'd, cou'd come near the topping Genius of the
> Men, and therefore why shou'd they envy or discourage her?
> Strength of Mind goes along with Strength of Body, and 'tis
> only for some odd Accidents which Philosophers have not yet
> thought worth while to enquire into, that the Sturdiest Porter is
> not the Wisest Man! (77)

Occasionally, Astell makes women also the butt of her wit as when
(again using the language of slavery) she bitingly complains that
women "are for the most part Wise enough to Love their Chains,
and to discern how very becomingly they set" (29). Her satire is

made particularly telling by her mastery of sentence form. Consider the elegant economy of the throw-away phrase in which she refers to "Lovers, who are not more violent in their Passion than they are certain to Repent of it" (43). Notice, too, the perfect balance and the laconic style here: "Women [...] are blam'd for that ill Conduct they are not suffer'd to avoid, and reproach'd for those Faults they are in a manner forc'd into" (65).

In conclusion, then, *Reflections* represents a number of "firsts" for Astell. Here for the first time, as we have seen, she engages fully in *contentio*, public rhetoric. Also for the first time she writes an epideictic work. Elements of praise and blame have certainly been present in her earlier works, just as elements of persuasion and information are to be found in this. But the overriding purpose of this work is to attack the public cultural values of her time, particularly as they concern women. *Reflections* is one of the more important of early feminist works, though its feminism belongs to its own time, not ours. And it is not only cultural values that she attacks, for this work includes a telling criticism of the political and philosophical values of her opponents, the rising Whig party. Here she first shows her powers in political rhetoric. The criticism begun in *A Serious Proposal, Part II* now blossoms. Her feminism and her politics work off each other, sharpen their edges against each other. She argues tellingly, forcefully, showing promise of the eloquence of her attack on her political opponents in her subsequent works, *The Christian Religion* and the political pamphlets.

Reflections is in many ways a more ambitious piece of discourse than either of the Proposals – wider in its scope, addressed to a more public, more heterogeneous audience, engaging more fully than ever before in the public debate about politics, engaging in a new kind of rhetoric, and extending her interest in feminist concerns to include married women. That Astell was able to accomplish so well her various purposes is proof of her consummate rhetorical skill.

7

The Christian Religion

n 1705 Mary Astell published her *magnum opus, The Christian Religion*. It is her longest work – well over 400 pages – and her most comprehensive and profound.[1] It brings together her ideas about philosophy, politics, education, and women's issues, and shows them to be consistent with one another, based as all of them are, fundamentally, on her Christian convictions. The work is divided into five sections. The first section, "Of Religion in general; and of the Christian Faith," she calls the theoretical part of the treatise, laying the groundwork of philosophy on which the remaining parts of the work are based. Having established the theory, she turns to Christian practice: section 2 deals with our duty to God, section 3 with our duty to our neighbour, and section 4 with our duty to ourselves. The fifth section is devoted to refutation, following the pattern of classical rhetoric. She also includes here a summary of the whole. In this chapter, though I shall make reference to the various issues Astell discusses, I am primarily interested in considering the work as a rhetorical project: To what rhetorical genre does the work belong? What is the context? Who are the audiences? And how does she accommodate her various purposes and audiences?

First, the question of genre: again, Astell adopts the letter form. Only *Some Reflections Upon Marriage* has so far not been in the form of a letter addressed to a particular audience. This work is written as a letter addressed to her friend Lady Catherine Jones. Astell does occasionally address the correspondent as "your Ladyship," but the subject matter, the organization, and the length suggest that it is in fact a treatise. Only in tone does it sometimes suggest a personal correspondence. The convention of the letter is, perhaps, wearing a little thin. It is a transparent device, probably adopted in this work to give some sense of focus and of personal address. Here her style is, as usual, conversational: it is voiced, and her tone is intimate, addressing the audience (for in spite of the letter form, she is manifestly addressing an audience of more than one) like familiar friends, sharing insights and taking them into her confidence. She wants, if possible, to give immediacy to her subject, as if it is the dominating topic of current conversation. As we have seen, she uses the death of the Duchess of Mazarin as the occasion of *Reflections*. *The Christian Religion* too is presented as an occasional work: "When I borrow'd *The Ladies Religion*, your Ladyship I believe had no suspicion of being troubled with such a long Address, nor had I any design to give you this trouble" (1). It is her reading of this book that she gives as the immediate occasion of her commencing the present work. Since Lady Catherine Jones was her friend and patron, it is probable that she addressed the work to her also to acknowledge her assistance and to honour her.

In thus using the letter genre for what is essentially a treatise, Astell is following a standard Renaissance convention, based on the example of Cicero.[2] In Astell's practice, the use of the letter genre implies the more conciliatory tone typical of *sermo*, instead of the masculine and adversarial *contentio*. Astell's later political pamphlets do adopt a contentious tone, as did *Reflections*. In those works she demonstrates a power of invective unsurpassed in her day. She has taken on the men, and she can match the best of them in a verbal fight. But her letters are always addressed to ladies, and to them she shows deference and tenderness. However, *The Christian Religion*, though ostensibly a letter to a lady, in fact addresses a much wider audience, including Astell's opponents, John Locke and Damaris Masham. In general, her tone is appropriate to *sermo*. It is true that when she is addressing the Masham/ Locke opposition, she can be quite sharp, but she never goes to the extremes of vituperative eloquence typical of *Reflections* and her political pamphlets.

Like *A Serious Proposal, Part II*, *The Christian Religion* is a work of instruction, with a very strongly developed persuasive element. It is in fact a treatise on the Christian life. In some respects it reprises and follows up her ideas in the second part of *A Serious Proposal*. However, whereas that work has primarily to do with education, this has a broader scope. Education itself is only part of the larger project of finding out how to live well. As Astell says:

> It is to little purpose to Think well and Speak well, unless we *Live well*, this is our Great Affair and truest Excellency, the other are no further to be regarded than as they may assist us in this. She who does not draw this Inference from her Studies has Thought in vain, her notions are Erroneous and Mistaken.

And all her Eloquence is but an empty noise, who employs it in any other design than in gaining Proselytes to Heaven. (*Serious Proposal II* 147)

In pursuance of this project, then, Astell continues her instruction of women to include directions for developing Christian spirituality. As she articulates it to "her Ladyship," her purpose is to put forward her own ideas as an alternative to what she considers the mistaken notions of the writer of *The Ladies Religion*. This work, which she professes to find very similar to Locke's *The Reasonableness of Christianity* (*Christian Religion* 83), is unacceptable because of its manifest deism and its emphasis upon the importance of morality as opposed to faith (F. Smith 115). She proposes to discuss "what I think a Woman *ought* to Believe and Practise, and consequently what she *may*" (3). However, although Astell identifies her reading of *The Ladies Religion* as the immediate occasion of her engagement in the project, this is not the only work she is concerned to challenge. During the years preceding the publication of *The Christian Religion*, there had been a number of addresses to such questions as these: What is the philosophical basis for belief? How does it relate to politics? And more specifically, what are the duties of the individual Christian believer? One of these works, *The Whole Duty of Man*, Astell praises as excellent. She believes it to have been written by a lady, though she does not specify the author.[3] She also has kind words to say of the author of *The Ladies Calling* and *The Gentleman's Calling* (*Christian Religion* 2), though she must have disagreed with his conviction of the natural inferiority of women and his recommendation of obedience, silence, and subjection (F. Smith 41ff.). But most of the works written at about this time Astell finds wanting: as well as *The Ladies Religion*, she is also concerned to refute certain arguments in other works, including, but not limited to, many of the works of John Locke: *An Essay Concerning Human Understanding* (1689), *The Reasonableness of Christianity* and *Vindication of the Reasonableness of Christianity* (1695), and *Two Treatises of Government* (1690). She also addresses the arguments in *A Discourse Concerning the Love of God* (1696), the attack by Damaris Masham on *Letters Concerning the Love of God*, her correspondence with John Norris. It is here, not in *A Serious Proposal, Part II*, that Astell answers the objections put forward by Masham in that work. She may have considered it to have been written by Locke, and it was indeed most probably strongly influenced by him. She also takes issue with some of the sermons of Archbishop Tillotson (403–07).

These works, then, provide the textual context in which she writes. Her ultimate purpose may be inferred from the epigraph, printed on the title page – a quotation from Jeremiah 6:16: "Thus saith the Lord, Stand ye in the ways and see, and ask for the Old Paths, where is the good Way, and walk therein, and ye shall find Rest to your Souls." This suggests that in this work Astell is responding to what she sees as an alarming tendency to latitudinarianism, to the reduction of the Christian faith to a kind of secular morality that ignores the mysterious elements that she holds to be essential. What she has in mind, then, is to set forth the basic principles, the philosophy of the faith, in opposition to the current ideas of more modern thinkers, and then to apply these principles to Christian living. She begins by setting forth the principles of the Christian faith, entailing a discussion of natural religion and of revealed religion in section 1. She concludes that although natural religion or reason could have told her that she, like all other human beings, was a sinner, without revealed religion she could not have known that "Adam's Sin was the cause of this" (50). Similarly, however much she desired forgiveness, she would not have known how it might be available: "For that GOD wou'd send His Son, at what time, and in what matter [*sic*] to Reconcile the World unto Himself, was what no Created Understanding cou'd ever have attain'd the knowledge of, unless GOD had thought fit to reveal it" (50).

She concludes, therefore, that although some truths may be established by reason and experience, others can come only by divine revelation. It is true that she must use reason to establish that revelation is genuine: she must "enquire [...] whether that which is call'd Divine Revelation, is so in reality, for thus far my own Reason is a proper judge" (13). Having satisfied herself in this respect, however, she must not allow reason to overrule revelation:

> Reason can judge of things which she can comprehend, she can determine where she has a compleat, or at least a clear and distinct Idea and can judge of a *contradiction in terms*, for this is within her compass; but she must not affirm in opposition to Revelation. (14)

Like Pascal, one of her intellectual heroes, Astell believed that reason and revelation each have their own particular sphere and must not trespass into the other's territory.[4] This position she had already clearly set forth in *A Serious Proposal, Part II*:

> There is not such a difference between Faith and Science as is usually suppos'd. The difference consists not in the Certainty but in the way of Proof: the Objects of Faith are as Rationally and Firmly Prov'd as the Objects of Science, tho by another way. As Science Demonstrates things that are Seen, so Faith is the Evidence of such as are Not Seen. And he who rejects the Evidence of Faith in such things as belong to its Cognizance, is an unreasonable as he who denies the Propositions in Geometry that are prov'd with Mathematical exactness. (103)

Having thus laid down the ground rules, the premises upon which their thinking should be based, Astell insists that people – all people, and especially women – must think for themselves and not rely upon what they have been told. Here, as in *Some Reflections Upon Marriage*, in thus preferring *logos* to the non-rational means of persuasion, *ethos*, and *pathos*, Astell shows herself to be a child of the Enlightenment. Although in many ways she looks back to the past – her epigraph, referred to above, is a case in point – in this emphasis upon reason she is typical of her age, though her allegiance is to the rationalism of Descartes, not to the empiricism of Locke. Her respect for reason is also consistent with her Neoplatonist philosophy: in *The Christian Religion* she refers to "the candle of the Lord" (17), this being the phrase used by the Cambridge Platonists to designate reason and to assert their belief that it is innate.

The conviction of women's intellectual powers – at least equal to those of men – is central to Astell's beliefs: "If GOD had not intended that Women shou'd use their Reason, He wou'd not have given them any, for He does nothing in vain" (6). As in *A Serious Proposal, Part II* (upon which this work expands), she insists that it is not enough for women simply to learn what they ought to do: they must also understand the reasons for the injunctions. Women have been too thoroughly trained in obedience, in deference to those who constitute themselves their superiors:

I therefore beg leave to say, That most of, if not all, the Follies and Vices that Women are subject to, (for I meddle not with the Men) are owing to our paying too great deference to other Peoples judgments, and too little to our own, in suffering others to judge for us, when GOD has not only allow'd, but requir'd us to judge for our selves. [...]

What is it that engages Women in Crimes contrary to their Reason, and their very natural Temper, but the being over-perswaded and over-rul'd by those to whose conduct they commit themselves? And how do they excuse these Crimes, but by alledging the examples and opinions of other People? (36,37)

It is in the context of setting forth these philosophical principles that Astell finds it necessary to refute some of the ideas of Locke. Yet in spite of her refutation, it is obvious that she respects him. She gives him the benefit of the doubt whenever possible, even to the point of accepting some of the ideas he puts forward. Ultimately, though, she finds his position inconsistent with both the evidence of Scripture and the traditions of the church as found in the earliest creeds. Locke has claimed (according to Astell) that "the coming of the Messiah, the Kingdom of Heaven, and the Kingdom of GOD are the same and was what John the Baptist Preach'd: And that this same Doctrine and nothing else was Preach'd by the Apostles afterwards" (71). Astell is not satisfied: "The former part of this Assertion we shall allow him, the latter is the point in question" (71). She then proceeds to prove her point by referring to the account in Acts 19 of the disciples at Ephesus who had been baptized only with John's baptism and had not received the Holy Ghost.[5]

Astell also takes issue with Locke for ignoring the doctrine of the Trinity "since his profess'd design is to speak of those Truths, and of those only which are absolutely requir'd to be believed to make any one a Christian" (75). Initiation into the Christian church, Astell points out, involves baptism in the name of all three Persons of the Trinity. Obviously, then, the doctrine of the Trinity is essential to Christianity. How then can Locke fail to mention it? Astell refutes Locke cogently, drawing on her profound and extensive knowledge of Scripture. She obviously respects him as a philosopher, but she cannot go along with his conclusions. What Locke is recommending, she believes, is not Christianity at all. The reasonableness of Christianity should not consist in removing all those elements that might promote conflict, which she sees as Locke's purpose:

> But, as appears to me, the Reasonableness of Christianity does not consist in avoiding such Arguments as Men object against, but in these two great Truths, viz. 1. That there is not any thing so Reasonable as to believe all that GOD has Reveal'd, and to practise all that he has commanded. 2. That GOD has given such proofs and evidences as are sufficient to satisfie any Reasonable Person, That the Christian Religion is a Divine Revelation. (65)

Naturally, one of the works Astell is most concerned to refute is Damaris Masham's *Discourse Concerning the Love of God*, which attacks Astell and Norris's *Letters Concerning the Love of God*. I have argued earlier that in *A Serious Proposal, Part II* Astell postpones her refutation of this work to a later occasion. It is here, in *The Christian Religion*, that she fully engages with her opponent. Most of this refutation is to be found in section 2, which deals with the duty of human beings toward God. As the titles of both Astell's and Masham's works suggest, the main issue is the question of love. In Astell's view, the chief duty of Christians toward God is to love him, and only him: their obedience is predicated on their love for him. This is, of course, very similar to the theology of Augustine of Hippo, that only God is to be loved for himself alone; other people and things are to be loved for his sake.[6] Masham finds this definition far too pietistic, accusing Astell of engaging in "Pompous Rhapsodies" (27) and suggesting as a better definition something more secular and grounded in empiricism: "Love simply [...] is that Disposition, or Act, of the Mind, which we find in our selves towards any thing we are pleased with" (51).

Taking a side swipe by way of the rhetorical device of paralepsis,[7] Astell proceeds with a *tu quoque* and then launches on a full-scale refutation:

> This is not the place to take notice how those who are so severe upon their Neighbours for being wanting (even in Private Letters writ without a design of being Publish'd)[8] in that exactness of Expression which is to be found in Philosophical Definitions, do themselves confound the notion of Love with the sentiment of Pleasure, by making Love *to consist barely in the act of the Mind*

towards that which pleases. I shall only observe, as more proper
to my present Business, That the Love of our enemies is by no
means consistent with that account of Love that is given by our
great Men [...] . (132)

Astell proceeds to refute Masham's argument by referring to
the commandment of Jesus Christ to love one's enemies (Matt.
5:44). Since "we cannot be pleas'd with our Enemies, consequently we cannot Love them" (132). Masham's definition of love
must be mistaken, then, since it is inconsistent with the words of
Jesus. The refutation of Masham's definition of love continues for
several pages, embracing also references to Locke's *Two Treatises
of Government*. Astell argues shrewdly and tellingly; however, it
is apparent that she and her opponents are basing their arguments
on different premises and therefore their minds will never meet.
Locke and Masham wish to argue from experience, Astell from
authority. For Astell, the authority of the revelation in Scripture is
paramount; for her opponents, it is not. Both sides cite Scripture,
but they do not give it the same weight.

   Not only are the two sides arguing from rather different premises; they also have fundamentally different values and tempera-
ments. Masham obviously finds Astell a pious prig: she has no
understanding of, no sympathy with, Astell's contemplative spirituality. For her, the world of sense is there simply to be enjoyed;
for Astell, that world is dangerous unless controlled by a primary
allegiance to the will of God. Their very different premises and
schemes of values are naturally played out in the discussion of the
political issues that concern them both. For Astell, the constraint
upon government must come from religion; for Masham it should
come from the people. Here is Astell's response to Masham's position:

> [W]hat but the Love of GOD can justly restrain Sovereign
> Princes from being Injurious, or excite them to be Just and
> Gracious to their People? Those who think the Awe of GOD's
> Sovereignty but a poor Restraint, and are therefore for Subjecting
> them to the Coertion [*sic*] of the People, against the Laws of this
> Nation as well as against the Doctrine of the Church, against
> Scripture, and Common Sense, shew too little regard to any
> Religion, whatever they may talk about it, to be look'd upon by
> any but a heedless Mob as its Defenders; and are in truth what

St Paul and his Fellow Christians were *falsly* accus'd of being, The *Men that have turn'd the World upside down.* (144)

Perhaps despairing of the possibility of persuading her opponents by reason, since their premises are so mutually incompatible, Astell resorts to irony:

> [A]s the World now goes, it is most for GOD's Service that we keep what we have got, and add as much to't as we can. For this enables us to be Patriots, to purchase Heads and Hands, and to Fight for Religion upon occasion; and in the mean while to do abundance of good to Mankind, by applying our selves to all their Inclinations whatever they be, that so we may bring them over to the Righteous side! (145)

Astell also answers Masham's attack upon monasteries. Conflating Astell's position in *Letters Concerning the Love of God* with her design to erect a Protestant monastery for women, put forward in *A Serious Proposal, Part I*, Masham had dismissed the suggestion as having no value, indeed as pernicious:

> As for Monasteries, and religious Houses, (as they are call'd) [they] serve only to draw in Discontented, Devout People, with an imaginary Happiness. For there is constantly as much Pride, Malice, and Faction, within those Walls, as without them; And (if we may believe what is said, and has not wanted farther Evidence) very often as much licentiousness. (126)

Connecting this attack with an earlier comment of Masham's – "if we had no Desires but after God, the several Societies of Mankind could not long hold together, nor the very Species be continued" (83) – Astell protests that she has been (wilfully?) misunderstood:

> [T]hat which they seem most affraid [*sic*] of, is dispeopling the World and driving Folks into Monasteries, tho' I see none among us for them to run into were they ever so much inclin'd; but have heard it generally complain'd of by very good *Protestants*, that Monasteries were Abolish'd instead of being Reform'd: And tho' none that I know of plead for Monasteries, strictly so call'd, in *England*, or anything else but a reasonable provision for the Education of one half of Mankind, and for a

safe retreat so long and no longer than our Circumstances make it requisite. As is so plainly exprest in what has been said in this business, that none can mistake the meaning, without great disingenuity and an eager desire to cavil. (142)

On the question of readership, there is no doubt that Locke and other philosophers of his persuasion were part of the intended audience. Astell implies as much when she refers to the fact that Locke died before the publication of *The Christian Religion*: "And to me the greatest difficulty of all, is in starting any Objection against an Author when he has left the World, and therefore can't explain and answer for himself, which is a misfortune I am already fallen into (with relation to Mr L.) by these Papers being so long in the Press" (408). However, Locke and others with whom she disagrees are by no means the primary audience she has in mind. Although much of what she says is equally applicable to men, and she does not exclude them from her audience, her reason for writing the work, as she states it at the beginning, is to provide an alternative to the false ideas in *The Ladies Religion*: she intends the work to be read by women. It is obviously appropriate, then, to look at the passages in which she specifically mentions women or issues of gender. These fall into three categories: references to Queen Anne, self-references, and more general references to questions of gender.

First, then, Astell's references to Queen Anne. Her satisfaction at having a woman on the throne is apparent in every work of hers published after Anne's succession. She hoped that under a female monarch the lot of women might improve: "May we not hope that She will not do less for Her own Sex than She has already done for the other; but that the next Year of Her Majesties Annals will bear date, from Her Maternal and Royal Care of the most helpless and most neglected part of Her Subjects" (143). These great hopes may have been inspired by looking back to the triumphs of Queen Elizabeth I's reign. That Queen had been herself a fine scholar and a superb rhetorician, and women's education, at least in the upper classes, had been encouraged by her example. If so, Astell was probably disappointed that so little was in fact achieved under Anne, who, unlike Elizabeth, was not a strong monarch.

Secondly, there are the self-references. These are more numerous and of greater significance. The first comes relatively early in the treatise: "Shall I then receive the Bounty of GOD in vain? GOD forbid! and therefore did I know or cou'd find out, a nobler Employment than the making my Calling and election sure, Woman though I am, I would employ all my Thoughts and Industry to compass it" (114). The force of this comment appears to be a recognition of the weakness and helplessness commonly ascribed to women, and perhaps a denial of it. Quite different is the self-reference that occurs toward the end, near the beginning of the final section, which sums up the whole: "Some perhaps will think there's too much of the Woman in it, too much of my particular Manner and Thoughts" (391). Here she refers not so much to her gender as to her distinctive personality. But later in the same paragraph she says something highly relevant to questions of gender: "[I]f these Papers shall survive me, by speaking Truths which no Man would say, they will appear to be genuine, and *no Man* will be blam'd for their Imperfections. I am sensible that by giving this account of Christianity according to its Truth and Purity, I have made a sort of Satyr on my self and others, whose Practice falls so very short of our Profession."

Here (irony aside) she obviously assumes that she is writing in a style specific to women. In general Astell makes very few concessions to differences of gender, her main thrust usually being that women are full human beings, whose capacities are no different from those of men. What, then, does she mean by "Truths that no Man would say"? An observation she makes further on in the passage may offer a clue:

> For Moral Discourses unless they are very particular do no good upon a Reader, every one being apt to justifie or excuse his own Conduct, and to believe he is unconcern'd. So that a Book is only so many words to no manner of purpose, except the Reader, even him whom the Author never so much as heard of, finds his own Picture in it, and is forc'd to say to himself, *I am the Man*. I design to do all the Good I can, which seems to me to be a Christian's Duty, and those who Won't suffer us to do it one way, must be content to receive it another. If any are offended at my manner of doing it, let them be pleas'd to show me a better, and I shall thankfully follow it. (393)

It seems from this passage that Astell believes that no man would write with such intimacy, such honesty, such self-disclosure. This particular style she sees as essentially feminine. Moreover, she sees it as a great advantage because it forces the readers to make direct application to themselves. The passage is especially interesting from a rhetorical point of view because it sheds light upon Astell's concepts of reception. The vividness and immediacy of which she speaks is part of the classical concept of *enargia*.[9] But Astell has added to it her own concept of the role of intimacy of style, of the importance of self-disclosure as a means of reaching the reader and forcing an application to the self.

The most extended passage of self-reference occurs a few pages later, where she compares her work favourably with other works of the same kind, slyly quoting from Locke's *The Reasonableness of Christianity*, and referring also to *The Ladies Religion* – she has, she asserts, written nothing inaccessible to the uneducated:

> No, not *the Day Labourers and Tradesmen, the spinsters and Dairy Maids*, who may easily *comprehend* what a Woman cou'd write. A Woman who has not the least Reason to imagine that her Understanding is any better than the rest of her Sex's. All the difference, if there be any, arising only from her Application, her Disinteressed and Unprejudic'd Love to Truth, and unwearied pursuit of it, notwithstanding all Discouragements, which is in every Womans power as well as in hers. And I assure you, Madam, she consulted no Divine, nor any other Man, scarce any Book except the Bible, on the Subject of this Letter, being willing to follow the thread of her own Thoughts. (403)

The force of this passage is that she believes she has done a much better job of informing the general public, especially those less educated, than any of her rivals or attackers, in part at least because she is a woman. The audience can understand without difficulty "what a Woman cou'd write."

Thirdly, there are references to women in general and to questions of gender. A number of these are complaints made about women themselves, rather than about the way they are treated. For example, she rather sourly complains about the worldliness of women of fashion: "For no time, no Care, no Pains, is thought too much for the acquisition of Honour, or Pleasure, Or Riches, tho' we may be taken from them very soon, and are sure we cannot long possess them. The making their Fortune as Men call it; or with us Women the setting our selves to purchase a Master" (113). Later, she complains again of the fashionable woman's lack of ambition to make herself "Wise and Good in her Generation," since she is "afraid of Censure, and dares not cross the vogue of the World, nor by doing what is unfashionable, hazard her Character tho' to improve it!" (315). And in exasperation, she exclaims that it is "easier to make some Ladies Understand every thing, than to perswade them that they are capable of Understanding any thing" (291).[10]

One the most important passages on women is found in section 4, *Of Our Duty to our Selves* (296) – the most important because it clarifies Astell's approach to the question of women's participation in public life:

> And since it is allow'd on all hands, that the Mens Business is without Doors, and their's is an Active Life; Women who ought to be Retir'd, are for this reason design'd by providence for Speculation: Providence, which allots every one an Employment, and never intended that any one shou'd give themselves up to Idleness and Unprofitable amusements. And I make no question but great Improvements might be made in the Sciences, were not Women enviously excluded from this their proper Business. (296)

Here is a particularly interesting twist on the customary confinement of women, and their exclusion from public affairs. Astell believes that a woman's person should be kept private: as she says in *A Serious Proposal, Part II*, women "have no business with the Pulpit, the Bar or *St Stephen's Chapel*" (143) (where Parliament met). Yet at the same time she believes that "the true Christian seeks a Reputation from Vertues of a Public, not of a Private Nature" (*Christian Religion* 325). However, a woman, by her very exclusion from appearing in public life, has a great opportunity to contribute to it. What Astell appears to be suggesting here is that scholarship ought to be the particular province of women, since they have both the intelligence and the leisure to engage in it and their contribution to the public good can be made from afar, without intruding their persons into the public world itself. As Ruth Perry has pointed out, "this (Cartesian) introspection which required leisure, isolation, and the willful doubting of all previous knowledge, was a mode of intellectual activity available to almost all literate middle-class and aristocratic women" ("Radical Doubt" 479). As we have seen, in using the genre of the ostensibly private letter for public purposes, Astell worked in the tradition of the Renaissance humanists. John Tinkler argues that this kind of writing was possible only to men of leisure: "[T]he literary *sermo* was above all the literature of *otium*" (287). Cicero produced his works of scholarship when he was out of political office, and "a surprising number of the humanist works we think of as most important were written at leisure" (Tinkler 287). Although Astell herself does not draw this parallel, it is interesting that she recommends women to use their leisure in pursuit of scholarship to an extent that men who are fully engaged with the business of the world cannot.

The references to women, however, are not numerous. Their very scarcity would suggest that Astell has more than women in mind as her audience, and that her purpose goes beyond a discussion of feminist concerns, important as these are, as it also goes beyond mere refutation of philosophers with whom she disagrees. The greater proportion of the whole work is devoted to a detailed discussion of Christian principles and how to put them into practice, and most of it is relevant to both women and men.

The Christian Religion gives the fullest, the most complete statement of Astell's ideas. To a modern audience, the title is misleading, suggesting a work exclusively devoted to theology. In Astell's time, however, and most especially in her own thought and practice, religion necessarily had implications for the whole of life, including philosophy, politics, education, and personal morality. In this work, too, she addresses her broadest audience yet. Although her address is purportedly to a single individual, Lady Catherine Jones, and her specific direction is to the ladies, she has in mind a much wider public. It includes, but is not limited to, those who disagree with her – Locke, Masham, and Tillotson. It might be argued that her political pamphlets and *Some Reflections Upon Marriage* are directed to a wider audience still; however, these address readers specifically engaged in the discussion of particular contemporary issues. *The Christian Religion* has a much wider view and a less ephemeral relevance.

Her style in this work shows little of either the devastating satirical bite of the political pamphlets and of *Some Reflections Upon Marriage* or the maternalism of *A Serious Proposal*. Of all her works, it is the most philosophical. Here she refutes the criticism of her opponents, something that the purpose of *A Serious Proposal, Part II* made inappropriate. Yet although the positions are closely and tellingly argued, the style remains intimate. Perhaps its foremost characteristic is its obvious sincerity: Astell not only believes, she deeply cares about the truths she is setting forth. One of the least regarded – it is still not available in a modern edition – *The Christian Religion* should nonetheless be considered Astell's greatest work.

8

Political Pamphlets

he Christian Religion is perhaps Astell's greatest work – the most profound and the most long-lasting – but from one point of view, her political pamphlets represent the most significant achievement of her career.[1] It is true that they are the least accessible to twenty-first-century readers, the issues they discuss having long since died. Yet they are important because they show a woman both participating in the kind of discussion traditionally limited to men and being respected and valued for the contributions she makes. Women had long been contributing to discussions of religious and educational matters. Their interest in these areas was acknowledged, and even those who did not approve of women writing might turn a blind eye to their activities in such fields. But politics was different. Political discussions, especially in the form of political pamphleteering, had the potential to sway public opinion and help set the agenda for parliamentary debate. That Mary Astell participated in such printed discussions as a celebrated contributor says much for her reputation during the early years of the eighteenth century and may be taken as a landmark in the progress of women toward full participation in public affairs.[2] With the publication of the political pamphlets, therefore, Astell's transition from *sermo* to *contentio* is complete.

Though a detailed discussion of the pamphlets is neither required nor indeed appropriate in the present context, some understanding of the issues involved is necessary for an appreciation of Astell's contribution.[3] And this presents a difficulty, for not only are the issues themselves long since outdated; the attitudes that lay behind Astell's convictions are hard for modern men and women to accept. Astell, who has been celebrated as the first English feminist, is – by modern standards – the opposite of typically feminist in her political ideas. She supported the Tories: in her pamphlets, therefore, we find her adopting typically Tory positions and resisting, sometimes ferociously, the very principles of liberalism that modern society has come to value.

In order to understand as far as possible the fervour of the pamphlet war, we must understand how radically the English nation had been affected by the civil war, and especially the death of Charles I, which for Astell and other Tories was something far worse than execution: "The Murder of King Charles I is the gentlest expression by which one can mention that execrable Action" (Astell, *Moderation* 81). The rancour had by no means vanished by the early 1700s: the hurt and the guilt were still there, exacerbated by the abdication of James II and the accession of William and Mary. Too many people, too many families, had suffered for the wars and their consequences to be easily forgotten.[4] The nation had polarized: those who supported the monarchy espoused the old political values, based in religion: the king was ordained by God and could not be deposed. The obligation to obey him (if only passively) remained, even if his policies displeased the people. As against this, the new men, the Whigs, asserted the power of the people. Astell and other Tories saw this as dangerously secular: God was being left out of the political equation and disaster would surely follow. For conservative thinkers such as Astell, order was an important issue. The hierarchical system guaranteed law and order and prevented the disastrous state of affairs in which might becomes right. The rejection of the divinely instituted hierarchy, with the king at the top, would put the whole structure of society at risk: "In a word, Order is a Sacred Thing, 'tis that Law which God prescribes Himself, and inviolably observes. Subordination is a necessary consequence of Order, for in a State of Ignorance and [De]pravity such as ours is, there is not any thing that tends more to Confusion than Equality" (*Moderation* 28).

It must be remembered that at this time religion was not a private matter: it was a highly public one, for both sides. Both Whigs and Tories – roughly corresponding to Dissenters and Anglicans – wanted to bring in what they thought was appropriate legislation. The issue was not at root religious: it was political. And what Astell and her party objected to was not the freedom of Dissenters to worship in their own way, but their political ambitions to put their ideas into practice for the whole nation. One of the most contentious issues in the early years of the eighteenth century was the question of Occasional Conformity. By law, only members of the Church of England could be elected to political office. Ambitious Dissenters, therefore, developed the practice of Occasional Conformity – that is, attending the Church of England services just often enough to qualify.[5] The practice drew public attention when the Lord Mayor of London attended both his own dissenting church and the Church of England on the same day. The Tories thereupon tried to bring in a bill against Occasional Conformity. According to the conservatives, "government ought to be in the hands of those whose birth and estates insured less self-interested motives and put them above common temptations" (Perry, *Celebrated* 197). They saw Dissenters who aspired to political office as power hungry men on the make. Occasional Conformity was the thin end of the wedge: allow the Dissenters into office, and the whole foundation of the body politic, the stability of the entire nation, would be jeopardized. Allowing Dissenters political power, therefore, was seen as a threat to the whole nation. It would involve, first of all, a possible shift of power from the old class of the nobility to the new bourgeoisie; furthermore, it would promote the power of parliament as against that of the monarch. Since the monarch was, according to Tory values, God's vice-regent, such a shift in power would be a direct insult to God. It would also, according to Astell, involve a shift in values toward materialism and even atheism. Religious belief might cease to be politically relevant. Astell saw allowing Occasional Conformity, then, as a dangerous move in the direction of a wholly secular society.

Astell's first political pamphlet, *Moderation Truly Stated* (1704), was directed to this particular issue. It was written as a contribution to the pamphlet war initiated by Daniel Defoe in *An Enquiry into the Occasional Conformity of Dissenters*, first published in 1698. However, Astell wrote in response not primarily to Defoe, but to *Moderation a Vertue* (1703) by the Welsh Presbyterian minister James Owen, a work much more moderate and reasonable in its approach and therefore more persuasive – and more dangerous to the Tory cause. Moderation was for Astell not a virtue: she regarded it as lukewarmness in religious matters. Her pamphlet, in fact, answers Owen's *Moderation a Vertue* as well as *Essays upon Peace and War* (1704) by Charles D'Avenant, who was regarded by Astell and other Tories as a turncoat. Her reply to D'Avenant was included as a preface to *Moderation Truly Stated* and is one of the best parts of the work.[6]

Astell's defence of the Tory position was admirable, and showed how powerful a woman's argumentation could be. She had researched the topic with her usual scholarly thoroughness, having acquainted herself with the details of the contemporary controversy and being familiar with current authors on both sides of the debate: "She appeared to know every word of Clarendon by heart, only just published, 1702–4. She turned Calamy inside out, with his account of the sufferings of the ejected nonconforming ministers at the Restoration, and discussed instead the way the Anglican clergy had been treated during the years of the Commonwealth" (Perry, *Celebrated* 195). She also demonstrates a wide knowledge of history, both ancient and modern, and acquaintance with some of the classical and Christian writers of antiquity: she refers to Tacitus and Tertullian and quotes Virgil in translation. She shows familiarity with more modern sources too, using not only well-known authors such as Machiavelli, but also politicians of an earlier age. She quotes Sir Francis Walsingham, "faithful Secretary," as she calls him, of Elizabeth I, to demonstrate that the problems arising "when Conscience exceeds its bounds and grows to be Faction" are not new (94). This formidable breadth of knowledge is effectively used in support of her position: she displays all her customary rhetorical brilliance, acutely addressing and answering the arguments of the opposition. Perry believes that the effectiveness of Astell's pamphlet is demonstrated by the number of prominent writers who replied to it, including James Owen, whose pamphlet she had attacked, Charles Leslie, and Defoe. However, they did not know at first to whom they were replying, for Astell maintained her usual anonymity. It was Dr. George Hickes who revealed her identity. In a letter dated December 9, 1704 to Dr. Charlett, master of University College, Oxford, he wrote: "And you may now assure your self, that Mrs Astell is the author of that other book against Occasional Communion, which we justly admired so much" (qtd. in F. Smith 158).

Her next contribution to the pamphlet war came primarily in response to Defoe's *More Short Ways with Dissenters* (1704). In *A Fair Way with the Dissenters* (1704), she answers Defoe (Mr. Short-Ways, as she calls him) point by point, undermining his arguments and demonstrating their inconsistency:

> Now give me leave to laugh a little, and 'tis at his telling us, That *The Scots have an undoubted Right to the Presbyterian Establishment* because forsooth! *'tis the Original Protestant Settlement of that Nation.* [...] But if Episcopacy is not to be restored in *Scotland*, against the Constitution of the Nation, by

the same Rule it is not to be destroyed in *England*, since it is our Constitution. (103)

Occasionally she pours scorn upon Defoe's writing: "Seventhly, Short-Ways is under a great mistake when he tells us, in his Admirable English, That 'The Barbarisms and Bloudy Doings us'd with the Episcopal Party in Scotland amounted to few'" (101). She concludes by asserting that she has successfully made her case against "the Secret Designs of the Dissenters, which are conceal'd under the Colour of Conscience" (112). Sympathetic though she was with any who were sincere in their objections, she believed that most of the occasional conformists were acting solely in the interests of ambition.

Just as Astell replies to two adversaries in *Moderation Truly Stated*, so she again addresses two in *A Fair Way with the Dissenters*. This time, her pamphlet was already in press when she read James Owen's *Moderation Still a Vertue* (1704). She therefore added a postscript that replied to his charges. One of these attacked her original pamphlet as being "Verbose and Virulent." She responds by nicely turning the tables, admitting the accusation and explaining her use of language as "answering the Dissenters Arguments against Schism and Toleration in their own Words [...] and their Virulency against the Government in Church and State as by Law established. [...] There you may find that those Expressions about Schism, which our Author is so offended at [...] are the very words of Mr Edwards the Presbyterian" (115). One of the most interesting parts of this postscript concerns her distinction between "Dissenters in Conscience" and "Dissenters in Faction," claiming that "the stater [that is, herself] has a true Compassion for Dissenters in Conscience [...] believing the greatest number of the Separation to be of this sort" (116).

Throughout her arguments in both pamphlets, she repeatedly insists that the issue is political ambition, not religious objection. As the postscript proceeds, she refers more frequently to that event which is the crux of all the arguments of the pamphlet war: the execution of King Charles I and whether or not it was justified. She denies that his conduct was any worse than that of previous monarchs; on the contrary, she points out that the events of the 1640s were preceded by a period of unusual peace. But even had he been "as bad as the worst of his revilers would represent him. What then? Neither the Laws of God nor of the Land, gave his subjects any Authority to use him as they did" (125). More than fifty years later, the execution of the king remained the great issue between the contending political parties.

Astell's next pamphlet is addressed directly to this issue. It was written in response to a sermon by Bishop White Kennett, *A Compassionate Enquiry into the Causes of the Civil War*, preached on the anniversary of the king's execution on January 31, 1704. Kennett was a Whig, and though ostensibly preaching in honour of the beheaded king, he tries to avoid placing the blame upon the parliamentary party that eventually executed him. He blames Charles's ministers for giving him bad advice, and he attributes the trouble to an understandable fear of the French influence and the real possibility that England would be returned to allegiance to the Roman Catholic church. Kennett was no doubt trying to make peace between the warring parties. It is indeed known that Queen Anne was all in favour of reaching a compromise that should bring an end to the hostilities created by the civil war. However, like many moderates, he pleased neither side: the Whig party thought he showed too much respect for the Stuart kings, and the Tories that he treated the republican rebels too gently. Mary Astell's pamphlet defends the position taken by Kennett but takes it much further. It is, Ruth Perry believes, a royalist manifesto (*Celebrated* 209).

The title of Astell's pamphlet, *An Impartial Enquiry into the Causes of Rebellion and Civil War* (1704), reflects that of the sermon to which she is responding, while subtly suggesting by her use of the word "rebellion" who was to blame. She begins by citing Kennett's sermon, recognizing that he is a priest in the Church of England and pointing out that the canons of the church enjoin obedience to the sovereign. As the discourse continues, it becomes clear that Astell rejects Kennett's attempts to reconcile the two sides: the Tories, the spiritual children of the Cavaliers, and the Whigs, who belong to the same political persuasion as the Roundheads. Astell is against any compromise since allowing any ground to the enemy would endanger the state. The fear of "popery," which according to Kennett lay behind much of the resistance to King Charles I, did not, she believes, arise from the actions of the king but was deliberately fostered by the parliamentary party: "The people THOUGHT themselves too much under French Counsels and a French Ministry?" she asks, quoting Kennett, and replies: "The Scots and Mr Pym told them so" (144). In other words, the

French threat, the threat of popery, was simply fabricated by the Parliamentary party, who were intent upon serving their own political purposes by wresting power from the sovereign.

> Strange! That such Principles shou'd be suffer'd in a Christian Nation, a Nation that has smarted so severely by them! But stranger yet, that any Prince shou'd Employ and Trust Men of these Principles! 'Tis certain he can have no hold of them; for whenever they get Power and Think that a Change will be for their Interest, they will never want Pretences to throw him out of the Saddle. (168)

Astell believes that popery itself is much less dangerous than presbyterianism. She acknowledges that "the People were wrought up into *Apprehensions and Fears of Popery*"; however, she denies that "the King and his Faithful Subjects were the cause of this" (176).

Since these events happened long before Astell herself was born, we may question why she is so strongly engaged with them. It might seem that an execution that had taken place fifty-five years previously would hardly merit such attention. Patricia Springborg is probably right in ascribing this interest to the similarity Astell perceives between the causes of the civil war and the political issues of her own time (*Astell, Political Writings*, 178). The cause of the civil war, Astell believes, was rebellion against the Christian principle of the authority of the monarch and its replacement with wholly secular principles. It is these principles that Astell sees as the great danger of the political tendencies of the early years of the eighteenth century:

> Was not one of the Causes of the Civil War, 'That small or rather no Authority or Power, that is allow'd the King [...] by the *Presbyterians'* or *Whiggs*, or whatever you call them? For they are all of the same Original, they act upon the same Principles and Motives, and tend to the same end, who place the Supreme Power originally in the People, giving them a Right, or at least an Allowance to resume it, whenever they believe they have a sufficient Cause; that is, in plain *English*, whenever they think fit, and are strong enough to put their *Thoughts* and *Fancies* in execution. (185)

The threat, then, is an immediate threat, since the contemporary Whigs hold the same political beliefs as the parliamentary party of fifty years ago.

The first three of Astell's political pamphlets were published in 1704.[7] The fourth and last one, *Bart'lemy Fair, or an Enquiry after Wit*, came out in 1709. It answers *A Letter Concerning Enthusiasm* (1708), written by Anthony Ashley Cooper, Lord Shaftesbury, who had been heavily influenced by Astell's old adversary, Locke. Astell did not know precisely who had written the pamphlet – in fact, she thought it had been produced by a member of the Kit-Cat Club, whose members were committed Whigs. The issue in this case was how to deal with religious fanaticism, or enthusiasm, as it was then called. Shaftesbury calls for mild measures, suggesting that the best way of dealing with religious fanaticism is not to persecute it – for such a response merely creates martyrs – but to laugh at it. He suggests that the opponents of Jesus Christ might have done better to lampoon him in a puppet show than to crucify him. In fact, ridicule has already been effectively used: he refers to the puppet show mocking the Puritans in Ben Jonson's *Bartholomew Fair*. But Astell sees in this approach not charitable willingness to spare the misdirected but a fundamental scepticism about all religious matters.

As with the earlier pamphlets, the position taken by Shaftesbury is one that most twenty-first-century readers find far more sympathetic than Astell's apparent intolerance. Yet Shaftesbury's toleration was founded upon a belief in the possibility of total objectivity, in which conclusions are reached on the basis of reason alone. Strongly as opinion in the twenty-first century supports the toleration advocated by Shaftesbury, there is growing scepticism about rational objectivity. Today, the importance of context and inherited cultural values is widely acknowledged. Here, surprisingly, Astell appears more in tune with postmodern approaches than her adversaries. As Ruth Perry notes, Astell knew that Shaftesbury's refusal to take context into account was a mistake:

> As she well knew, no one was ever unencumbered by previous commitments. [...] No one was ever as free as Shaftesbury's line of reasoning required humans to be in order to judge the truth for themselves. [...] She understood very well that the "Bart'lemy Fair method" could only work in the most ideal circumstances – circumstances that had never yet obtained in the real world. (*Celebrated* 227)

Yet, according to Perry, it is unlikely that Astell's arguments carried conviction at the time, in a society increasingly given over to materialism, scepticism, and the denial of spiritual values. Indeed, according to Van C. Hartmann, it was precisely because she saw how destructive of society the new commercial values would be that Astell was moved to write so eloquently against them: "Astell's pamphlet illustrates the unsettling impact that the new capitalism was having on social relations and human identity, especially for women, and thus helps us understand the essential continuity between High Church Tory conservatism and Astell's progressive feminism" (244).[8]

By 1709 opinion was increasingly supportive of this new commercialism that ignored the older values of community, and Astell's influence declined. In the earliest years of the eighteenth century, however, her clear vision and the ability to convey it powerfully to her audience gave her opinions considerable weight. Among the many pamphlets published on the issue of Occasional Conformity in these years, hers are distinguished by superior scholarship. She had read all the relevant books and documents, had studied all the arguments, and above all was thoroughly familiar with the historical background. As Florence Smith argues, "[T]he strength of her argument lies in the historical method she pursues in going back to original sources" (152). All authorities on Astell agree that she was highly respected by the conservatives of her own time, especially the clergy. Ruth Perry believes that in engaging in political discussion, Astell "wrote as a celebrity" (*Celebrated* 185). She had by this time (1704) demonstrated her skill in argumentation and devastatingly scathing satirical wit, and her writing was highly valued by her own party. As Myra Reynolds observes, "[S]he was beyond [...] most men of her day in her command of satire and irony" (299). Her reputation grew: "She became a figure in London society. Her pamphlets were widely read and discussed" (Perry, *Celebrated* 210). Perry quotes an (anonymous) Tory pamphleteer who praised the "'Heroine [...] Mrs A'___l' who, he says, 'hath maintain'd her Position not only with the Air of a Disputant, but the Spirit of a *Christian*'" (210). And Henry Dodwell, professor of ancient history, praised her "'excellent and ingenious writings'" (qtd. in Perry, *Celebrated* 211). Such respect, however, did not stop Astell from disagreeing at times with her supporters. As she had begun her career by questioning one of the arguments of John

Norris, so she continued, refusing to submit to any position that failed to commend itself to her reason.

Her consummate skill as a writer can still be enjoyed today, long after the issues of which she so passionately wrote have been forgotten. In the pamphlets, Astell uses a more colloquial, conversational style than in her earlier work. There she had used a voiced style and an intimate tone, it is true, but still one of some formality, especially in diction. No such considerations of propriety withheld her in her pamphleteering: she took as her model the style of other writers in the pamphlet war and wrote accordingly. The style she adopts for polemic is colloquial, ringing with immediacy. For example, this is how she begins *A Fair Way with the Dissenters*:

> WELL! If in Disputes in Print and Disputes at *Billingsgate*, which, as they are manag'd, are equally scolding, he were to carry the day who rails loudest and longest; Wo be to the poor Church and its Friends, they could never shew their Faces or hold up their Heads against the everlasting Clamour of their Adversaries. (87)

In thus referring to Billingsgate, the fishmarket notorious for bad language, Astell appeals to popular knowledge and popular prejudice. Again, in refuting Defoe's anonymously published *More Short-Ways with the Dissenters*, she adopts an exceedingly informal conversational style:

> Sixthly, *Short-Ways* will have it that my Lord *Clarendon's* History tells us that *K. Charles I. brought all the Calamities of Civil war upon on his own head.* Bless me! what hideous Spectacles Prejudice and Prepossession are upon a Reader's nose! But when our brother *Short-Ways* has laid these aside, has wip'd his Eyes, and is willing to see clearly, I would then advise him to another Perusal of that excellent and useful History, which he will find to be point blank against his Assertion [...] . (101)

This informality extends occasionally to her use of colloquial vocabulary – for example, in this passage from *An Impartial Enquiry into the Causes of Rebellion and Civil War*, where she uses the slang word "bubbled" for "deceived," or "taken in":

> But sure we of this age, who have this dismal tragedy so fresh in our Memories, must be the greatest Fools in nature, if we

suffer our selves to be bubbled any more by Men of the same Principles, and by the same Artifices so often detected, and so justly abhorr'd. (138)

Oddly, however, this use of colloquial vocabulary is part of a style that can only be identified as grand. This, after all, is persuasive writing at its most urgent. There is an appeal to the emotions characteristic of the grand style, revealing itself in the use of rhetorical tropes and schemes.[9] The following passage from *An Impartial Enquiry*, for example, demonstrates her use of the rhetorical question, the exclamation, and irony:

> Is it not an Inconsistency to deplore the Fate of *Char.* I and to justify that of other Princes? If we think their Fall to be Just, and his to be Unjust and Deplorable, we may in time come to abhor those Principles that brought him to the Block, and the practices that flow from them, as being equally destructive of the Best, as well as the worst Princes; and then what will become of the Peoples Right to shake off an Oppressor? Must we take that dull way which *David* took, and which the old-fashion'd Homilies talk of, Wait God's time, and let him go down to the Grave in Peace? Why at this rate we may tamely have our Throats cut; and sure it is better to be beforehand with him! (148)

She also makes use of the long periodic sentence, gradually building the tension to a climax. In the following passage, she castigates the reign of William III (much approved by the Whigs):

> As little did we hear of *Illegal Acts* and *Arbitrary Power*, of *Oppression* and *Persecution*, in a Reign that tugg'd hard for a Standing Army in time of Peace; that had Interest to suspend the *Habeas Corpus* Act several times, tho' it be the great Security of the *English* Liberties; that outed 7 or 8 Reverend Prelates, the Ornament and Glory of the English Church, besides several of the inferiour Clergy, and Members of the Universities, and that only for *Conscience sake*, and because they cou'd not swallow such new Oaths, as they believ'd to be contrary to the old ones: And tho' 12 of them were thought so deserving, that there was a Provision made in their Favour, even by that Act that depriv'd them of their Freeholds and Subsistance, of the Rights

as *English-men* and Ministers of God's Church, yet not one of them enjoy'd, in that Human, Charitable and Religious Reign! the Advantages which the *Body of the Good-natur'd* English *People* design'd them. (194)

This stylistic expertise serves her well as a polemicist and gives a sharp edge to her attack. She has a keen eye for the inconsistencies of her opponents' arguments and a biting, satirical wit. Particularly successful is her refutation of Dr. D'Avenant, who had changed his political opinions: as Florence Smith says, "[I]n a skillful manner she wove together the Doctor's opinions with comments of her own so as to bring out the change in his views" (139). She is adept at turning the arguments of her opponents against them, a skill she shows particularly in refuting Biblical evidence brought forward by the opposition: her thorough familiarity with Scripture allows her to put the citations in context and offer convincing alternative interpretations.

After 1709, Astell produced no new works. Indeed, *Bart'lemy Fair* itself was something of an afterthought. Since she had been so successful, so highly regarded, the question must arise as to why she wrote no more. But perhaps a more relevant question to ask is why the early years of the eighteenth century provided her with exactly the right context for her work. What circumstances provided her with the opportunity to use her talents in the political arena? A number of them no doubt contributed, but pre-eminent among them must be the succession in March 1702 of Queen Anne. In "A Prefatory Discourse to Dr D'Avenant," which introduces *Moderation Truly Stated*, she refers to the Queen as "the Light of England. She is the breath of our nostrils, we know not how to live if this fails us" (xxviii). The new reign brought a new hope to many of the conservative persuasion, but for Astell there were added reasons to look eagerly to a better future.

In the first place, Anne was a Stuart, daughter of the deposed James II. Her sister, Mary II, who had reigned before her, was also of course a Stuart; but her sister's husband, William of Orange, had refused to be a mere consort and had insisted upon the holding the monarchy in his own right jointly with his wife. Many among the Royalist party objected strongly to this arrangement: William III had, in their view, no claim to the throne whatever. Some of them, including Astell's friend and patron, William Sancroft, Archbishop of Canterbury, had refused to swear allegiance to him.

William's Protestantism was not of a kind to appeal to Anglicans of Astell's rather High Church stamp, and the exclusion of non-jurors in his reign angered the conservative party. With the accession of Anne, many hoped that matters might improve, and it did indeed seem that they might. Anne herself was inclined to the Tory position politically, and "was known to be sympathetic to the High Church position, had spoken for it, and was herself a conservative Anglican" (Perry, *Celebrated* 188). Astell, therefore, may have been looking forward to Anne's support of the political and religious causes that were so dear to her. The conservative party might come again to predominate, and the convictions of the High Church Anglicans would flourish under the approval of the monarch. The conservatives, therefore, were riding high at the time of Anne's accession, and were already moving to regain some of the power and influence they had lacked in the previous reign.

But for Astell there was even more cause for hope, arising from the fact of Anne's being a woman. Her delight in this instance of a woman's power comes to the fore in several of her works at this time, including, as we have seen, *The Christian Religion*. In *Moderation Truly Stated*, a woman lectures two men on the impropriety of their sneering remarks about women:

> [I]n a Lady's reign, and even in Books that you Dedicate to her Majesty, you take upon yourself to tell the World that in this Kingdom no more Skill, no more Policies are requisite, than what may be comprehended by a Woman. *As if there were any Skill, and Policy that a Woman's Understanding could not reach. So again, if women do anything well, nay should a hundred thousand Women do the Greatest and most Glorious Actions, presently it must be with a Mind (forsooth) above their Sex! Now if Women be such despicable Creatures, pray what's the plain English of all your fine Speeches and Dedications to her Majesty, but Madam we mean to flatter you?* (liii)

To Astell, the accession of a woman who was also a Stuart, a conservative and a High Church Anglican appeared to promise a new world, or rather a return to the old one of the early seventeenth century. She hoped and believed that Anne would be another Elizabeth. Indeed, she suggests, though not perhaps wholly seriously, that all our monarchs should be queens, since so many of the best have been women (lv). She cites Isabella of Castile, Margaret of Denmark, and Zenobia of Palmyra (29). Astell's anticipation of the Queen's support for women had begun even before she came to the throne. It was rumoured that Princess Anne, as she then was, had been prepared to endow Astell's proposed Protestant monastery for women with ten thousand pounds (Perry, *Celebrated* 134). Whether or not it was indeed she who came forward – only to be discouraged by the counsel of Bishop Burnet – Mary Astell no doubt at one time had hopes of her royal support, for it was to her that she dedicated Part II of *A Serious Proposal*. By the end of the first decade of Anne's reign, however, some of these hopes had been disappointed. In the first instance, the Queen found it wise to try to make peace between the warring political factions. Then she came increasingly under the influence of her Whig courtiers, especially the ladies, to whom she listened more and more. It is true, however, that the mere fact of her being on the throne apparently encouraged her female subjects. As Ruth Perry points out, the reigns of Elizabeth I and of Victoria similarly encouraged women (*Celebrated* 188). But Anne was not a strong monarch, as Elizabeth I had been, and not as influential as Victoria was to become.[10] The position of women did not greatly change during her reign. Indeed, already in *An Impartial Enquiry*, published in 1704, Astell is inclined to fault Anne for being too conciliatory:

> [H]er only fault, if Duty and Respect will allow that Expression, consists in too much of the Royal Martyr's Clemency and Goodness; Her Majesty's Reign having left us nothing to wish, but that she had less of K. *Charles* and more of the Spirit of Q. *Elizabeth*, since a Factious People can no way be kept in bounds, but by a sprightly and vigorous Exertion of just Authority. (195)

The early years of the eighteenth century, then, gave Astell a unique opportunity to participate in public discussion of matters very close to her heart. The pamphlets represent her crowning achievement, the summit of her success. True to her own conviction that the greatest Christian virtues are public ones, she finally emerged as a political thinker whose work was taken seriously. The experience of producing her earlier works had trained her in strenuous argumentation and had given her a command of style seldom equalled in her day. When in 1709 she turned her attention again toward education, it must have been with a feeling that she had already made an important contribution to public life.

Part III

Mary Astell's Rhetorical Theory

9

Rhetorical Theory I

Mary Astell was not only a distinguished practitioner of rhetoric; she was also a theorist, and her rhetorical theory is one of the most important contributions she made to the rhetorical tradition. Astell's rhetorical theory is to be found in chapter 3 of *A Serious Proposal to the Ladies, Part II*. It is put forward in ninety-six pages (in the original edition) of detailed discussion and includes a great deal of highly practical advice. The first fifty-four pages of this discussion are devoted not specifically to rhetoric, but to logic. However, this forms an important part of her theory of rhetoric, for Mary Astell appears to have followed Petrus Ramus in confining rhetoric proper to matters of style: *inventio* and to some extent *dispositio*, the discovery and arrangement of the arguments, she treats therefore under logic, seeing it as the essential preliminary to rhetoric.[1] The whole discussion is remarkable for its accessibility to her primary audience of women: there is nothing in it to frighten them. At the same time, it is never condescending, and Astell maintains the discussion at a level that accommodates those more advanced in philosophical thought than her scantily educated ladies. She never makes the mistake of confusing lack of education with lack of intelligence. The ideas she puts forward make strong demands upon the understanding; it is Astell's compelling clarity that renders them accessible. But as we have seen, although her primary audience was women, she also had a broader audience in mind, including those contemporary philosophers and theologians with whose positions she disagreed. In this chapter, then, I shall discuss Astell's theory of logic and try to establish not only some of her sources, but also the extent to which she transcends them.

Perhaps the most important element in Astell's rhetorical theory, both for *inventio* and *dispositio* – which she treats under logic – and for her style, is that thinking and writing are natural:

> As to the *Method* of Thinking [...] it falls in with the Subject
> I've now come to, which is, that *Natural Logic* I wou'd propose.

I call it natural because I shall not send you further than your Own Minds to learn it, you may if you please take in the assistance of some well chosen book, but a good Natural Reason after all is the best Director, without this you will scarce Argue well, though you had the Choicest Books and Tutors to Instruct you, but with it you may, tho' you happen to be destitute of the other.[2] (117)

What is immediately apparent here is Astell's debt to Descartes. His influence is apparent throughout her theory of logic and extends also to her theory of style. Having enunciated Descartes's principle of the naturalness of human thought, its givenness, she turns to a discussion of another of his principles: the importance of clear and distinct ideas. Her discussion of the difficulty of arriving at conceptions of sufficient clarity involves a consideration of the deficiencies of language itself.[3] She shares with other thinkers of her time a dissatisfaction with the fluidity of the meanings of words, an instability that inhibits exactness and clarity: "Thus many times our Ideas are thought to be false when the Fault is really in our Language" (122). Constant vigilance is required if the slipperiness of language is to be overcome:

The First and Principal thing therefore to be observed in all the Operations of the Minds is, That we determine nothing about those things of which we have not a Clear Idea, and as Distinct as the Nature of the Subject will permit, for we cannot properly be said to Know any thing which does not Clearly and Evidently appear to us. (122)

She then turns to Descartes in order to nail down exactly what is meant by clear and distinct ideas:

That (to use the words of a Celebrated Author) may be said to be "clear which is Present and Manifest to an attentive Mind; so as we say we see Objects Clearly, when being present to our Eyes they sufficiently Act on 'em, and our Eyes are dispos'd to regard 'em. And that Distinct, which is so Clear, Particular, and Different from all other things, that it contains not any thing in it self which appears not manifestly to him who considers it as he ought." (123)

This direct quotation from Descartes she documents in the margin, citing his *Principes de la Philosophie* and giving the page number. Clarity for Astell is "the best eloquence" (142), and obscurity one of the faults most to be avoided; and the achievement of the one and avoidance of the other require, first of all, clear thought – clarity at the level of *inventio*: "Obscurity, one of the greatest faults in Writing, does commonly proceed from a want of Meditation, for when we pretend to teach others what we do not understand our selves, no wonder that we do it at a sorry rate" (138).

Closely related to Descartes's insistence on clarity and distinctness is the principle of attention. In fact, according to Thomas M. Carr, "the clarity and distinctness of self-evidence are functions of attention" (39). He quotes from Descartes's *Principes*: "I call clear that which is present and manifest to an attentive mind" (qtd. in Carr 39). For Descartes, what draws and maintains attention is admiration, in its seventeenth-century sense of wonder, more than a flattering regard. Referring to Descartes's *Les Passions de l'âme*, Carr asserts: "[Descartes] not only includes admiration among his six primitive passions in which all others find their source (3.1006), he labels it the first of all the passions (3.999). This admiration is 'a sudden surprise of the soul which brings it to consider with attention objects that seem rare and extraordinary to it'" (53). Astell too stresses the importance of admiration, though she sees its application more particularly to matters of style: "[W]hatever it is we Treat of our Stile shou'd be such as may keep our Readers Attent, and induce them to go to the End. Now Attention is usually fixt by Admiration, which is excited by somewhat uncommon either in the Thought or way of Expression" (144). The debt to Descartes is obvious, though at this point unacknowledged.

Also unacknowledged is Astell's most important debt to Cartesian principles: the six rules she gives for *inventio* and *dispositio*. A comparison of these rules with the four given by Descartes in *Discourse on Method* demonstrates his influence. Here are Descartes's rules:

> I believed that the following four rules would be sufficient, provided I made a firm and constant resolution not even once to fail to observe them:
>
> The first was never to accept anything as true that I did not know evidently to be so; that is, carefully to avoid precipitous

judgment and prejudice; and to include nothing more in my judgments than what presented itself to my mind with such clarity and distinctness that I would have no occasion to put it in doubt.

The second, to divide each of the difficulties I was examining into as many parts as possible and as required to solve them best.

The third, to conduct my thoughts in an orderly fashion, commencing with the simplest and easiest to know objects, to rise gradually, as by degrees, to the knowledge of the most composite things, and even supposing an order among those things that do not naturally precede one another.

And last, everywhere to make enumerations so complete and reviews so general that I would be sure of having omitted nothing. (10)

Here are Mary Astell's six rules:

RULE I Acquaint our selves thoroughly with the State of the Question, have a Distinct Notion of our Subject whatever it be, and of Terms we make use of, knowing precisely what it is we drive at.

RULE II Cut off all needless Ideas and whatever has not a necessary connexion to the matter under Consideration.

RULE III To conduct our Thoughts by Order, beginning with the most Simple and Easie Objects, and ascending by Degrees to the Knowledge of the most Compos'd.

RULE IV Not to leave any part of our Subject unexamin'd. *[...] To this Rule belongs that of* Dividing the Subject of our Meditations into as many Parts as we can, and as shall be requisite to Understand it perfectly *[...]*

RULE V Always keep our Subject Directly in our Eye, and Closely pursue it thro all our Progress.

RULE VI To judge no further than we Perceive, and not to take any thing for Truth, which we do not evidently Know to be so. (128)

It is immediately apparent that Astell's rules of logic have been inspired by Descartes. But what is important to note here is the way Astell accommodates his directions to her primary audience of women. Since they are less educated than the audience for which he wrote, she adds advice that she believes they especially need to follow. In particular, the women need to guard against hastiness and lack of focus. For example, in her commentary on Rule II, she warns them about

> those causeless Digressions, tedious Parentheses and Impertinent Remarques, which we meet with in some authors. For, as when our Sight is diffus'd and extended to many objects at once, we see none of them Distinctly; so when the Mind grasps at every Idea that presents it self, [or] rambles after such as relate not to its present Business, it loses its hold and retains a very feeble Apprehension of that which it shou'd Attend. (126)

The length of Astell's commentary on this rule suggests that she sees digression as a particular danger for her audience. It is significant that what she says here sounds very much like a description of conversation, where one subject frequently leads naturally into another. This form of communication would, of course, have been practised constantly by the women in her audience; therefore, they need to guard against transferring the characteristics of oral communication too freely to their written discourse. She had herself fallen into this error and been reproved for it, as we have seen, by John Norris.

Astell comments on other rules too. Especially interesting is her comment on Rule IV, derived from Descartes's Rule IV, for here she feeds in ideas of decorum:

> [A] Moral Action may in some Circumstance be not only Fit but Necessary, which in others, where Time, Place and the like have made an alteration, wou'd be most Improper; so that if we venture to Act on the former Judgment, we may easily do amiss, if we wou'd Act as we ought, we must view its New Face, and see with what Aspect that looks on us. (127)

This is a particularly good example of Astell's accommodation of Descartes's ideas to her own audience. Obviously, propriety was of great concern to her high-born ladies, as it was to Astell herself. Completeness for Astell and her audience includes, as it does not for Descartes, a study of the rhetorical situation: a change in time and place will involve a reconsideration of the facts, a different selection from them, perhaps, and a new presentation.

Rule V adds to those given by Descartes, and again it is apparent that Astell sees her audience to be in need of this particular piece of advice. As with Rule II, there is a danger of wandering attention, distraction, inattention to detail, so that the thinking becomes superficial and logically disconnected. Having directed her readers to keep the subject in view, she goes on: "[...] there being no better Sign of a good Understanding than Thinking Closely and Pertinently, and Reasoning dependently, so as to make the former part of our Discourse a support to the Latter, and *This* an Illustration of *That*, carrying Light and Evidence in ev'ry step we take" (127). This instruction in the process of logical argumentation is particularly necessary for her audience of women who would be far more comfortable with a narrative than with an argumentative approach.

Astell's rules for thinking – that is, *inventio* – are combined with instructions for *dispositio*. Thus, Rule III is "to conduct our Thoughts by Order, beginning with the most Simple and Easie Objects," and Rule IV, which introduces *divisio*, stresses the importance of recapitulation and the drawing of conclusions at the end of each part of the discourse. She reiterates and extends this advice in her later discussion of rhetoric. In fact, she finds it ultimately impossible to separate the method of thinking from organization, and organization from style. Thus in her praise of clarity in style, she speaks of the importance of "Exactness of Method; [...] by putting every thing in its proper place with due Order and Connexion, the Readers Mind is gently led where the Writer wou'd have it" (138).

Astell's rules, then, though well accommodated to her own audience, owe an obvious debt to Descartes. Yet in giving these rules, Astell does not quote him or even name him. She introduces them by giving a general acknowledgement: "which Rules as I have not taken wholly on Trust from others, so neither do I pretend to be the Inventer of 'em" (126). Obviously she is drawing upon many different sources and using them to create her own theory rather than simply reproducing them. Who then were some of these others to whom she refers? We may suspect that many of the authors she had read contributed to her theory, but we can be sure only of the influence of those whom she cites. Two of the more important of these are Antoine Arnauld and Pierre Nicole, the authors of *The Art of Thinking*. It was available to her in English, and she probably read it in translation. However, since she cites it by its French title as well, she may have used both the translation and the original.

The Antoine Arnauld whose work informed Astell's theory of logic (there were many of the Arnauld family who bore that name) was born in 1612 and lived until 1694. His collaborator, Pierre Nicole, was thirteen years younger.[4] Arnauld taught in the Little Schools of Port Royal for which he and Pierre Nicole wrote their famous *L'art de penser*, which was published in 1662 (Dickoff xxviii). Interestingly, given the importance of *L'art de penser* to Astell's theory, Port Royal des Champs was a Cistercian institution founded in 1204 to provide an education for women. In 1223 it was granted the privilege of serving as a retreat house for seculars and was therefore open to many among the pious, both men and women, who had not taken religious vows. Blaise Pascal, whose *Soul of Geometry* was a key influence on the Port Royal Logic (Springborg, *Mary Astell* 190 n.114), was a retreatant there.

Sometime in the mid-1650s, Arnauld began to collaborate with Pierre Nicole, and the two frequently worked together from then on.[5] In 1641 Arnauld was asked as a theologian to comment on Descartes's *Meditationes de prima philosophia* (Dickoff xxxv). In 1648 Descartes himself asked Arnauld's opinion of the *Meditationes*. As a result of the earlier request (in 1641), Arnauld had studied the *Meditationes* and was attracted to Descartes's philosophy. Accordingly, when he and Pierre Nicole came to write *L'art de penser* in 1661, they drew heavily on Cartesian philosophy, supporting it but also to some extent redirecting it in the light of Augustinian theology.

Thomas Carr's discussion of the eloquence of Port Royal usefully clarifies the relationship between the Cartesian and Augustinian elements in *L'art de penser*:

> Arnauld [...] was attracted by the distinction between the pure intellect and sense perception in Cartesian epistemology. As early as 1641[...] Arnauld had noted the convergence of Descartes' philosophy with that of Augustine. Indeed the

explicit discussion of eloquence in terms of Cartesian attention that is inaugurated in the *Logique de Port Royal* is a product of Nicole and Arnauld's allegiance to Descartes' psychophysiology coupled with their Augustinian stress on concupiscence. At each step, Cartesian elements are re-oriented by a theological imperative. [...] The distinction between the two kinds of thought (pure intellect and sense perception) takes on a religious colour absent in Descartes when Arnauld and Nicole cite Augustine's teaching that, since the Fall, humans find it more pleasurable to attend to the product of the senses represented by corporal images than to pure ideas. (65)

This Christian interpretation of Descartes's philosophy attracted Astell because it brought together and reconciled two of her most deeply held beliefs: her belief in human reason and her belief in God. The whole of *A Serious Proposal, Part II* is based on the assumption that reason and faith inform one another and that if they are functioning as they ought, they must produce both impeccable morality and religious devotion. A brief comparison of her ideas on this subject with those of Descartes and of Arnauld and Nicole demonstrates the extent to which her thinking was grounded in her theological convictions and suggests that she took her ideas on thinking not simply from Descartes, but from Arnauld and Nicole's conflation of Cartesian philosophy with Augustinian theology.

I begin, then, with Descartes. The obvious objection to Descartes's theory of the naturalness of human reason – a theory taken up by Mary Astell – is the fact of human error. Descartes himself answers this objection by attributing error in part at least to immaturity: "Descartes warns against hasty judgments and preconceived notions in the first rule of the *Discours* because the prejudices of prolonged childhood that present such obstacles to his philosophy are the accumulated residue of hasty judgments made before the will was mature" (Carr 38). Arnauld and Nicole, though they do not dispute Descartes's attribution of error to immaturity, obviously do not think it sufficient to cover all cases. In chapter 9 of part I of *L'art de penser*, they develop Cartesian ideas of the prejudices of childhood being responsible for errors in reasoning as these apply to the study of physics; but in chapter 10, they turn their attention to ethics, and here they draw upon Augustine's doctrine of concupiscence (73). They apparently consider physics to be neutral, something to which human passions do not apply. But ethics is not neutral; the study of ethics is extremely vulnerable to errors arising from human sinfulness. They therefore make a distinction between scientific knowledge and ethical or human knowledge: for the latter, the theological perspective of Augustine is required. Earlier, in part 1, Arnauld and Nicole have introduced the idea that the Fall of man has undermined the powers of the intellect: "The images of material things enter the brain through the senses and – as St Augustine frequently remarks – man since the Fall has so accustomed himself to considering only material things that most men believe they can conceive only what they can imagine, that is, what they can represent to themselves by means of material images" (32). In chapter 10, they resume the argument: "Though in God alone is true happiness found and though only in the pursuit of God is the pursuit of happiness, still the corruption of sin has impelled man to seek happiness in a multitude of things" (73). It is this distortion of the nature of true happiness that has twisted the moral sense and given rise to errors of judgement in ethics.

Throughout *The Art of Thinking*, Arnauld and Nicole frequently cite Augustine and use theological instances and examples to clarify their arguments. It is this bringing together of Cartesian philosophy and Augustinian theology that Mary Astell draws upon in her own theory of logic, a theory that emerges from her discussion of the relationship between the understanding and the will. She believes that each must inform the other, but her underlying conviction is that intellectual failures are fundamentally the result of sin.[6] She does reluctantly allow that some intellectual incapacity may be innate: "[S]ome minds are endow'd by their Creator with a larger Capacity than the rest" (111). However, she urges her audience to be very sure of their disability before they give up: "Yet e'er we give out let's see if it be thus with us in all Cases: Can we Think and Argue Rationally about a Dress, an Intreague, an Estate? Why then not upon better Subjects?" (111). It is much more likely that disinclination for intellectual pursuits arises from deficiencies in the will rather than in the understanding. She works out this thesis in the first two chapters of the book; in the third she shows its practical application. In doing so, she shows in detail how the mind is inhibited by failures in morality. For example, the claim of each successive scholar to hold a monopoly on the truth strikes her as absurd (107). It is wrong to claim a personal and privileged enlightenment, or to try to use one's knowledge for personal aggrandizement. It is not by such practices – inspired by pride – that truth may be found; nor do they contribute to the moral and spiritual health of those who use them.

Astell cites *The Art of Thinking* at various points in chapter 3 of *A Serious Proposal, Part II*. She begins her discussion of logic by acknowledging her debt to this work and quoting from it: "For as a very Judicious Writer on this Subject (to whose Ingenious Remarks and Rules I am much obliged) well observes, 'These Operations [of the Mind] proceed meerly from Nature, and that sometimes more perfectly from those who are altogether ignorant of Logic, than from others who have learn'd it'" (117).[7] She refers to the work again in her discussion of sophisms. She declines to list all these, suggesting instead that her readers consult *The Art of Thinking*, giving the part and chapter numbers to make the consultation easy for them (133).

Yet in spite of this obvious – and fully acknowledged – debt to *The Art of Thinking*, what comes across most clearly is the difference between that work and Astell's *Serious Proposal, Part II*. Astell draws upon Arnauld and Nicole, Descartes, and even her old enemy, John Locke, but she does not in any sense imitate them. She uses them as material out of which she creates something new. She transmutes and transcends her sources, and the work is her own. Partly this difference is brought about by the different rhetorical situation: the audience is different from the anticipated audiences of her sources, and her purpose is unlike theirs. These changes promote a wholly different tone: Descartes, Arnauld and Nicole, and Locke, however accessible they try to make their ideas, write as philosophers in philosophical style; Astell's tone, though somewhat more formal than the one she uses in *A Serious Proposal, Part I*, is still conversational. She adopts the commonsense stance of the mentor, even the mother, not aspiring to the dignity of the authority. Yet all this she achieves without sacrificing the depth of intellectual approach to her subject or overlooking its complexity.

Astell concludes her discussion of logic by demonstrating how to apply her method to the consideration of specific questions. She takes two standard questions: "Whether there is a God or a Being Infinitely Perfect" and "Whether a rich Man is Happy." In the first of these, the arguments she uses show that she was familiar with the discussion between Stillingfleet and Locke on questions of this kind, and as Patricia Springborg points out, the reference to the watchmaker is evidence that she also knew the arguments of Descartes.[8] In fact, it is obvious that Astell has read Descartes's argument for the existence of God in *Principes de la Philosophie*. What is remarkable here is not so much her grasp of the philosophical principles involved as her ability to make the steps in the argument plain to the amateur:

> For in the first place, what ever has any Perfection or Excellency (for that's all we mean by Perfection here) must either have it of it self, or derive it from some other Being. Now Creatures cannot have their perfections from themselves because they have not their Being, for to suppose that they Made themselves is an Absurdity too ridiculous to be seriously refuted, 'tis to suppose them to Be and not to Be at the same time, and that when they were Nothing, they were able to do the greatest Matter. Nor can they derive either Being or Perfection from any other Creature. For tho some Particular Beings may seem to be the Cause of the Perfections of others, as the Watch-maker may be said to be the Cause of the Regular Motions of the Watch, yet trace it a little farther, and you'll find this very Cause shall need another, and so without End, till you come to the Fountain-head, to that All-Perfect Being, who is the last resort of our Thoughts, and in whom they Naturally and Necessarily rest and terminate. (130)

Astell's intention in this passage is to demonstrate to her readers that they do not have to be trained as philosophers in order to argue philosophically. This kind of discussion should be for them both interesting and possible. In the first place, she hopes to arouse their curiosity about such questions: how much more worthwhile it is to discuss the existence of God than what dress to wear at the next party. Then she wants to demonstrate that such mental activity is not beyond their powers. She therefore makes her argument as simple as possible to show her readers that they can reason effectively merely by using the method she has just laid out for them.

Astell's theory of logic, then, is her own distillation of the thoughts of some of the foremost philosophers of the seventeenth century – Descartes, Arnauld, and Nicole – combined with her own good sense and her understanding of the needs and capacities of her primary audience of women. She draws, therefore, on all available sources but she never merely repeats their ideas. What is of the greatest importance to her in this particular work is to give her audience of ladies what they require in order to embark on the life of the mind. Guided by their needs, therefore, she simplifies the theories of those philosophers whose work on the subject she has herself studied and offers her audience a workable procedure for them to follow.

aving dealt with *inventio* and *dispositio* under logic, Astell turns her attention to rhetoric, by which (as a Ramean) she means *elocutio*: issues of style, tone, and accommodation of the audience. In this chapter I shall look at a number of issues that are important to consider in order to understand Astell's theory in the context of the late seventeenth century and to establish the significance of her contribution to rhetoric in that period. First I shall place Astell in terms of the new ideas current in her time: the plain style movement and, in particular, the new approach of the Cartesians. Among these, the most important influence on Astell's theory of *elocutio* is that of Bernard Lamy: drawing upon his work, she grounds her theory of style in the practice of morality. A comparison of his theory with hers will illuminate not only areas of agreement but also, and more importantly, the ways in which her theory departs from that of her main source. I shall also address the question of Astell's ambivalence toward rhetoric and try to account for it. Doing so will involve some discussion of the relationship between Bernard Lamy's *The Art of Speaking* and Arnauld and Nicole's *The Art of Thinking*. I shall then consider some possible influences coming from the period of classical rhetoric. And finally, I shall try to determine the extent to which Astell's theory may be considered feminist.

As in her theory of logic, the guiding principles of Astell's theory of *elocutio* are typical of the Cartesian sources upon which she draws. The first of these is that writing and speaking, like thinking, are natural, a birthright of each human being. She had begun her instruction on thinking with the promise that she would not "send you further than your Own minds to learn it" (117). She now reiterates this principle at the beginning of the section on rhetoric: "As Nature teaches us Logic, so does it instruct us in Rhetoric much better than Rules of Art" (137).[1] The other Cartesian principle that underlies her theory of both logic and rhetoric is that of clarity: as clarity of thought is of the first importance in thinking, so clarity of expression is the pre-eminent virtue of style. And these

two important principles are linked: "[A]s Thinking conform-
ably to the Nature of Things is True Knowledge, so th'expressing
our Thought in such a way, as more readily, and with the greatest
Clearness and Life, excites in others the very same Idea that was in
us, is the best Eloquence" (142). Clear thinking, as we saw in the
last chapter, is linked with clear diction. In this commitment to
simplicity, she shows herself to be in sympathy with the promot-
ers of the plain style who had led a revolt against the grand style
of rhetoric throughout the seventeenth century. As early as 1605,
Bacon had complained that "men began to hunt more after words
than matter" (26), being preoccupied with the niceties of style rather
than with the truth of content. Throughout the century, Bacon's
objections had been echoed by the new philosophers, who found
the language inappropriate for the new demands being made upon
it. Among these, significantly, were Arnauld and Nicole. Astell
quotes from *The Art of Thinking* at the end of her introductory
paragraph on rhetoric (meaning *elocutio*), referencing the quotation
in the margin: "All that's useful in this Art is 'the avoiding certain
evil ways of Writing and Speaking, and above all an Artificial and
Rhetorical Stile, Compos'd of false Thoughts, Hyperboles and
forc'd Figures which is the greatest fault in Rhetoric'" (137).

How, then, are these "evil ways of Writing and Speaking" to
be avoided? Astell's advice is to apply the principles of morality to
the arts of discourse. Throughout *A Serious Proposal, Part II*, she
has argued for the interdependence of the understanding and the
will: just as ignorance contributes to unethical behaviour, so inad-
equacies of thinking arise from moral deficiencies. In the passage
on rhetorical theory, she shows how this relationship plays out in
detail. The "evil ways" are not just technically bad: they are actually immoral, and are caused by moral failure. As she explains it,
to avoid faults in writing it is necessary to eradicate "those Vicious
Inclinations from whence the most distastful faults of Writing
proceed" (142). She identifies pride, vanity, deceitfulness, laziness
and contempt for the audience as the moral flaws most likely to
lead to faults in writing:

> For why do we chuse to be Obscure but because we intend to
> Deceive, or wou'd be thought to see much farther than our
> Neighbours? One sort of Vanity prompts us to be Rugged
> and Severe, and so possess'd with the imagin'd Worth and
> Solidity of our Discourse, that we think it beneath us to Polish

it; Another disposes us to Elaborate and Affected ways of Writing, to Pompous and improper Ornaments; and why are we tediously Copious but that we fancy every Thought of ours is extraordinary? (143)

Unwarranted attacks on other writers are motivated by revenge and often demonstrate a prideful unwillingness to be corrected. Problems of coherence arise from lazy thinking: we cannot express ourselves clearly, she points out, if we have not fully thought out what we want to say.

The cure for these evils, however, is not mere resistance to temptation but something much more positive. For most important of all, and governing all the details of her advice, is the principle of love:

> [T]he way to be good Orators is to be good Christians, the Practice of Religion will both instruct us in the Theory, and most powerfully enforce what we say of it. [...] Besides, being True Christians we have Really that Love for them which all who desire to perswade must pretend to; we've that Probity and Prudence, that Civility and Modesty which the Masters of this Art say a good Orator must be endow'd with. (142)

Astell demonstrates how this theory works in practice. In particular, the writer must be careful not to humiliate the audience, but on all occasions to spare their feelings, to let them "fancy if they please, that we believe them as Wise and Good as we endeavour to make them" (141). Thus encouraged, the readers will "conclude there's great hopes they may with a little pains attain what others think they Know already, and are asham'd to fall short of the good Opinion we have entertain'd of 'em" (141). It is important, then, to avoid being dogmatic, and above all to avoid boastfulness and bullying. The reader must always be treated lovingly and with great respect.[2]

The idea that the practice of rhetoric should be based on moral principles is consistent with the approach she has taken throughout *A Serious Proposal, Part II*. But her rhetorical theory at this point is informed, as she herself acknowledges, by Bernard Lamy's *The Art of Speaking*. Like Astell, Lamy connects the art of speaking with the principles of morality. As John T. Harwood explains, "Lamy's rhetorical system is never unrelated to his ethical and theological beliefs" (145). Astell's debt to Lamy, whose work she cites, is obvious throughout her discussion. Both ground their rhetorical theory in the fundamental Christian virtue of love: says Lamy, "Those who are really pious, have no need to counterfeit; their charity shows it self quite through their discourse" (360). Both identify pride as a block to communication: nothing, says Lamy "is so invincible an obstacle to perswasion as arrogancy and boldness" (353). Astell makes the same point: "There's nothing more improper than Pride and Positiveness" (141). Both Lamy and Astell insist, moreover, that the Christian speaker should avoid humiliating the audience not simply because it is uncharitable to undermine their self-esteem, but also because it is ineffective. Lamy believes that effective persuaders "with such art conceal their triumph, that the vanquish't person is scarce sensible of his defeat, but rather thinks himself victorious over that error to which he was before a slave" (355). Astell makes the same point, and we hear echoes of Lamy even in her diction as she makes it: "And since many would yield to the Clear Light of Truth were't not for the shame of being over-come, we shou'd Convince but not Triumph, and rather Conceal our Conquest than publish it. We doubly oblige our Neighbours when we reduce them into the Right Way, and keep it from being taken notice of that they were once in the Wrong" (141).

In basing her instruction in rhetoric on the principle of Christian love, then, and in identifying writing errors with moral flaws, Astell appears to have been strongly influenced by Lamy: we hear echoes of him throughout the discussion. However, it is important not to overestimate his influence. At every point where she uses him, Astell makes the argument her own, accommodating it to her primary audience of women and expressing it in her own way. Furthermore, she by no means always agrees with Lamy. Some of these disagreements are technical – for example, Lamy believes the arts of speaking and writing to be essentially dissimilar:

> The good Qualities of the Mind are not always concomitant with the qualities of a good Imagination, and happy Memory; which causes a great difference betwixt Speaking and Writing well. Oftentimes those who write well upon premeditation speak ill *Ex tempore*: To write well there is no need of a prompt, hot, and fertil Imagination. Unless our Wit be very bad indeed, upon serious Meditation we shall find what we ought, and what we might say upon any subject proposed; those who speak

easily and without premeditation, receive that advantage from a certain fertility and fire in the Imagination, which fire is extinguished by repose and cold contemplation in a Study. (309)

Astell, on the other hand, like Quintilian, sees a mutually supportive relationship between speaking and writing. They facilitate one another:

> I have made no distinction in what has been said between Speaking and Writing, because tho they are talents which do not always meet, yet there is no material difference between 'em. They write best perhaps who do't with the gentile and easy air of Conversation; and they Talk best who mingle Solidity of Thought with th'agreeableness of a ready Wit.[3] (143)

Another point on which Astell is in less than full agreement with Lamy concerns the human appetency for truth. In the course of his defence of the use of the passions in persuasion, Lamy justifies the appeal to the emotions on the grounds that reason is not enough. His supporting arguments, however, show his ambivalence on the question. On the one hand, he seems to admit that there is a natural love of truth; on the other, he appears to believe that it seldom comes into operation:

> Were men Lovers of Truth, to propose it to them in a lively and sensible way, would be sufficient to perswade them: But they hate it, because it accommodates but seldom with their Interests, and is seldom made out, but to the discovery of their Crimes: In so much that they are affraid [*sic*] of its lustre, and shut their Eyes that they may not behold it. They stifle the natural love that Men have for it, and harden themselves against the salutiferous strokes that she strikes upon the Conscience. (246)

Lamy appears to have little trust in humankind: original sin rather than grace seems to predominate in the soul. This suspiciousness colours much of his rhetorical theory and even to some extent undermines his professed belief in the importance of charity. Mary Astell's love for her audience, on the other hand, is obvious throughout all her works addressed specifically to women (though not those addressed to a wider public). She has a higher regard than does Lamy for the moral potential of people in general: "Truth is so very attractive, there's such a natural agreement between our Minds and it, that we care not to be thought so dull as not to be able to find out by our selves such obvious matters" (141). This difference in their attitudes is most clearly seen in the passages where they theorize relationships with the audience. Astell's theory is infused with tenderness, an almost maternal desire to spare the audience pain: we must not take the stance of the wise addressing the ignorant, but attempt only to "explain and illustrate what lay hid or might have been known before if they had consider'd it, and supposes that their Minds being employ'd about some other things was the reason why they did not discern it as well as we" (141). Lamy is very different. Even his theory as to the importance of charity is tainted with suspicion: "One may put on the face of an Honest man, only to delude those who have a reverence for the least appearance of truth; yet it follows not but we may profess love to our Auditors, and insinuate into their affections, when our love is sincere, and we have no design but the interest and propagation of truth" (359). There is no such suspicion of motive in Astell's theory.[4]

This suspicion, the rather grudging and limited trust in the honesty of both orators and audiences, probably arises from Lamy's conception of persuasion according to the traditional rhetorical model of warfare. Never far from his mind, it seems, is the conviction that the orator is primarily interested in winning. His vocabulary reflects a preoccupation with conflict: "If Postures be proper for defence, in corporal invasions; Figures are as necessary, in spiritual attacks. Words are the arms of the Mind, which she uses, to disswade or perswade, as occasion serves" (226). The whole of chapter 4 of the second part of *The Art of Speaking* is devoted to a discussion of eloquence according to this model, and the first section is entitled "Figures are the Arms of the Soul. A Comparison betwixt a Soldier Fighting and an Orator Speaking." Lamy finds exact parallels between the two activities and explores them in great detail.

In fairness to Lamy, it is important to remember that the audience he was addressing was masculine, and since most young men were trained in the arts of warfare, the comparison would have made sense to them and perhaps helped them to understand some of the rhetorical strategies. Yet the hostility does seem to infect Lamy himself, and a certain resentment toward unsympathetic or turgid audiences manifests itself in his writing. Astell, on the other hand, makes no use of warfare as means of explication. Furthermore, she does not share Lamy's underlying lack of trust in audiences, nor does she recommend it to her ladies. And her relationship with her own primary audience in this work is a tender one. She can become annoyed with them, it is true, and blame them for their resistance to instruction, but she never treats them as the enemy. The adversarial stance, though in some of her own writings she adopts it, is not one that she recommends to her audience of women.

It is this rejection of the metaphor of warfare as useful and appropriate for her ladies' understanding of rhetoric that constitutes one of Astell's most important contributions to rhetorical theory. Military comparisons would make no sense to her primary audience, who had no direct experience of battle. The kind of rhetorical activity for which she is preparing her audience of women is not *contentio* but *sermo*. It is to this private or semi-public kind of rhetoric that her theory applies, and she therefore advises an attempt always to bring about a win/win situation. The audience is to be reassured by a belief in their own intelligence, even if it means that the orator must conceal their mistakes from them. The orator's reward is not consciousness and acknowledgement of victory, which is morally dubious, but the innocent and spiritually valuable satisfaction of knowing that good has been done to others.

In spite of her disagreements with him, however, the importance of Lamy as a source for Astell's rhetorical theory cannot be doubted. Why, then, does she begin the passage with a quotation, not from Lamy, but from Arnauld and Nicole? And why does she appear at the beginning of the discussion to dismiss rhetoric as trivial? The answer to these questions involves some discussion of the relationship between *The Art of Thinking* and *The Art of Speaking*, and in particular some consideration of the author of the second work, Bernard Lamy. Its title suggests that the author wished it to be strongly associated with *The Art of Thinking*, the Port Royal Logic produced by Arnauld and Nicole, and because it was at first published anonymously, it is very likely that Astell mistakenly believed it to have been written by the same authors. As we shall see, this misapprehension might explain the slight but noticeable inconsistency in Astell's own attitude to rhetoric. It is therefore important to understand the circumstances of its original publication and why the author chose to remain anonymous.

Bernard Lamy belonged not to Port Royal, as did Arnauld and Nicole, but to another institution, the Congregation of the

Oratory of Jesus.[5] He also held a teaching position at the college of Anjou. Like Arnauld and his collaborator and friend, Pierre Nicole, Lamy was a Jansenist – and therefore Augustinian – in his theological allegiance, and hostile to the Jesuits. He was also, like Arnauld and Nicole, a Cartesian, and he perceived, as they did, the connection between the theology of Augustine and the philosophy of Descartes. Following Descartes, he believed in making scholarly work available in the vernacular: like *Discourse on Method, The Art of Speaking* was written in French. It was this open support of Descartes that brought Lamy to the attention of the authorities in 1675, for Descartes's work had been officially condemned as tending toward scepticism, and in 1665 had been placed on the Index, a list of works Roman Catholics were not allowed to read. Lamy's open avowal of Cartesian principles had endangered his Order:

> Lamy's adhesion to Cartesianism became a matter of public scandal. The official policy of the Oratory, as dictated by royal edict, was to remain faithful in philosophy classes to the Aristotelianism of Saint Thomas and to avoid any hint of the new doctrines. Orders were given requiring suspected Cartesians like Lamy to submit their lecture notes for examination by doctors of the Sorbonne. Propositions considered injurious to the state were found in which Lamy supposedly preferred democratic government to hereditary monarchy. A *lettre de cachet* exiled Lamy to a monastery near Grenoble and forbade him to teach or to preach. (Carr 128)

Lamy was reinstated in 1676, but at the time of the publication of *L'art de parler* in 1675, he was still in disgrace. Because he was keeping a necessarily low profile at the time, the work was published anonymously and did not bear his name until the French third edition of 1688. The original edition was translated into English almost immediately and published in 1676; it was attributed to "Messieurs du Port Royal" – that is, Arnauld and Nicole. In neither of the subsequent English editions of 1696 and 1708 – which were almost exact reprintings of the first – was Lamy named as author. Since Mary Astell cites the English translation (although she at least once refers to Arnauld and Nicole's *L'art de penser* by its French title), she almost certainly used this rather than the French original. She therefore most probably did not know that the two works had not both been produced by the scholars of Port Royal.

In fact, Lamy, though he shares some of Arnauld and Nicole's reservations about rhetoric, and like them bases his ideas in Cartesian philosophy, is much more sympathetic to it than are the authors of *L'art de penser*. There are, of course, areas of strong agreement between them, one of the strongest being the Cartesian principle of the naturalness of speaking. Lamy believes this to be the guiding principle of effective *dispositio*: "[T]hey speak most clearly and intelligibly, who speak most simply, and most according to the natural order and impressions upon their Mind" (Lamy 196). As is apparent in the quotation from their work with which Astell begins her discussion, Arnauld and Nicole so strongly believe in natural eloquence and so greatly resist late Renaissance models of rhetoric that they attempt to exclude from it any function other than, a merely corrective one. Carr, it is true, believes that "the grudging concessions they make to traditional rhetoric for the sake of sermons can be extended to legitimize a more wide-ranging eloquence than they admit" (63). Nevertheless, he concedes that their advice about rhetoric is "invariably negative" (86). "Their treatment of the emotions is perfunctory. The only role allowed them is that of supporting the ideas of the orator. [...] No effort [...] is made to follow up on Descartes' suggestions about the passions' potential for strengthening attention" (86).

It is this negative attitude to rhetoric that Mary Astell appears at first to share. Yet though she begins her discussion with a forceful rejection of the preoccupation of late Renaissance rhetoric with a virtuoso display of proficiency in the traditional tropes and schemes, as the discussion proceeds it seems that she is not as hostile to it as might first appear. Because she believed *The Art of Speaking* to have been written by the same authors as *The Art of Thinking*, she may not have noticed this gradual slippage into a more positive attitude to rhetoric. It is, however, apparent to the reader that she is increasingly taking Lamy, rather than Arnauld and Nicole, as her guide. For example, in spite of the condemnation of the rhetorical style cited above, later in the passage she is by no means wholly against the use of figures of speech. In fact, she refers her readers to *The Art of Speaking* for a full treatment of them (144). Interestingly, she immediately associates the use of the figures, which engage the emotions, with retaining the reader's attention: "He who wou'd take must be Sublime in his Sense, and must cloath it after a Noble way" (144). She concedes that "if Ornament be wholly neglected, very few will regard us" (140). The perfect orator considers that "as mere Flourish and Rhetorick are good for nothing, so neither will bare Reason dull and heavily express'd perform any great matter [...] and thinking it not enough to run 'em down with the strength of Reason, he draws them over to a Voluntary Submission by th' attractives of his Eloquence" (145). In this recognition of the value of a certain amount of ornament, she agrees not only with Lamy, but also with Descartes himself (Carr 87) rather than with Arnauld and Nicole.

As the discussion of rhetoric continues, we find that the influence of Lamy increases. Particularly important is the fifth section of *The Art of Speaking*, entitled "A Discourse in which is given an Idea of the Art of Persuasion." Lamy's definition of persuasion is wide: to quote Thomas Carr, Lamy holds that rhetoric is not "limited to the pulpit, the law courts, or negotiations – the traditional areas of *la grande eloquence* – persuasion takes place in all areas of life, whenever we seek to bring others around to our views" (Carr 129). Of course this idea of rhetoric is not a new one: it reproduces Plato's definition of rhetoric as "the art of influencing men's minds by means of words, whether the words are spoken in a court of law or before some other public body or in private conversation" (261). Later rhetorical tradition, however, had often restricted it to public discourse. Lamy's inclusion of everyday discourse within the scope of rhetoric is naturally particularly attractive to Mary Astell, who believes that "Women have no business with the Pulpit, the Bar or *St Stephen's Chapel*" (*A Serious Proposal, Part II* 143). She is educating her readers to participate in "Private Conversation" (143) and of course in writing.

Given this theoretical base, what methods does Astell recommend to her readers? First, they are to trust their own judgement, believing that the arts of expression are fundamentally natural. The abandonment of the belief that rhetorical expertise involves the learning of Latin and a rigorous apprenticeship to the methods of logic, as well as the memorization of the figures of rhetoric, has effectively opened the world of the intellect to women, and Astell's women readers can reap the benefits of this revolution of thought. They do not even have to learn modern languages, much less ancient dead ones. This means that they can teach themselves. Naturalness and simplicity are the rhetorical virtues she holds up to her readers, along with clarity, to which they both contribute; and these virtues are to be directed and supported by a genuine love for the audience. However, she does not wholly reject traditional rhetoric: as we have seen, her ladies should not neglect any rhetorical devices that might aid in focusing attention by exciting wonder and making the reception of the discourse pleasurable and thus persuasive. She therefore refers them to Lamy's exposition for specific instruction.

Although she does not believe that rhetoric can be learned by rule, she does support the judicious use of models. Since no writer has a perfect style, the best procedure is to choose a number of models, imitating what is good in each while avoiding the faults. There follows a passage that might have been inspired by the *Rhetorica ad Herennium*, a discussion of how each of the styles can degenerate: the grand style can "fly out of sight and by being Empty and Bombast become contemptible," the simple style can easily slide into the "Dull and Abject;" the severe style can be dry, and the florid vain.[6] The apprentice writer must therefore exercise her judgement in the use of models. Above all, she must put into the practice of her writing the Christian virtues, particularly the most important one, the love of God and of the audience, for God's sake.

It remains to pursue somewhat further the complex question of her sources. We know that she drew heavily upon Descartes, Arnauld and Nicole, and Lamy because she cites them. She also refers her readers to Locke's *Essay on Human Understanding*. Yet these authorities seem insufficient to explain her thorough knowledge of the principles of classical rhetoric, and we may speculate that she used a variety of other sources as well. Erin Herberg has demonstrated Astell's debt to Aristotelian and Ciceronian rhetoric, and also suggests the influence of Plato, mediated principally by the Cambridge Platonists in whose traditions she was trained by her uncle. Of all the rhetorical authorities, however, I believe it is to Augustine that Astell owes most. Her seventeenth-century sources were of course strongly influenced by him: not only Arnauld, Nicole, and Lamy, but also the Cambridge Platonists who drew upon his philosophy. Norris, indeed, quotes liberally from Augustine in his correspondence with Astell in *Letters Concerning the Love of God*. So strongly does her theory recall Augustine's, however, that one is tempted to believe she had access to *On Christian Doctrine* or *The Confessions*.

For example, her insistence that the emotional element in language is important not only to stimulate the audience to act upon the message but also to ease communication and maintain their interest is strongly reminiscent of Augustine. He allows the grand style on occasions when it is necessary to stimulate the audience to action: "But when something is to be done and he is speaking to those who ought to do it but do not wish to do it, then those great things should be spoken in the grand manner in a way appropriate to the persuasion of their minds" (*On Christian Doctrine* 4.19.38). Augustine also allows the use of the moderate style:

> That which the moderate style urges, that is, that eloquence itself be pleasing, is not to be taken up for its own sake, but in order that things which may be usefully and virtuously spoken, if they require neither a teaching nor a moving eloquence, may have a knowing and sympathetic audience which may assent more readily to that which is being said because of the delight aroused by that eloquence. (4.25.55)

What is most impressive about Astell's rhetorical theory, however, is not her ingenuity in drawing upon and blending ideas from various sources, but her originality in putting her own spin on them. She reconstitutes the theories of her sources, adapting them to her primary audience of women, and in doing so brings them out of the public into the private sphere. The theories of Augustine were formed with a view to instructing the Christian preacher, those of Aristotle and Cicero to prepare the student for a career in politics or law. Similarly, the audiences to whom her modern sources, Arnauld and Nicole and Lamy, addressed their discourse were predominantly masculine. Her ladies, on the other hand, debarred as they were from public speaking (and in Astell's view rightly so), would be concerned with the rhetoric of *sermo* rather than *contentio*. It is to this private, or semi-private rhetorical tradition that Astell makes her important contribution to rhetorical theory. Not that she necessarily believes that women's discourse should be confined forever to the private sphere: though she does not hold with their speaking in public, certainly in *The Christian Religion*, as we have seen, she recommends that through print they make a contribution to public discussion. Indeed, before long she will do so herself, and will prove to be as effective in *contentio* as any of her adversaries. Yet in *A Serious Proposal, Part II*, she is instructing beginners; obviously they will start with the practice of *sermo*, private or semi-public speaking and writing, and it is to *sermo* that her theorizing relates.

This matter of the theorizing of *sermo* brings us to the important question of the extent to which Astell's theory may be seen as feminist. The question can be approached in a number of different ways. Obviously, the theory is feminist inasmuch as it is addressed to women (the primary audience in *A Serious Proposal, Part II*) and is formulated in response to what Astell sees as their greatest need. However, as we have seen, it does not derive from feminine sources, nor does it arise in the context of a community of females. Indeed, it might be argued that it is the very lack of such a community that stimulates Astell to write in the first place. Although she did have one or two like-minded women friends, these were not sufficient to create a community of discourse. Astell's hope, as she expressed it in a letter to John Norris, was that she might be able to educate her friends to the point where they could become intellectual companions (Norris and Astell 49–50).[7]

We may also see as feminist her stress upon consideration for the audience, correcting them gently, preserving their self-esteem: "[W]e should Convince," she asserts, "but not Triumph." Indeed, she believes "we should [...] rather Conceal our Conquest than publish it" (141). In this tenderness toward the audience we may hear a forecasting of the rhetoric of care typical of certain twentieth-century approaches. To quote Amanda Goldrick-Jones: "Much North American feminism now equates this 'ethic of care' with women's ethical and moral voice, so much so that the notion of women's 'different voice' has become a powerful governing trope" (30). Astell's recommendations seem very similar to the approach of feminists such as Nel Noddings, and as suggested earlier, they seem to be grounded in her motherly care for the women she addresses.

However, in spite of the obvious similarity, ultimately Astell's theory is at odds with these modern positions in certain significant ways. An important element in much of the late twentieth-century discussion of the ethics of care is the notion of difference. The title of Carol Gilligan's book is *In a Different Voice*, and the authors of *Women's Ways of Knowing* hold that women even think differently from men: what they call "separate knowing" is typically masculine; "connected knowing" is typically feminine (Belenky et al. 104).[8] But the whole thrust of Astell's argument throughout all her works is that women are not significantly different from men: she wants to establish the essential similarities, not the differences. In her time, much of the discrimination against women was founded upon this very idea of difference, and except in certain areas Astell therefore challenges it. She recognizes some differences, it is true: in *A Serious Proposal, Part II*, she rather sourly intimates that mothers are morally superior to fathers (150); and in *The Christian Religion*, she claims that women are more open than men, more prone to self-disclosure (391). Then of course issues of propriety constrain women's practice: it is not appropriate for them to speak in public, and Astell's own policy was to remain officially anonymous in her writings. But these few exceptions aside, she believes that women are by nature much the same as men.

We should not assume, therefore, that Astell suggests that it is simply because they are *women* that her readers should be tender with their audiences. Her own practice refutes such an assumption: as we have seen, in *Some Reflections Upon Marriage* and the political pamphlets, nobody could be less sparing of her audience. In these works she engages in verbal warfare – full *contentio* – and does it very well. If Astell means her theory to apply to all rhetoric, then her theory is at odds with her practice. However, I think it is clear that Astell means her theory to apply specifically to *sermo*. As we have observed, she never writes into the void but always addresses a particular audience in a particular rhetorical situation. Her primary audience in *A Serious Proposal, Part II* is upper-class women, and it is to them, in relation to the kind of rhetoric that they will use, that she directs her advice; and for the foreseeable future, they will be engaged not in *contentio* but in *sermo*. It is a question, not of *gender*, but of *genre*, and as Erin Herberg has pointed out, Astell's theory is equally appropriate for men (156). Whatever the gender of the speaker, the less public form of rhetoric demands a relationship with the audience quite different from that which is appropriate to *contentio*.

It is indeed in this theorizing of *sermo* that Mary Astell makes her most important contribution to rhetorical theory. In her own time, it was important in offering instruction in rhetoric to women in a way that accommodated their particular needs and interests. It made accessible a body of theory that might otherwise have been impossible for many members of her audience to grasp. By relating rhetorical theory to moral practice, she brought it into line with concepts that her audience of women readily understood. In the longer term, her theory is interesting and relevant because it shows the application of traditional rhetorical principles not only to *contentio* but also to *sermo*. Perhaps even more important, it shows where these principles fail to apply: by challenging the propriety of the accepted adversarial practices of *contentio* to the more private *sermo*, she makes explicit the difference between them. The particularity of her recommendations on the tender consideration of the audience brings rhetorical theory into the sphere of the intimate and – with some reservations – may be seen as anticipating the rhetoric of care that is typical of the work of some of the most influential twentieth-century feminists. Inasmuch as she puts forward a theory of *sermo*, Mary Astell's theory of rhetoric is as relevant today as it was in her own time.

Conclusion

It is time to revisit the questions asked at the beginning, to evaluate what the evidence shows about Mary Astell's importance in the history of rhetoric, particularly women's rhetoric. What is there of lasting interest in her writings and her theories? Can they cast light on the progress of women's rhetoric in general, and have her ideas any practical application in the twenty-first century? Finally, what benefit, if any, can modern feminist scholars derive from the study of one of the earliest of their kind in England? In addressing these questions, I shall recapitulate the themes in this study and bring them to bear in finding answers. To this end, I shall review her address to the problems of *ethos*, her development as a writer, her achievements both as a practitioner and as a theorist, her standing as an educator and as a feminist, and finally her contributions to women of our own time.

One of the most interesting aspects of Astell's career is her negotiation of the difficulties presented by the woman writer's lack of a good *ethos*. The low view of women, combined with the strong – indeed, growing – sense of the bourgeois culture that they should not intervene in the public life of the community but should stay at home and mind house and children made it difficult for any woman writer to gain a respectful hearing. A woman venturing into print required great courage and self-confidence, which the society of the time did nothing to promote. Mary Astell drew the strength to embark on her career as a writer from various sources, none of them mainstream. The earliest influence on her was no doubt that of her Neoplatonist uncle. She therefore was brought up to believe not in the low view of her sex that belonged to Aristotelian philosophers but rather the much more positive ideas of the Platonists. This positive approach was strengthened by the contribution of the Cartesians: encouraged to think of her identity as grounded in the soul, not the body, released from the necessity of studying Latin and the complexities of scholastic logic, Astell had an opportunity to participate in the life of the mind that had rarely been open to her sex before. Beyond this modern development, however, she looked to the medieval model that honoured the unmarried woman and tried to bring it back. What lay behind her work, therefore, was a rich web of philosophy and theology, old and new, that gave her the superb confidence that is one of most remarkable features of her writing.

Astell's development as a writer has a particular interest because it illustrates one woman's progress from the kind of private writing long recognized as appropriate to her sex to a full participation in the genres traditionally belonging to men. As we have seen, Astell moved from the practice of *sermo* to the practice of *contentio*. She began her career as a writer by engaging in correspondence with a prominent philosopher. Already in her time, intellectually ambitious women had begun the practice of using the private letter to further their education by corresponding with learned men. In this Astell was not unusual. What was unusual was the publication of such letters. Astell certainly did not intend them for publication and agreed to it only at the insistence of John Norris. And the benefit she derived from this correspondence was not the launching of her career as a writer: though begun earlier than *A Serious Proposal*, the *Letters* were published later, and on her part very reluctantly. What she gained was training in the rhetoric of scholarship: she put herself into the hands of Norris, who was delighted to instruct her. Her style was already well developed, and Norris praised her for it, but her treatment of subject matter was grounded in the practice of conversation and therefore tended toward the superficial. Norris taught her to discuss each topic thoroughly, a lesson she later passed on to her female readers in *A Serious Proposal, Part II*.

Profiting from her instruction by Norris, and no doubt encouraged by her success – his praise must have been deeply reassuring – she went on to produce *A Serious Proposal to the Ladies*, also in the form of a letter, but this time addressed to women. Her audience is not yet the general public: specifically, in the title itself, she restricts her intended audience, and thus positions herself still within *sermo*, defined as either private or semi-public discourse. With *A Serious Proposal, Part II*, she further broadens her audience: though still using the letter form, she abandons the second person address in favour of a more formal inclusive "we." Her audience in this work takes in members of the interested public and includes some rebuttal of the criticisms made by John Locke/Damaris Masham, who must therefore also be seen as part of her intended readership, though her primary audience remains the ladies of the title. It is in her next work, *Some Reflections Upon Marriage*, that she abandons the form of the letter, and addresses a general audience. This is an important step: for the first time she goes fully public, challenging common opinion on the nature, the status, and the rights of women. Her *magnum opus*, *The Christian Religion*, is again presented as a letter; but it is in fact a philosophical treatise. Astell is not the first to use the form of a supposedly private letter with a public audience in mind: Cicero, for example, had led the way in this respect. Her audience in this work is again primarily, though not exclusively, women. However, the genre, philosophy, is traditionally a masculine preserve. Finally, we have the political pamphlets, in which Astell emerges into full *contentio*. Her audience in these is the general educated public, including particularly the major politicians and political theorists of the day. In these papers she proves herself one of the most skilled polemicists of her time, a formidable warrior on the Tory side, able to take on the men at their own game and on their own terms, and win. We see in Astell's progress as a practising rhetorician, then, a woman moving out of the acknowledged women's sphere of private and semi-public discourse into the fully public world of philosophy and political debate. Her considerable success in public pamphleteering is a landmark in women's entry into public political discourse.

What was it that made her so successful? She was not the first woman to write passionately in support of women's education; she was not the first woman to engage in philosophical discussion. Even in producing political pamphlets, other women had gone before her. Yet none achieved her celebrity status. In part, I believe, her success was the result of her acute awareness of topical issues, her accurate reading of the rhetorical situation. All her works are in the best sense of the word occasional, created in response to a particular exigency. She never wrote into the void. The correspondence with John Norris was initiated to satisfy her curiosity about a current issue in his philosophy. Both parts of *A Serious Proposal* addressed the immediate problem of the material, intellectual, and spiritual poverty of women, particularly those who were unmarried. *Reflections* challenged public opinion on the question of the plight of married women, which Astell saw as another burning issue, made topical by the death of the Duchess of Mazarin. Even the most philosophical of her works, *The Christian Religion*, was occasioned by the popularity of a book lent to her by Lady Catherine Jones, one that she considered dangerously in error, moving her to produce her own work to address what she saw as an immediate theological and social crisis. As for her political pamphlets, they were the most occasional of all, belonging to the then hot topic of the relationship between politics and religion.

Along with this accurate perception of what interested the public went an unusually strong talent for argumentation and a particularly effective use of the language, a powerful style. Its two most prominent features are its clarity and its basis in conversation. Its perspicuity is most remarkable, because hardest to achieve, in her philosophical works: that is, much of *A Serious Proposal, Part II* and *The Christian Religion*. Yet it is not a cold clarity: the writing demonstrates a high degree of intellectual passion, and the relationship with the audience remains in these works warm and familiar. The most memorable characteristic of her style, though, is that it is formed by her experience of conversation. What this means is that we notice above all its sound: it is voiced, informed by the rhythms and patterns of speech. There is always in her writing the sense of a human being talking, a distinct personality. She never retreats into the impersonal, the distanced.

There is, however, distinct variation in tone according to whether she is addressing a semi-public audience of women or the full general public, consisting mostly of men. With her predominantly female audience she is all tenderness and consideration – reassuring, nurturing, comforting, treating them gently, building their self-esteem, minimizing their faults, and in every conceivable way encouraging them. On the other hand, when her audience is the general public, principally men, her style is very different. In these works – that is, *Reflections* and the political pamphlets – she is on the attack. As sincere in her rejection of what she sees as false as she is passionate in her commitment to truth, she goes into battle, armed with all her powers of eloquence, and flays the opposition without mercy. She is out to draw blood, and she succeeds: her words sting and scald. In an age given to vituperation, no one did it better. In these works she fights not for the satisfaction of winning a rhetorical argument, but to prevent what she sees as the serious damage her opponents are doing to the whole culture, and most particularly women. She is fighting against an increasingly secular world that values money above people, a new culture that she sees as disastrous. As Van C. Hartmann observes, she gives "a perceptive feminist response to the new forms of inequality and dehumanization being promulgated by emergent capitalistic economics and Whig liberalism" (244).

In evaluating Astell's rhetorical achievement, we notice that she is successful in all three of the categories of speech distinguished by classical rhetoricians according to their primary purpose: teaching, praising (or blaming), and persuading. *A Serious Proposal, Part I* and the political pamphlets are primarily persuasive pieces. Though very different in tone, each puts forward a particular position and argues strongly in support of it. *A Serious Proposal, Part II* and *The Christian Religion* are largely informative, both combining philosophy and education in different proportions. Astell's concern in these is to teach. As for *Reflections*, it falls within the category of the epideictic, the rhetoric of praise and blame. It is sheer invective, using irony, the mock encomium, and all the other devices of satire to make its point. There is a good deal of vituperation in the pamphlets as well.

Successful as she is in all the categories of rhetoric, however, it is not her practice alone that entitles Astell to an important place in the history of women's rhetoric. She is also a theorist. As we have seen, her practice moves from *sermo* to *contentio*, from the private to the fully public. Her theory, on the other hand, moves from the public to the private, applying the received rhetorical theory of *contentio* to *sermo*. As Erin Herberg shows, Astell draws upon the precepts of the rhetorical tradition as it appears in Plato, Aristotle, and Cicero; an even more important source for Astell is Augustine.[1] She also uses theorists much closer to her own time: Descartes, Poullain de la Barre, Arnauld and Nicole, and Lamy. All these authorities were concerned with public discourse, but she uses them to theorize *sermo*. As Cicero had observed, *sermo*, though an important genre, had never been adequately theorized (1.132), and the situation had not greatly improved since his time. Astell, then, does for English rhetoric what Madeleine de Scudéry had done earlier in the century for French: she takes the principles of the theory of *contentio* and applies them to *sermo*, for it is with *sermo* that her ladies will begin their practice of rhetoric.[2] She perceives where the theory is applicable to the probable rhetorical exigencies of her own audience and applies it to their situation. But in accommodating traditional rhetorical theory to the requirements of her audience of women, Astell also challenges it: the adversarial stance appropriate to *contentio* is by no means suitable in a private or semi-public situation. While borrowing from the theories within the rhetorical tradition, then, she yet makes significant changes, insisting on the importance of respect and consideration for the audience – qualities not usually much valued by rhetoricians in the masculine tradition. She thus anticipates the rhetoric of care of late twentieth-century feminist rhetoricians.[3]

It is important to remember, however, that Astell's rhetorical theory is included as part of the instruction to the women who were the principal intended readers of *A Serious Proposal, Part II*, and that therefore her emphasis on the rhetoric of care applies only to *sermo*, not to *contentio*; for unless we recognize this limitation, we shall see Astell as something of a hypocrite. In her semi-public works, she follows her own advice and is tender and considerate toward her audience, but nothing could be less tender than her relationship with the opposition in *Reflections* or her political writings. We must understand, therefore, that her rhetorical theory is limited in its application. Furthermore, it is necessary to note that this is emphatically not primarily a question of gender: Astell is not taking the position that her ladies ought to be deferential in their own practice of rhetoric simply because they are women. In a semi-public or private context, treating the audience with the utmost courtesy and respect is as important for men as for women. The difference is in the rhetorical situation and in the genre used, not in the gender of the speaker or writer. It is this which principally distinguishes her from the late twentieth-century feminists who see the rhetoric of care as a specifically feminine characteristic.

Astell's achievement as a rhetorician, both in her theorizing and her practice, is, then, considerable. It remains to consider her influence, both on the men and women of her own time and on subsequent generations. In her day, Astell was certainly a celebrity. Her influence was acknowledged by many of the more notable *literati* of the day, both those who shared her philosophical and political positions and those who did not. Many admired her, some attacked her, but whether by praise or blame, her importance was recognized. As we have seen, she was highly valued by John Norris, who praised her "moving Strains of the most natural and powerful Oratory" (Norris and Astell n.p.) and by George Hickes, who referred to her *Moderation Truly Stated* as a book that he and his friend Dr. Charlett "justly admired so much" (qtd. in F. Smith 158). John Evelyn, most famous for his diaries, speaks of her in his *Numismata*, published in 1697, referring to "the satisfaction I still receive by what I read of Madam Astell's of the most sublime" (265). John Dunton calls her "the divine Astell" (qtd. in Perry, *Celebrated* 99). Another admirer was Thomas Burnet: in a letter written to the Electress Sophia in 1697, he refers to Astell as "a young Ladie of extraordinary piety and knowledge" (qtd. in Reynolds 303). And George Wheeler in 1698, as well as Robert Nelson in 1715, praised her ideas about women's education (F. Smith 72, 76). Ruth Perry has shown that Astell's influence on ideas about the education of women persisted throughout the eighteenth century, affecting even such prominent writers as Samuel Richardson and Samuel Johnson: Astell's *Serious Proposal* was the inspiration for Sir Charles Grandison's disquisition on a Protestant nunnery and in Johnson's *Rasselas*, one of the heroines, Princess Nekayah, wishes to "found a college of pious maidens" (qtd. in Perry, *Celebrated* 111).

There were others who disagreed with her politics or philosophy yet took her seriously enough to reply to her: Damaris Masham, almost certainly prompted by John Locke, replied to *Letters Concerning the Love of God* and *A Serious Proposal to the Ladies*; Charles Leslie, James Owen, and Daniel Defoe all replied to her *Moderation Truly Stated*, the pamphlet so much admired by George Hickes. Then there were those who simply held her up to ridicule, but even these in doing so implicitly acknowledged the significance of her opinions and influence. Best known of the satirical attacks on her is that of Steele in Tatler 32, where she is represented as the school mistress Madonella. Steele was possibly acting in the interests and at the behest of Swift and others, who resented her attack on the Kit-Cat Club in her 1709 pamphlet, *Bart'lemy Fair*. Steele writes in the tradition of the attack on learned women made popular by Moliere's *Les Femmes Savantes*. While he is at it, Steele includes Elizabeth Elstob and Mary de la Riviere Manley as objects of ridicule, depicting them as instructors in Madonella's school. Astell's *Serious Proposal* was sufficiently well-known for readers to make the association between her and Madonella without difficulty.

Most telling of all, however – if imitation is the sincerest form of flattery – is the borrowing of her ideas, sometimes amounting to outright plagiarism, by well-known men of the time. To recapitulate the discussion in the chapter on *A Serious Proposal, Part I*: Gilbert Burnet, who had probably persuaded Princess Anne not to endow Astell's Protestant monastery on the grounds that it had too much the flavour of Roman Catholicism, very shortly afterwards proposed such an institution himself (Hill 118). And Daniel Defoe, though arguing against her proposal, then borrowed her ideas – without acknowledgement (Springborg, *Mary Astell* xiii). The worst of these borrowings was perpetrated by the compiler of *The Ladies Library*, published in 1714. Astell believed this was Richard Steele, who had satirized her as Madonella. In the preface to the 1722 edition of Bart'lemy Fair, she claimed that he had "transcribed above an hundred pages into his Ladies Library, verbatim" – of course, without acknowledgement (Springborg, *Mary Astell* xxxviii n.49). Only recently has it been established that the compiler was in fact, not Steele but George Berkeley (Springborg, *Mary Astell* xxxviii n.47).

Well known as Astell obviously was to the men of letters of her day, we may nonetheless speculate that her most important influence was upon other women. Some of these can be identified, and Ruth Perry gives an account of them in chapter 4 of *The Celebrated Mary Astell*. Of these, perhaps the most important, if not the best known, is Elizabeth Elstob, the expert in Old English, whose scholarly ambitions were supported and encouraged by her reading of *A Serious Proposal* while she was still a young girl. She, like Astell, wished to encourage scholarship among women, and her Anglo-Saxon grammar was prepared especially to promote it: written in English instead of Latin, it was therefore accessible to women readers whose ignorance of Latin would have prevented them from studying earlier works on the subject. Another woman who was much encouraged by Astell's precepts and example was Mary, Lady Chudleigh, most famous for *The Ladies Defence*, a reply to Sprint's offensively misogynist *The Bride-Woman's Counsellor*. Not only did she cite Astell in this work, but she also wrote a poem in praise of "Almystrea" (an anagram on "Mary Astell"), as did her friend, Elizabeth Thomas. If women such as Chudleigh and Thomas were inspired by Astell's ideas, other women admired her command of the language: in a letter to Astell's friend, Lady Elizabeth Hastings, Lady Schomberg refers to "Mrs Astell's eloquence" (Perry, *Celebrated* 99).

Not all the women influenced by Astell necessarily adopted her ideas. As we have seen, Damaris Masham was moved to respond to Astell because she so strongly disagreed with her. And Judith Drake, who was probably encouraged by Astell's example to write *An Essay in Defence of the Female Sex*, nonetheless does not approach the problems of women's situation in quite the same way. What this suggests is a healthy measure of independent thinking: we do not find anything like an Astell school of thought, women who simply played follow-the-leader without working out the social problems for themselves.

The best known among the women influenced by Astell was Lady Mary Wortley Montagu. As a young girl, Lady Mary was inspired by Astell's writings, and when she met her in person they became great friends. Mary Astell loved Lady Mary and admired her intelligence and her sparkling personality (though she could not always approve of her conduct); she even wrote at least one poem in praise of her (Perry, *Celebrated* 270ff). Lady Mary is most famous for her *Embassy Letters*, written while her husband was ambassador to Turkey in 1717 and 1718. These she refused to publish during her lifetime, it being thought indecorous for a lady of the nobility to do so. However, at the insistence of Mary Astell, she agreed to have them published after her death, which occurred in 1762. In anticipation of this event, Astell wrote a preface, which was duly included in the publication of the *Letters* in 1763, more than thirty years after Astell herself had died.[4]

We see, therefore, that Astell's influence on her century was considerable and lasted some time beyond her own era: Ruth Perry asserts that "by mid eighteenth century, some years after her death, Astell's powers as a writer were still admired" (*Celebrated* 215). Yet Perry also acknowledges that "no other woman writer picked up where Astell left off" (330). The status of women was no longer a burning issue, and the age lost interest in it. Women writers indeed there were, but they occupied themselves principally with novels and poetry; they were not politically engaged, as Astell had been in the earlier years of the century. Yet even so, her influence was not lost. Her friend Elizabeth Elstob – for whose Anglo-Saxon grammar Astell had raised subscriptions – introduced her to a new generation of women: Sarah Chapone, Mrs. Delany, and Mrs. Dewes, who were part of a group later known to us as the blue-stockings. Encouraged by Elstob, they read Astell's works and modelled themselves upon her.

It would naturally be of great interest to know whether or not Mary Wollstonecraft read Astell. Many of their complaints about women's lot were similar, and it seems probable that the later Mary would have had access to the earlier Mary's work. However, evidence that Wollstonecraft knew Astell's work has not been forthcoming, and as Regina Janes rightly points out, their solutions to the problems were grounded in very different systems of belief. The foundation of Mary Astell's hopes and convictions was religious, that of Mary Wollstonecraft, secular: "The religious center that provided Astell with a focus from the beginning served Wollstonecraft only briefly, and in its place she put, when she had found them, the rights of man" (Janes 131).

In spite of the regard of those of her friends who survived into the mid-eighteenth century and kept her memory alive, Astell's reputation faded. Rescued for a time by George Ballard's book on the learned ladies of Great Britain, it nonetheless failed to survive except in odd works and occasional entries in dictionaries and encyclopaedias.[5] Not until Florence Smith's important biography of Astell was published in 1916 did her reputation begin to revive, and even then it was not until the latter part of the twentieth century that scholars such as Bridget Hill and Ruth Perry introduced her to feminist awareness. Between her death and the earlier part of the twentieth century, her reputation went underground, and her influence is almost untraceable. We may suspect it is there, unacknowledged and even unrecognized, but there is little proof.

Something must be said about Astell's contribution to women's education and to feminism in early modern times.[6] She was not the first learned woman to argue for the proper education of girls. What distinguishes her is the thorough philosophical basis she provides for her *Serious Proposal*, especially in *Part II*, and for that other great work of instruction, *The Christian Religion*. In these three works she shows women not only how they should live, but why. A philosophical idealist, she grounds every suggestion in a firm philosophical position, tellingly argued and forcibly and eloquently presented. This same philosophical grounding undergirds her position as a feminist. She argues strongly for women's rights, not only in the three works mentioned above, but also in *Some Reflections Upon Marriage*. As a feminist, she is one of the earliest of the time to recognize that women could lead satisfactory and productive lives without becoming wives and mothers if proper provision could be made for their education and social accommodation. The Protestant monastery she proposed could provide educational preparation and social support for a useful and satisfying way of life independent of men. It is this positive vision of the good life beyond the constraints of contemporary ideals of womanhood that puts Astell's work above mere complaint. She is not, in the end, arguing for the mere correction of the state of affairs, but for a new vision of who and what women truly are and what they should see as their destiny.

It is in the light of this vision that we must see the importance of her political writings, especially the pamphlets. Part of her vision for women is that they should participate in government and scholarship. Their minds are not less well-endowed than those of men, and she argues in *The Christian Religion* that simply because women are not engaged in the day-to-day administration of public affairs, they have the leisure to think things out in depth and therefore to offer wise advice. It is true that she does not foresee the full public participation of women in government, though given her admiration of the female monarchs of the country, Queen Elizabeth and Queen Anne, we may surmise that she would have had no objection to it. For herself, she believes that her own place in society makes it necessary for her to maintain her anonymity: it was this sense of social decorum that prevented her friend Lady Mary Wortley Montagu from publishing at all during her lifetime. Astell did not aspire to be known by name; her ambition, for herself as for other women of her own kind, was to make a difference, in politics and in social conditions. The influence that women could in this way bring to bear upon the society of their time would not only fulfill their own needs but also justify their existence.

This is what Astell herself was attempting to do in her political pamphlets. It is a measure of her importance – even her importance as a feminist – that she did not confine her interest to the betterment of women's condition. Strongly as she argued for such improvement, she was concerned for the whole of her society, not simply the women in it. She is therefore important to posterity as a model: this is how a woman can live, this is how she can make a useful contribution to the public good. If, as twentieth-century feminists have argued, women need a sense of their own history of achievements, Mary Astell is a highly important figure, as inspiration and as model. Some of the problems she addressed may no longer be current, though the materialism that she saw as a social evil in her time is even more developed in ours. It is true that the specific political issues at stake in her time are no longer relevant, but her participation in them is.

There is another important lesson that we can learn from the example of Mary Astell. One of the distinguishing characteristics of her thought is that it stems both from medieval ideology and from modern philosophy. She can speak to our time because she was not, ultimately, confined to hers. She looked back beyond the Protestant bourgeois era and received inspiration from the feudal

Catholic past. But she also derived inspiration from the new ideas of Descartes and his followers, and from the Cambridge Platonists of the seventeenth century. This ability to combine the good of both the old and the new shows that she was not the slave of mere intellectual fashion. If her work is relevant to future ages, it is because she was not confined in thought or aspiration to her own time, and it is this timelessness that allows her to speak with such relevance to our condition today.

Appendix A

The following passage continues the discussion of Patricia Springborg's contention that *A Serious Proposal to the Ladies, Part II* is primarily a response to Damaris Masham's *A Discourse Concerning the Love of God*. For the earlier part of this discussion, see chapter 5.

Springborg believes that

> Astell takes seriously Masham's claim that to deny the relative autonomy of individual cognition is gratuitous Platonist quietism. To deny the Creator who made us the power to endow us with independent cognition is both to deny God essential attributes and to ignore New Testament exhortations to take responsibility for our own salvation. The consequence of 'seeing all things in God', is a form of sollipsism that allows the self as the only object of real knowledge, thus denying the role of human interaction in understanding and in implementing a programme for a Christian life. It logically leads to the nunnery.

> In *A Serious Proposal, Part II*, Astell appears to concede Masham's first charge and tries to address the second. She declares the proposition of Malebranche endorsed by John Norris that 'we see all things in God' is, if not true, at least pious. And she denies that her house of retirement for women was ever intended as other than a primarily academic establishment. (Springborg, *Mary Astell* xvi)

What Astell actually says, however, is this:

> Above all things we must be throughly convinc'd of our entire Dependence on GOD, for what we *Know* as well as for what we *Are*, and be warmly affected with the Sense of it, which will both Excite us to Practise, and Enable us to Perform the

rest. Tho' we are Naturally Dark and Ignorant, Yet in *his Light we may* hope to *see Light*, if with the Son of *Syrac* we petition for *Wisdom that sits by his Throne to labour with me*, and Sigh with *David* after his *Light and Truth*. For then he who is The Light that Lightneth everyone that comes into the World, the Immutable Truth, and Uncreated Wisdom of His Father, will Teach us in the way of Wisdom and lead us in right Paths, he will instruct us infinitely better by the right use of our own Faculties than the brightest Human Reason can. For in him are all the Treasure of Wisdom and Knowledge which he Liberally dispenses to all who Humbly, Honestly and Heartily ask 'em of him. To close this Head: Whatever the Notion That we see all things in GOD, may be as to the truth of it, 'tis certainly very commendable for its Piety [...]. (*Serious Proposal II* 116)

Springborg reads this last sentence as conceding Masham's point: "Astell appears to accept Masham's critique in *Discourse Concerning the Love of God* (1696) of the Malebranchean principle of 'Seeing all things in God,' to which Astell had subscribed in her *Letters Concerning the Love of God* (1695). But in *The Christian Religion* (1705) she reindorses Malebranche's principle" (*Astell, Political Writings* 189n93).

As I read it, however, Astell does not concede Masham's point: she simply refuses to discuss it in detail. All the rest of the passage quoted above supports the idea of our seeing all things in the light of God. The last sentence suggests only that she declines in this particular work to discuss it further. Now if, as Springborg believes, *A Serious Proposal, Part II* is essentially a philosophical disquisition addressed to other philosophers, this evasion is inexcusable, and might well suggest a concession of the point or at least an inability to refute it. But if, as I believe, Astell's main purpose is to deepen the understanding of her primary audience of women, her avoidance of the question makes sense. It makes *rhetorical* sense, for a thorough refutation would involve reference to philosophical principles that sidetrack her from her main purpose of instruction. All her readers need to know to get the point of the present discourse is that "tis certainly very commendable for its Piety." Astell in fact does address the question in a later work, *The Christian Religion*: Springborg speaks of her as *completing* her answer to Masham/Locke in that work. I believe, on the contrary, that she postpones her refutation to this later, more philosophical work.[1] In support of this contention, we should note that the passage Springborg quotes from Locke (cited in chapter 4 above) concerning "the Day-Labourers and Tradesmen, the spinsters and Dairy Maids" is quoted verbatim and responded to specifically by Astell in *The Christian Religion* (403). A further indication that it is *The Christian Religion* that constitutes Astell's refutation of Masham can be found in John Norris's *An Admonition concerning two late Books called "Discourses of the Love of God."* He attached this essay to volume 4 of his *Practical Discourses*, which he published in 1698. Here he declines to refute *A Discourse Concerning the Love of God*, on the grounds that "a kind pen" had undertaken to do so, the kind pen being that of Mary Astell (Acworth 177). He thus speaks of her defence as to come: *A Serious Proposal, Part II* had already been published in 1697, and if it was that work which was to be seen as the primary response to Masham's attack, he would surely have said so.

Appendix B

Annotations in books in Lady Mary Wortley Montagu's library, Sandon Hall, Stafford (Owner, the Rt. Hon. the Earl of Harrowby; archivist, Michael Bosson). The following are thought to be annotations made by Mary Astell. [Mary Astell] in Bayle, *Pensees Diverses* 4th ed., 1704 (flyleaf):

> I ask pardon for scrolling in Yr Laps Book. The Author is so disingenuous & inconsistent yt no lover of Truth can read it without a just Indignation. Under pretence of exposing Popery (ye common Cant) & answering his own Chimeras abt Comets, he rakes togather all ye vile suggestions his great reading afforded, agst Xtianity & indeed agt all Religion. They are his true but <?wilful edsmns??> & sly insinuations, such as show his malice, not his Judgmt. I suppose ye other Volumes are like. <?> read ym/ Pensees de Pascal are profound <?> solid, just full of noble sentiments, good Sense & true reasoning, clearly yet conscisely express'd in proper language. This Pensees Divers of Bailes wch seems to me to be writ in opposition to ye other, tho covertly, is a loose, rambling, incoherent rapsody, wch all ye affectation of Method, Reasoning & Exactness, full of words, wth every thing strain'd to a latent ill meaning or else vry impertinent, Trifling, or worse.
>
> The *Equivoque* is ye grand figu<re> yt adorns the whole work; the force of his Argumts les in confounding w<t> ought to be distinguish'd. Thus he every where confounds ye <?Round> with ye *Real* Man, ye *Practical* Atheist with ye *Speculative*; if the<re> be any one who does in reality disbelieve in GOD, among ye many who wou'd fain persuade ymselves there is none, because they are obnox <?>.

(<> signifies uncertain reading.)

Contributed by Professor Isabel Grundy of the University of Alberta

Bibliography

Acworth, R. *The Philosophy of John Norris of Bemerton*. Hildesheim: Georg
  Olms, 1979.
Aristotle. *The Politics of Aristotle*. Ed. and trans. Ernest Barker. Oxford:
  Clarendon, 1948.
———. *Rhetorica*. Trans. W. Rhys Roberts. New York: Random House, 1984.
Armstrong, Nancy, and Leonard Tennenhouse, eds. *The Ideology of Conduct:
  Essays on Literature and the History of Sexuality*. New York: Methuen, 1987.
Arnauld, Antoine, and Pierre Nicole. *The Art of Thinking*. Trans. and intro.
  James Dickoff. Indianapolis: Bobbs-Merrill, 1964.
Astell, Mary. *Bart'lemy Fair: Or an Enquiry after Wit in which Due Respect Is
  Had to a Letter Concerning Enthusiasm. To my Lord XXX by Mr Wotton*.
  London, 1709.
———. *The Christian Religion as Profess'd by a Daughter of the Church of England
  in a Letter to the Right Honourable T.L. C.I*. London, 1705.
———. *A Fair Way With the Dissenters And Their Patrons. Not Writ by Mr.
  L____y, or any other Furious Jacobite whether Clergyman or Layman; but by
  a Very Moderate Person and Dutiful Subject to the Queen*. London, 1704.
———. *An Impartial Enquiry into the Causes of Rebellion and Civil War in this
  Kingdom in an Examination of Dr. Kennett's Sermon, Jan. 31, 1703/4 and
  Vindication of the Royal Martyr*. London, 1704.
———. *Letters Concerning the Love of God, between the Author of the Proposal to
  the Ladies and Mr. John Norris*. London, 1695.
———. *Moderation Truly Stated: Or a Review of a Late Pamphlet, Entitul'd
  Moderation a Virtue, or The Occasional Conformist Justified from the
  Imputation of Hypocrisy*. London, 1704.
———. *A Serious Proposal to the Ladies for the Advancement of Their True and
  Greatest Interest*. London, 1694.
———. *A Serious Proposal to the Ladies, Part II, Wherein a Method is Offer'd for
  the Improvement of Their Minds*. London, 1697.
———. *Some Reflections Upon Marriage, Occasion'd by the Duke & Duchess of
  Mazarine's Case*. 3rd ed. London, 1706.
Augustine of Hippo. *On Christian Doctrine*. Trans. D. W. Robertson.
  Indianapolis: Bobbs-Merrill, 1958.
Bacon, Francis. *The Advancement of Learning and New Atlantis*. Oxford:
  Clarendon, 1974.
Bald, R. C., ed. *Six Elizabethan Plays*. Boston: Houghton, 1963.
Ballard, George. *Memoirs of Several Ladies of Great Britain Who Have Been
  Celebrated for Their Writings or Skill in the Learned Languages, Arts and
  Sciences*. Ed. Ruth Perry. Detroit: Wayne State UP, 1985.
Barash, Carol. "'The Native Liberty ... of the Subject': Configurations of
  Gender and Authority in the Works of Mary Chudleigh, Sarah Fyge
  Egerton, and Mary Astell." Grundy and Wiseman 55–69.

Baumlin, James S., and Tita French Baumlin, eds. *Ethos: New Essays in Rhetorical and Critical Theory.* Dallas, TX: Southern Methodist UP, 1994.

Baumlin, Tita French. "'A good (wo)man skilled in speaking': *Ethos*, Self-Fashioning and Gender in Renaissance England." Baumlin and Baumlin 229–63.

Belenky, Mary Field, Blythe McVicker Clinchy, Nancy Rule Goldberger, and Jill Mattuck Tarule. *Women's Ways of Knowing: The Development of Self, Voice, and Mind.* New York: Basic Books, 1986.

Benson, Thomas W., and Michael H. Prosser, eds. *Readings in Classical Rhetoric.* Davis, CA: Hermagoras Press, 1988.

Bizzell, Patricia. "Feminist Methods of Research in the History of Rhetoric: What Differences Do They Make?" *Rhetoric Society Quarterly* 30.4 (2000): 5–18.

Bizzell, Patricia, and Bruce Herzberg, eds. *The Rhetorical Tradition: Readings from Classical Times to the Present.* 2nd ed. Boston: Bedford/St Martin's, 2001.

Bordo, Susan. "The Cartesian Masculinization of Thought." *Signs* 11.3 (1986): 439–54.

Bridenthal, Renate, and Claudia Koonz, eds. *Becoming Visible: Women in European History.* Boston: Houghton, 1977.

Brody, Miriam. *Manly Writing: Gender, Rhetoric and the Rise of Composition.* Carbondale: Southern Illinois UP, 1993.

Bryson, Cynthia B. "Mary Astell: Defender of the 'Disembodied Mind.'" *Hypatia* 13.4 (1998): 40–62.

Burton, Robert. *The Anatomy of Melancholy.* Rpt. London: G. Bell & Sons, 1926.

Carr, Thomas M., Jr. *Descartes and the Resilience of Rhetoric: Varieties of Cartesian Rhetorical Theory.* Carbondale: Southern Illinois UP, 1990.

Cassirer, Ernst. *The Platonic Renaissance in England.* Trans. James Pettegrove. Austin: U of Texas P, 1953.

Cavendish, Margaret. *Plays.* London, 1662.

———. *Plays, Never Before Printed.* London, 1668.

Chudleigh, Lady Mary. *The Ladies Defence.* London, 1701.

[Cicero]. *Ad C Herennium. (Rhetorica ad Herennium).* Trans. Harry Caplan. Loeb Classical Library. Cambridge: Harvard UP, 1913.

———. *De Officiis.* Ed. and trans. Walter Miller. Loeb Classical Library. Cambridge: Harvard UP, 1913.

Copleston, Frederick, SJ. *A History of Philosophy.* Vol. 5. Garden City, NY: Doubleday, 1963.

Cragg, Gerald R. *The Cambridge Platonists.* New York: Oxford UP, 1970.

Cunningham, Lawrence, and John Reich, eds. *Culture and Values: A Survey of the Western Humanities.* Vol. 2. Fort Worth, TX: Harcourt, 1994.

Daybell, James, ed. *Early Modern Women's Letter Writing, 1450–1700.* Basingstoke, UK: Palgrave, 2001.

Descartes, René. *Discourse on Method and Meditations on First Philosophy.* Trans. Donald A. Cress. Indianapolis: Hackett, 1980.

Dickoff, James. Introduction. *The Art of Thinking.* By Antoine Arnauld. Indianapolis: Bobbs-Merrill, 1964. xxxvii–li.

Donawerth, Jane. "As Becomes a Rational Woman to Speak: Madeleine de Scudéry's Rhetoric of Conversation." Wertheimer 305–19.

———. "Conversation and the Boundaries of Public Discourse in Rhetorical Theory by Renaissance Women." *Rhetorica* 16.2 (1998): 181–99.

———. "The Politics of Renaissance Rhetorical Theory by Women." Levin and Sullivan 257–74.

———, ed. *Rhetorical Theory by Women before 1900*. Lanham, MD: Rowman and Littlefield, 2002.

Donne, John. *The Poems of John Donne*. Ed. Herbert Grierson. London: Oxford UP, 1933.

Ede, Lisa, Cheryl Glenn, and Andrea Lunsford. "Border Crossings: Intersections of Rhetoric and Feminism." *Rhetorica* 13.4 (1995): 401–41.

Elyot, Thomas. *The Defence of Good Women*. Ed. Edwin Johnston Howard. Oxford, OH: Anchor Press, 1940.

Evans, G. Blakemore, ed. *The Riverside Shakespeare*. Boston: Houghton Mifflin, 1974.

Evelyn, John. *Numismata, or, a Discourse Concerning Medals*. London, 1697.

Ezell, Margaret J. M., ed. *The Poems and Prose of Mary, Lady Chudleigh*. New York: Oxford UP, 1993.

Frankforter, A. Daniel, and Paul J. Morman, trans. and eds. Introduction. *The Equality of the Two Sexes by François Poullain de la Barre*. Lewiston, NY: Edwin Mellen, 1989, vii–xlx.

Gilligan, Carol. *In a Different Voice: Psychological Theory and Women's Development*. Cambridge: Harvard UP, 1982.

Glenn, Cheryl. *Rhetoric Retold: Regendering the Tradition from Antiquity through the Renaissance*. Carbondale: Southern Illinois UP, 1997.

Goldie, Mark. "The Revolution of 1689 and the Structure of Political Argument: An Essay and an Annotated Bibliography of Pamphlets of the Allegiance Controversy." *Bulletin of Research in the Humanities* 83.4 (1980): 473–564.

Goldrick-Jones, Amanda. "Feminist (Re)Views and Re-Visions of Classical Rhetoric." *Proceedings of the Canadian Society for the History of Rhetoric* 5 (1993–94): 25–40.

Grundy, Isobel, and Susan Wiseman, eds. *Women, Writing, History 1640–1740*. London: B. T. Batsford, 1992.

Halsband, Robert, ed. *Complete Letters of Lady Mary Wortley Montagu*. Vol. 1. Oxford: Clarendon Press, 1965.

Harth, Erica. *Cartesian Women: Versions and Subversions of Rational Discourse in the Old Regime*. Ithaca: Cornell UP, 1992.

Hartmann, Van C. "Tory Feminism in Mary Astell's *Bart'lemy Fair*." *Journal of Narrative Technique* 28.3 (1998): 243–65.

Harwood, John T., ed. *The Rhetorics of Thomas Hobbes and Bernard Lamy*. Carbondale: Southern Illinois UP, 1986.

Henderson, Judith Rice. "Erasmus on the Art of Letter-Writing." Murphy 331–55.

Herberg, Erin. "Mary Astell's Rhetorical Theory: A Woman's Viewpoint." Sutherland and Sutcliffe 147–57.

Heywood, Thomas. "A Woman Killed with Kindness." Nethercot, Baskervill, and Heltzel 811–45.

173

Hill, Bridget. "A Refuge from Men: The Idea of a Protestant Nunnery." *Past and Present* 117 (1987): 107–30.

Hiscock, Andrew. "'Here's no design nor plot, nor any ground': The Drama of Margaret Cavendish and the Disorderly Woman." *Women's Writing* 4.3 (1997): 401–20.

Hutton, Sarah. "Damaris Cudworth, Lady Masham: Between Platonism and Enlightenment." *British Journal for the History of Philosophy* 1.1 (1993): 29–54.

Isocrates. *Antidosis.* Excerpted in *Readings in Classical Rhetoric.* Ed. Thomas W. Benson and Michael H. Prosser. Davis, CA: Hermagoras Press, 1988. 47–52.

Jamieson, Kathleen Hall. *Eloquence in an Electronic Age: The Transformation of Political Speechmaking.* New York: Oxford UP, 1988.

Janes, Regina. "Mary, Mary, Quite Contrary Or, Mary Astell and Mary Wollstonecraft Compared." *Studies in Eighteenth-Century Culture* 5 (1976): 121–39.

Jonson, Benjamin. *Epicoene or the Silent Woman.* Bald 207–96.

Keller, Evelyn Fox. *Reflections on Gender and Science.* New Haven: Yale UP, 1985.

Kelly-Gadol, Joan. "Did Women Have a Renaissance?" Bridenthal and Koonz 137–64.

Kelso, Ruth. *Doctrine for the Lady of Renaissance.* Urbana: U of Illinois P, 1978.

Kersey, Shirley Nelson, ed. *Classics in the Education of Girls and Women.* Metuchen, NY: Scarecrow, 1981.

Knox, John. *The First Blast of the Trumpet against the Montrous Regiment of Women.* Geneva, 1558. STC 15070.

Lamy, Bernard. *The Art of Speaking* (1676). Harwood 165–377.

Lanham, Richard A. *A Handlist of Rhetorical Terms.* Berkeley: U of California P, 1968.

Layser, Henrietta. *Medieval Women.* New York: St Martin's Press, 1995.

Levin, Carole, and Patricia A. Sullivan, eds. *Political Rhetoric, Power and Renaissance Women.* Albany: State U of New York P, 1995.

Lewis, C. S. *The Allegory of Love: A Study in Medieval Tradition.* London: Oxford UP, 1936.

Lilley, Kate, ed. *Margaret Cavendish Duchess of Newcastle: The Description of a New World Called the Blazing World and Other Writings.* New York: New York UP, 1992.

Locke, John. *An Essay Concerning Human Understanding.* London, 1689.
———. *The Reasonableness of Christianity.* London, 1695.
———. *Two Treatises of Government.* London, 1690.
———. *Vindication of the Reasonableness of Christianity.* London, 1695.

Luckyj, Christina. *"A Moving Rhetoricke": Gender and Silence in Early Modern England.* Manchester: Manchester UP, 2002.

Lunsford, Andrea A., ed. *Reclaiming Rhetorica: Women in the Rhetorical Tradition.* Pittsburgh: Pittsburgh UP, 1995.

Maclean, Ian. *The Renaissance Notion of Woman.* Cambridge: Cambridge UP, 1980.

Makin, Bathsua. *An Essay to Revive the Antient Education of Gentlewomen.* London, 1673.

Marcus, Leah S. "Shakespeare's Comic Heroines, Elizabeth I and the Political Uses of Androgyny." Rose 135–53.

Masham, Damaris. *Discourse Concerning the Love of God*. London, 1696.

McLaughlin, Eleanor Commo. "Equality of Souls, Inequality of Sexes: Woman in Medieval Theology." Ruether 213–66.

Meynell, Hugo A. *Grace, Politics and Desire: Essays on Augustine*. Calgary, AB: U of Calgary P, 1990.

Middleton, Thomas. "More Dissemblers Besides Women." *The Works of Thomas Middleton*. Ed. A. H. Bullen. Vol. 6. New York: AMS Press, 1964. 376–481.

———. *Women Beware Women*. Ed. Roma Gill. London: Ernest Benn, 1968.

Milton, John. *Paradise Lost. The Poetical Works of John Milton*. Ed. H. C. Beeching. London: Oxford UP, 1938.

More, Thomas. *Letters*. Ed. Elizabeth Frances Rogers. New Haven: Yale UP, 1961.

Murphy, James J., ed. *Renaissance Eloquence: Studies in the Theory and Practice of Renaissance Rhetoric*. Berkeley: U of California P, 1983.

Nethercot, Arthur H., Charles R. Baskervill, and Virgil B. Heltzel, eds. *Elizabethan Plays*. New York: Holt, 1971.

Noddings, Nel. *Caring: A Feminine Approach to Ethics and Moral Education*. Berkeley: U of California P, 1984.

Norris, John. "An Admonition concerning two late Books called 'Discourses of the Love of God.'" In *Practical Discourses*, n.p.

———. *Reflections upon the Conduct of Human Life*. London, 1690.

———. and Mary Astell. *Letters Concerning the Love of God*. London, 1695.

———. *Practical Discourses*. 4 vols. London: 1698.

O'Faolain, Julia, and Lauro Martines, eds. *Not in God's Image: Women in History from the Greeks to the Victorians*. New York: Harper, 1973.

Owst, G. R. *Literature and Pulpit in Medieval England*. Oxford: Basil Blackwell, 1961.

Patrides, C. A., ed. *The Cambridge Platonists*. London: Edward Arnold, 1969.

Pernoud, Régine. *Pour en finir avec le Moyen Age*. Paris: Editions Seuil, 1977.

Perry, Ruth. *The Celebrated Mary Astell: An Early English Feminist*. Chicago: U of Chicago P, 1986.

———. "Mary Astell and the Feminist Critique of Possessive Individualism." *Eighteenth-Century Studies* 23.4 (1990): 444–57.

———. "Radical Doubt and the Liberation of Women." *Eighteenth-Century Studies* 18.4 (1985): 472–93.

Peter, John. *Complaint and Satire in Early English Literature*. Oxford: Clarendon Press, 1956.

Plato. *Phaedrus and Letters VII and VIII*. Trans. and intro. Walter Hamilton. Harmondsworth: Penguin, 1973.

Plett, Heinrich F. "The Place and Function of Style in Renaissance Poetics." Murphy 356–75.

Poullain de la Barre, François. *The Equality of the Two Sexes*. Trans. Daniel Frankforter and Paul J. Morman. Lewiston, NY: Edwin Mellen, 1989.

Powicke, P. J. *The Cambridge Platonists: A Study*. Hildesheim: Georg Olms, 1970.

Puttenham, George. "The Arte of English Poesie." G. Gregory Smith 3–193.

Quintilian. *Institutio Oratoria*. Trans. H. E. Butler. Cambridge: Harvard UP, 1920.

Redford, Bruce. *The Converse of the Pen: Acts of Intimacy in the Eighteenth-Century Familiar Letter.* Chicago: U of Chicago P, 1986.

Reynolds, Myra. *The Learned Lady in England, 1650–1760.* Gloucester, MA: Peter Smith, 1964.

Roberts, James Deotis. *From Puritanism to Platonism in Seventeenth Century England.* The Hague: Martinus Nijhoff, 1968.

Rose, Mary Beth, ed. *Women in the Middle Ages and the Renaissance: Literary and Historical Perspectives.* Syracuse: Syracuse UP, 1986.

Ruether, Rosemary Radford, ed. *Religion and Sexism.* New York: Simon, 1974.

Schaef, Anne Wilson. *Women's Reality.* San Francisco: Harper & Row, 1985.

Shakespeare, William. *Macbeth.* Evans 1306–42.

———. *Troilus and Cressida.* Evans 443–98.

Schiebinger, Londa. *The Mind Has No Sex? Women in the Origins of Modern Science.* Cambridge: Harvard UP, 1989.

Scudéry, Madeleine de. *Conversation on the Manner of Writing Letters.* Donawerth, *Rhetorical Theory* 90–99.

———. "On Conversation." Donawerth, *Rhetorical Theory* 84–90.

Smith, Florence. *Mary Astell.* New York: AMS Press, 1966.

Smith, G. Gregory, ed. *Elizabethan Critical Essays.* Vol. 2. London: Oxford UP, 1904.

Smith, Hilda. *Reason's Disciples: Seventeenth-Century English Feminists.* Urbana: U of Illinois P, 1982.

Springborg, Patricia, ed. *Astell, Political Writings.* Cambridge: Cambridge UP, 1996.

Springborg, Patricia. *Mary Astell, A Serious Proposal to the Ladies: Part I, 1694, Part II, 1697.* London: Pickering, 1997.

———. "Mary Astell, Critic of Locke." *American Political Science Review* 89.3 (1995): 619–33.

Sprint, John. *The Bride-Woman's Counsellor.* London, 1699.

Sutherland, Christine Mason. "Aspiring to the Rhetorical Tradition: A Study of Margaret Cavendish." Wertheimer 255–71.

———. "Love as Rhetorical Principle: The Relationship Between Style and Content in the Rhetoric of St. Augustine." Meynell 139–54.

———. "Mary Astell: Reclaiming Rhetorica in the Seventeenth Century." Lunsford 93–116.

———. "Outside the Rhetorical Tradition: Mary Astell's Advice to Women in Seventeenth-Century England." *Rhetorica* 9.2 (1991): 147–63.

———. "Reforms of Style: St. Augustine and the Seventeenth Century." *Rhetoric Society Quarterly* 21.1 (1991): 26–37.

———. "Women in the History of Rhetoric: The Past and the Future." Sutherland and Sutcliffe 9–31.

———, and Rebecca Sutcliffe, eds. *The Changing Tradition: Women in the History of Rhetoric.* Calgary, AB: U of Calgary P, 1999.

Swearingen, C. Jan. "Plato's Women: Alternative Embodiments of Rhetoric." Sutherland and Sutcliffe 35–46.

Swift, Jonathan. "A Modest Proposal." Cunningham and Reich 271–75.

Thompson, Karl F., ed. *Classics of Western Thought*. 4th ed. Vol. 2. San Diego: Harcourt, 1988.

Tilney, Edmunde. *A Brief and Pleasant Discourse of Duties in Mariage Called the Flower of Friendshippe*. London, 1568.

Tinkler, John. "Renaissance Humanism and the *genera eloquentiae*." *Rhetorica* 5.3 (1987): 279–309.

Truelove, Alison. "Commanding Communications: The Fifteenth-Century Letters of the Stonor Women." Daybell 42–58.

Van der Weyer, Robert. *The Little Gidding Way*. London: Dartman, 1988.

Vives, Juan Luis. *The Instruction of a Christen Woman*. Trans. Richard Hyrd. London, 1529.

Wertheimer, Molly Meijer, ed. *Listening to Their Voices: The Rhetorical Activities of Historical Women*. Columbia, SC: U of South Carolina P, 1997.

Wiesen, David S. "St. Jerome as Satirist." *Cornell Studies in Classical Philology*. Vol. 34. Ithaca: Cornell UP, 1964.

Woodbridge, Linda. *Women and the English Renaissance: Literature and the Nature of Womankind, 1540–1620*. Urbana: U of Illinois P, 1986.

Notes

Notes to Introduction

1   However, it should be noted that Astell is included in the second edition of Bizzell and Herzberg's *The Rhetorical Tradition*.

2   I have previously dealt with Mary Astell's rhetoric in "Outside the Rhetorical Tradition: Mary Astell's Advice to Women in Seventeenth Century England," *Rhetorica* 9.2 (1991): 147–163; "Mary Astell: Reclaiming Rhetorica in the Seventeenth Century" in *Reclaiming Rhetorica* and "Women in the History of Rhetoric: The Past and the Future" in *The Changing Tradition*.

3   The three most important biographies of Astell, to which I am heavily indebted, are those by George Ballard, Florence Smith, and Ruth Perry.

4   "[O]riginally [the hostmen] had been a guild of hostelers, the official hosts of feudal Newcastle" (Perry, *Celebrated* 29).

5   There is no good evidence that Astell ever considered marriage. However, there was a rumour referred to by George Ballard that she suffered a "disappoiontment in a marriage contract with an eminent clergyman" (Ballard 385). It seems likely, however, that this was no more than spiteful gossip invented by those who resented her virulent attack upon the marriage customs of the time.

6   At the time "ladies" designated women of the upper classes. It is these whom Astell addresses in her proposals.

7   This is Elstob's Grammar. At the time, publication costs were often covered by selling copies in advance. This practice was known as subscription.

8   "Mrs" was at this time a title used for an adult woman. It did not indicate that the woman was married.

9   For an argument reconciling Astell's feminism with her Toryism, see Hartmann.

10   A notable exception is Jane Donawerth's "Conversation." Donawerth deals most usefully with Astell's rhetoric in this essay.

11   For a good discussion of the importance of conversation in women's rhetoric see Donawerth, "Conversation."

12   The history of the letter is a complicated one. During the Middle Ages, the highly formal letter of the *ars dictaminis* was a dominant form of rhetoric. The relationship between the *ars dictaminis* and the letter writing practices of the early humanists is discussed in Tinkler. See also Henderson.

13   A voiced style is one whose rhythms and structures are close to those of conversation, The reader "hears" the voice in the text.

Notes to Chapter 1

1   See excerpt from *Antidosis* in Benson and Prosser 47–52.
2   On this subject, see Owst; see also Peter.
3   On this subject, see Woodbridge.
4   On the question of women's possible independence, see Layser 154–65.
5   For further discussion of Augustine's principle of love, see Sutherland, "Love as Rhetorical Principle."
6   The contemplative way, *via contemplativa*, the withdrawal from the world of the early medieval monastic movement, is set against the active way, *via activa*, engagement with the world, preferred generally in the Renaissance.
7   In "'A Good (wo)man skilled in speaking'" (231) Tita French Baumlin draws upon Stephen Greenblatt's *Renaissance Self-Fashioning*.
8   For a discussion of the effeminate style, see Brody. See also Jamieson. As Jamieson points out, the idea that the articulate woman must be infertile persisted until at least the late twentieth century. She records that "in the early 1970s Representative Patricia Schroeder [...] told a hostile constituent, 'Yes, I have a uterus and a brain, and they both work'" (69).
9   For a full discussion of Elizabeth I's negotiation of her ethos as a public speaker, see Baumlin 243–252. See also three essays on Elizabeth I in Levin and Sullivan: Ilona Bell, "Elizabeth I – Always Her Own Free Woman" (57–84); Lena Cowen Orlin, "The Fictional Families of Elizabeth I" (85–112); Dennis Moore, "Dutifully Defending Elizabeth: Lord Henry Howard and the Question of Queenship" (113–38).
10 In the seventeenth century, another woman who exploited what she chose to portray as her androgyny was Margaret Cavendish, Duchess of Newcastle; however, in her own time it worked to some extent against her. Though married to a nobleman, she enjoyed none of the political power of a queen, and the hermaphroditic nature she liked to claim (because of her propensity for going public) often served only to make her appear ridiculous. Elizabeth I was androgynous not simply because she engaged in public speaking, but because she was doing a man's job; and if she was to do that man's job properly, she had to speak in public. Margaret Cavendish's situation was entirely different. In her case we must also take into account the connection she made between gender and genre: as she mixed the roles of men and women, so did she combine genres and ignore traditional distinctions between them. Her singularity too, though it appeared to her own contemporaries to be a disadvantage, was part of her own project for getting herself noticed. For a discussion of Cavendish's claim to hermaphroditic activities, see Kate Lilley's introduction to her *Margaret Cavendish Duchess of Newcastle*, ix–xxxiv. For a discussion of Margaret Cavendish as a rhetorician, see Sutherland, "Aspiring to the Rhetorical Tradition."
11 Even silence, however, could be ambiguous. For a thorough discussion of this question see Luckyj 51–52.

Notes to Chapter 2

1   References to *Some Reflections* are to Springborg's 1996 edition; those to *A Serious Proposal, Parts I and II* are to Springborg's 1997 edition.

2   It is uncertain whether or not Astell had read Plato. George Ballard believes that she had (385), but Florence Smith disputes his claim (7).

3   See for example Bordo; Schaef 1–20; Schiebinger 147–148.

4   For further discussion of the importance of Descartes in this matter, see Harth.

5   Poullain's position as an ardent feminist is somewhat compromised by his having written, in 1675, a refutation of his own earlier argument: *De l'excellence des hommes contre l'Egalité des sexes*. This suggests that he was merely engaging in the rhetorical exercise of arguing on two sides of a question. But whether it was sincere or not, this work was not nearly so well known at the time. Even in France it did not affect his reputation as a feminist: Pierre Bayle cites him as such in his *Dictionnaire historique et critique*.

6   Linda Woodbridge observes that "all the works of the formal controversy [the debate about women] use *exempla* – historical and/or literary examples, usually biblical and classical in origin" (14).

7   For further discussion of this question, see Sutherland, "Women in the History of Rhetoric" 25ff.

8   The parallels Astell draws between political and domestic issues will be discussed at greater length in the chapter on *Some Reflections Upon Marriage*.

9   "Women have no business with the Pulpit, the Bar or St Stephens Chapel [where Parliament sat]" *(Serious Proposal, II* 143).

Notes to Chapter 3

1   References are to the 1695 edition.

2   For a discussion of the importance of Descartes' ideas to women, see Harth; and Frankforter and Morman.

3   For an account of the origins of Emmanuel College, see Powicke.

4   It is important to remember, however, that Plato's concept of love is not a Christian one, since it disvalues the body in a way inconsistent with the religion of an incarnate God.

5   For more discussion of the history of the Cambridge Platonists, see Cassirer; Cragg; Patrides; and Roberts.

Notes to Chapter 4

1   References are to Springborg's 1997 edition.

2   For information on Elstob, see Hilda Smith 139ff.

3   It is apparent from the Introduction to *A Serious Proposal, Part II* that Astell knows that her original proposal has been read by the ladies, since she reproaches them for praising the work but still neglecting to embark on their education. It is to help them do so that she writes the second part of the proposal. See also Ballard: "These books [i.e., Astell's *Proposals, Parts I and II*] contributed not a little towards awakening

their [the ladies'] minds and lessening their esteem for those trifling amusements which steal away too much of their time and towards putting them upon employing their faculties the right way in pursuit of useful knowledge" (382).

4 Ferrar founded the Little Gidding community for his female relations. It did not survive for more than about thirty years.

5 On the revival of the Little Gidding community in the twentieth century, now open to both women and men, see Van der Weyer. See also www.littlegiddingchurch.org.uk.

6 This practice is in accordance with her own theory, as stated in *A Serious Proposal, Part II* (141). She recommends to her ladies, potential practitioners of *sermo*, the greatest care and tenderness in dealing with the audience.

Notes to Chapter 5

1 References are to Springborg's 1997 edition.

2 For a discussion of the application of the formal oratorical categories, forensic, deliberative and epideictic, to the less formal letter-writing genre, see Henderson 355.

3 The general reading public in Astell's day would exclude many lower-class men and almost all lower-class women. These either could not read or would lack the inclination or opportunity to buy Astell's work.

4 For a full discussion of the ideas of Damaris Masham, see Hutton.

5 For a discussion of the question of the supposed authorship of *A Discourse Concerning the Love of God*, see the introduction to Springborg, *Mary Astell* xvi.

6 See Springborg, *Astell, Political Writings* xx, where Springborg refers to Astell's "long and carefully thought-out reply to Masham."

7 For a further discussion of Springborg's contention, see Appendix A.

8 For a discussions of the debate between Locke and Stillingfleet on the question of the Trinity, see Springborg, *Mary Astell*, cited above, 186n50.

9 Here is what she says: "As to what is to be done by way of Exercise, not to enter too far into the Philosophy of the Passions, suffice it briefly to observe: That by the Oeconomy of Nature such and such Motions in the Body are annext in such a manner to certain Thoughts in the Soul, that unless some outward force restrain, she can produce them when she pleases barely by willing them, and reciprocally several Impressions on the Body are communicated to, and affect the Soul, all this being perform'd by the means of Animal Spirits. The Active Powers of the Soul, her Will and Inclincations are at her own dispose, her Passive are not, she can't avoid feeling Pain or other sensible Impressions so long as she's united to a Body, and that Body is dispos'd to convey these Impressions. And when outward Objects occasion such Commotions in the Bloud and Animal Spirits, as are attended with those Perceptions in the Soul, which we call the Passions, she can't be insensible of or avoid 'em, being no more able to prevent these first Impressions than she is to stop the circulation of the Bloud, or to hinder Digestion. All she can do is to Continue the Passion as it was begun, or to Divert it to another

Object, to Heighten or to let it Sink by degrees, or some way or other to Modifie and Direct it. The due performance of which is what we call Vertue, which consists in governing Animal Impressions, in directing our Passions to such Objects, and keeping 'em in such a pitch, as right Reason requires" (161).

Notes to Chapter 6

1 References are to Springborg's 1996 edition.
2 Patricia Springborg sees this work as she sees *A Serious Proposal, Part II* – that is, as principally a work of politics: "Mary Astell's *Some Reflections Upon Marriage* is a truly political work whose target is less the injustice of traditional Christian marriage than the absurdity of voluntarism on which the social contract theory is predicated" (*Astell, Political Writings* xxviii). Again, I have to disagree: although there is certainly a strong political element inasmuch as Astell uses the analogy of the state to discuss issues of domestic power relations, I think the discerning reader will perceive the subject to be the abuse of women rather than the inconsistencies of the Whigs.
3 Patricia Springborg points out that Astell is here referring to Locke's *Two Treatises*. See Springborg, *Astell, Political Writings* 19n21.
4 For additional discussion of this issue, see Sutherland, "Women in the History of Rhetoric" 23ff.
5 "Demean" at this time means "behave."
6 To give a very basic definition of the enthymeme: it is a truncated syllogism. One part of the syllogism is omitted, on the assumption that the audience will fill it in. The audience thus participates in constructing the argument. The rhetorician must understand what part of the syllogism can be omitted. That is, he or she must have a thorough understanding of the values and cultural practices of the audience.

Notes to Chapter 7

1 The references in this chapter are to the 1705 edition of *The Christian Religion*.
2 For Cicero's ideas on this question see *De Officiis* 1.132.
3 On the question of the authorship of *The Ladies Calling*, see Florence Smith 41n10.
4 For Astell's admiration of Pascal, see Appendix B. For more discussion of the similarity between Astell and Pascal, see Sutherland, "Women in the History of Rhetoric" 24.
5 These disciples had not heard of Jesus Christ. They had received the "baptism of repentance" of John the Baptist, but it was necessary for them to be baptized in "in the name of the Lord Jesus" in order to receive the Holy Ghost (Acts 19, 1–6).
6 "Thus there is a profound question as to whether men should enjoy themselves, use themselves, or do both. For it is commanded to us that we should love one another, but it is to be asked whether man is to be loved by man for his own sake or for the sake of something else. If for

his own sake we enjoy him; if for the sake of something else, we use him. But I think that man is to be loved for the sake of something else." Augustine of Hippo 18.

7   Paralepsis: "A speaker emphasizes something by pointedly seeming to pass over it" (Lanham 68).

8   The reference is to *Letters Concerning the Love of God*, Astell's correspondence with John Norris. Originally written as private letters, these were later published in 1695 at the insistence of Norris.

9   Enargia. "Vivid description" (Lanham 40).

10   Astell presumably is referring here to the women's lack of confidence in their own judgement.

Notes to Chapter 8

1   References to *Moderation Truly Stated* (1704) and to *Bart'lemy Fair* (1709) are to the original editions of those years. Those to *A Fair Way with the Dissenters* and to *An Impartial Enquiry into the Causes of Rebellion* are to Springborg's 1996 edition.

2   Astell was not the only woman to participate in public discussion: there were many others, including, for example, Elinor James, and Astell's opponent, Damaris Masham. She was, however, the most celebrated in her own day, and arguably the best of them. Unfortunately this participation of women in public discussion was short-lived. It was not resumed until long after the time of Mary Astell.

3   For a good introduction to the issues involved, see Springborg, *Astell, Political Writings* xi–xxix.

4   In 1688, James II, who had become a Roman Catholic, left the country and was replaced by his daughter, Mary II, and his son-in-law, William III, who reigned jointly. Many people, however, believed that, as the anointed king, James II could not be deposed, and therefore refused to swear allegiance to the new king and queen. They were known as non-jurors. William Sancroft, Archbishop of Canterbury, who assisted Mary Astell, was one of them.

5   For a clear and brief explanation of Occasional Conformity, see Florence Smith 131. For a full discussion of the pamphlet warfare following the Revolution of 1689, see Goldie.

6   Dissenters were those who adhered to churches other than the Church of England. Their theology tended to the extremes of Protestantism. Although the Roman Catholics were also politically disabled, they were not thought of as Dissenters.

7   The first three pamphlets were published in 1704, before *The Christian Religion*, 1705. However, since Astell refers (*Christian Religion* 408) to the book's having been "so long in press," it is probable that it was written before the 1704 pamphlets, certainly before the death of Locke in October, 1704.

8   For a thorough account of Astell's position, see Hartmann.

9   The grand style is designed to stimulate the emotions by using such devices as vibrant diction, simile, metaphor, various patterns of repetition

and elaborate sentence structures such as the periodic, which rises to a climax. A master of this style in modern times was Martin Luther King Jr.

10 For a good introduction to the issues involved, see Springborg, *Astell, Political Writings* xi–xxix. For an account of the importance of Queen Anne to contemporary women writers, see Barash.

Notes to Chapter 9

1 Petrus Ramus (1515–1572) had argued that in the interests of efficiency, *inventio* and *dispositio* should be taught only under logic, not, as hitherto, under both logic and rhetoric.

2 References are to Springborg's 1997 edition.

3 For a discussion of the criticism of language in the seventeenth century, see Sutherland, "Reforms of Style."

4 "In 1662 *La Logique ou L'art de penser* appeared anonymously. Doubtless various of the Messieurs de Port Royal, especially Nicole, contributed to the text; still, Antoine Arnauld is generally credited with its authorship" (Dickoff xxxvii). Dickoff's translation is published under the name of Arnauld alone, but as both Harwood and Carr always cite Nicole as co-author, I have found it best to follow their practice.

5 For information on Nicole, see Carr 64n7.

6 This matter is more fully discussed in the chapter on *A Serious Proposal to the Ladies, Part II*.

7 In fact, though Astell's moral approach is heavily influenced by Arnauld and Nicole, the rules themselves are more obviously like those of Descartes, though there is some similarity between hers and those in *L'art de penser*. (See Arnauld 310 and 336). For the possible influence of Blaise Pascal, see Springborg, *Mary Astell* 190.

8 See Springborg, *Mary Astell* 190n118 and 191n121.

Notes to Chapter 10

1 Here again, references are to Springborg's 1997 edition.

2 Astell follows this principle herself when she addresses the ladies. In her political pamphlets, however, and in *Some Reflections Upon Marriage* she spares the feelings of the opposition not at all.

3 It should be borne in mind that Astell's audience of women would be concerned primarily with the rhetoric of *sermo*, in which a conversational model is especially appropriate. Lamy's audience of men would be more concerned with *contentio*.

4 It is possible that Astell is in this respect influenced by the milder philosophy of the Cambridge Platonists with their strong emphasis on the importance of love and their belief in the human spirit as the "candle of the Lord."

5 For information on this matter, see Harwood's introduction to his edition of Lamy.

6 See [Cicero] *Rhetorica Ad Herennium* 4.7.10–11.16.12, 253–69.

7   Her friends Lady Ann Coventry and Lady Elizabeth Hastings were not
     permanently resident in Chelsea where Astell lived. Elizabeth Elstob did
     not move to London until the early eighteenth century.
8   For discussions of varieties of feminist rhetoric and rhetorical research,
     see Bizzell; and Goldrick-Jones. Goldrick-Jones cites the following
     composition theorists as inspired by feminist theories of the "ethics of
     care": Cynthia Caywood, Gillian Overing, Elizabeth Flynn, Catherine
     Lamb, Lisa Ede, and Andrea Lunsford.

Notes to Conclusion

1   See Donawerth, "Conversation."
2   For a discussion of Madeleine de Scudéry's theory, see Donawerth, "As
     Becomes a Rational Woman."
3   It is worth noting, however, that among the early theorists of rhetoric,
     Augustine was remarkable for his insistence on the necessity of caring
     for the audience. For a discussion of his stance on this question, see
     Sutherland, "Love as Rhetorical Principle."
4   For Mary Astell's Preface, see Appendix III in Halsband 466–68.
5   For an account of references to Astell's works up until the earlier
     twentieth century, see the Bibliographical Note included as Appendix I
     in Florence Smith's Mary Astell, 167–72.
6   For the interconnectedness of rhetoric and feminism, see Ede, Glenn,
     and Lunsford.

Notes to Appendix A

1   For confirmation of this judgement, see Hutton 36.

Index

A

Acworth, R., 49

admiration, 127

An Admonition concerning two late Books called "Discourses of the Love of God" (Norris), 167

"An Anatomie of the World: The First Anniversary" (Donne), 10

Anatomy of Melancholy (Burton), 17, 60

androgyny, 20, 21, 22

Anglicans, 110, 121

Anne, Queen, 31, 102, 114, 120, 121–22, 159, 163

anonymity, 4, 51, 150, 163

Aristotle, 147, 148, 157
  Politics, 19
  Rhetorica, 3, 4, 8
  on women, 5, 27

Arnauld, Antoine. *The Art of Thinking*, 69, 131–36, 137, 138, 143–45, 148, 157

The Arte of English Poesie (Puttenham), 8–9

The Art of Speaking (Lamy), 69, 137, 139–46, 148, 157

The Art of Thinking (Arnauld, Nicole), 69, 131–36, 137, 138, 143–45, 148

Astell, Mary
  anonymity of, 51, 150, 163
  attacks on cultural values, 92
  audience of, 61–62, 66, 75–76, 80, 102, 106, 125, 129, 134, 136, 137, 141–43, 148, 150, 154–55, 156–58
  Bart'lemy Fair, or an Enquiry after Wit, 116–17, 120, 159
  The Christian Religion, xx, 35, 49, 50–51, 71, 93–107, 109, 121, 148, 150, 155, 156, 157, 162, 166–67
  colloquial vocabulary of, 118–19
  conversational style of, xx, 45–46, 93–94, 118–19, 156
  correspondence with Norris, 42, 44–52, 129, 147, 149, 154, 155, 158, 165
  death of, xv
  development as writer, 154–56
  education of, xi–xii, 26, 27, 42, 54
  egalitarianism of, 70
  employment of, xii–xiii
  A Fair Way with the Dissenters, 112–14, 118
  as feminist, xvi, 82, 89, 109, 149, 162
  feminists on, xvi–xvii
  friends of, xiv, 46–47, 50
  headship of charity school, xv
  as High Church, 121
  An Impartial Enquiry into the Causes of Rebellion and the Civil War, 114–16, 118–19, 122
  influence of, 158–61
  intellectual isolation, 47, 50
  interest in politics, 88

Epicoene, or The Silent Woman (Jonson), 20
epideictic writing, 79, 90, 92
Erasmus, Desiderius, 14, 15
Errington, Mary, xi
Essay concerning Human Understanding (Locke), 95, 147
An Essay in Defence of the Female Sex (Drake), 160
Essays upon Peace and War (D'Avenant), 111
Essay to Revive the Antient Education of Gentlewomen (Makin), 54
ethics, 133
ethos, 3–4, 36, 97
    categories, 4–5
    of Elizabeth I, 23
    false, 4
    intrinsic vs. extrinsic, 3–4, 80, 83
    women and, 25
Evelyn, John. *Numismata*, 158
The Excellencie of Good Women (Rich), 19
experience, 30–31

A Fair Way with the Dissenters (Astell), 112–14, 118
Falkland, Lettice, Viscountess, 61
Fall of man, 132, 133
Fell, Margaret, 25
The Female Academy (Cavendish), 60
feminism, 27, 89, 90, 92, 158, 162, 163
Les Femmes Savantes (Molière), 159
Ferrar, Nicholas, 61
feudalism, 12, 14
Finch, Anne, Viscountess Conway, 41
The First Blast of the Trumpet against the Monstrous Regiment of Women (Knox), 21
The Flower of Friendshippe (Tilney), 17
Fox, Margaret Fell, xvii
Frankforter, Daniel, 28
freedom, 11, 87, 88
Fuller, Thomas, 60

Gelindo, Beatrix, 14
gender, 103, 104. *See also* men and women
    genre vs., 150, 158
Genesis 2, 6, 16
Gilligan, Carol. *In a Different Voice*, 149
Glanville, Joseph, 41
Glenn, Cheryl, 20
    Rhetoric Retold, xvii
Goldrick-Jones, Amanda, 149
goodwill, 5
grammar, 77